The Palaces
of
Medieval England

The Palaces
of
Medieval England
c. 1050–1550

Royalty, nobility, the episcopate
and their residences from
Edward the Confessor to Henry VIII

Thomas Beaumont James

London

I dedicate this book to my wife Muffie,
whose fund of knowledge of publishing and of good advice
has improved the end product very considerably.

© Tom Beaumont James 1990

First published 1990

Typeset by Enset (Photosetting).
Midsomer Norton, Bath, Avon
and printed and bound in Great Britain by
The Alden Press, Oxford
for the publishers
B.A. Seaby Ltd.
7, Davies Street
London W1Y 1LL

Distributed by
B.T. Batsford Ltd.
P.O. Box 4, Braintree, Essex CM7 7QY

ISBN 1 85264 030 8

British Library Cataloguing in Publication Data
James, Thomas Beaumont
   The palaces of medieval England, c. 1050–1550:
   royalty, nobility, the episcopate and their
   residences from Edward the Confessor to Henry VIII.
   1. England. Palaces, history
   I. Title
   942

ISBN 1–85264–030–8

Contents

Preface

To stand in the great hall of Clarendon palace, now an overgrown ruin, and to imagine the confrontation which took place between Henry II and Thomas Becket at the Wiltshire palace in 1164 is a stirring experience. Medieval palace sites offer opportunities to recreate many such scenes from the Middle Ages and from the early Tudor period, and herein lies one of their major attractions. No single book has so far sought to draw together the rich material of documents and archaeology which relate to these exotic sites. A work of this length can do no more than open windows on to wide and shadowy vistas, and focus on the patches of knowledge revealed by various people who have studied individual sites and particular palace dwellers, royal, noble and episcopal.

Few of those who read this book will ever live in a palace, and the great buildings described here have for the most part almost entirely disappeared. The aim of this text and its supporting illustrations is to breathe life into buildings which were once the centres of English life, but which are now in very many cases ruined or put to other uses. Of the royal palaces of the Middle Ages only Windsor is still used as a royal residence, although Hampton Court survives largely intact as an ancient monument open to the public. Medieval noble residences have also largely disappeared, although occasionally, as in the case of Dartington, some buildings are still in use. Similarly, few bishops now reside in their medieval or early Tudor palaces: the Reformation and its aftermath put an end to that. Paradoxically therefore, ruination and change of use make medieval palace sites more readily accessible than they might be if they were still private residences.

This book seeks to explore the archaeology and surviving architecture of English medieval palaces, and to cast some light on the aspirations of the palace builders. This is attempted not only by reference to the vital events (births, marriages and deaths) of certain individuals who enjoyed palace life between 1042 and 1547, but also to events which shaped their experience.

Winchester
June 1989

Acknowledgements

Many people have contributed to this book through giving advice, imparting specialist knowledge, and in many other ways. The magnificent volumes on the King's Works by Howard Colvin (who dug at Clarendon in 1939) have been indispensable for royal residences, together with other materials he has published on palaces and their surroundings. As the text shows, my previous work on Clarendon paved the way for this more general investigation, and John Charlton's kindness in providing his materials on Clarendon, and his advice on many other matters, can again be detected here. Although the work was already well advanced when a conference on medieval palaces took place at Oxford in December 1987, much benefit was derived from the papers delivered by the participants there, and from subsequent correspondence with individual speakers. Much of the background reading was undertaken during a lecture tour of Australia in 1986, in the magnificent libraries at the universities of Adelaide, Canberra, Melbourne and Sydney, where I was most warmly welcomed. To my colleagues in the History and Archaeology Division at King Alfred's, who have freely answered many questions and provided many insights, and to the generations of students who have been exposed to palaces, I offer my thanks.

Alex Turner has patiently recreated various drawings for me, and has taken photographs on my behalf. The King Alfred's College Research Fund has been generous in support for travel and materials. My friends Chris Given-Wilson, Edward Roberts and John Steane have been especially kind in reading drafts and giving much from their wealth of specialist knowledge of the royal household, the Winchester bishopric pipe rolls, and on the archaeology of the royal family respectively. To them I owe an especial debt of gratitude.

My immediate and extended family (including of course the Wolvesey Jameses, the only members of the family currently living in a palace, and whose chapel survives from the Middle Ages) have again been very long suffering and supportive of this project as of previous ones, and I thank them most warmly.

Winchester
June 1989

Chapter 1
Palaces

Medieval palaces were principally royal and episcopal residences, although at one time and another certain members of the highest rank of the nobility also used the term for their buildings. Nobles with palaces were usually closely linked to the monarch, as brothers, uncles and relations by marriage, or grew close to the king by bearing onerous responsibilities for defending border areas of the realm. A palace was not usually fortified, although some castles such as the Tower of London and Windsor were furnished with palatial accommodation. In essence the palace was the manor writ large, with a great hall, or halls, chambers, chapels, kitchens and other offices. Apart from scale, a major difference between the local manor and the palace complex was the way in which the palace provided an opportunity for the élite to display their wealth in sumptuous architecture, in concert with interior and exterior decoration, to most lavish specifications. Innovation is frequently found in palace building, whether in scale as found at King William Rufus's huge great hall at Westminster from the eleventh century, or in pure experiment such as Henry II's Sicilian-style retreat with interconnecting pools at Woodstock from the twelfth century.

Élite living was not confined to a small group of palaces. Furthermore, Kings, bishops and nobles in the Middle Ages were highly mobile and spent time at a range of residences of their own: palaces, castles, town houses and hunting lodges. Kings in particular enjoyed the right to stay with bishops and nobles, a right which was frequently exercised. In a sense the palace might be said to exist at whichever residence a monarch, bishop or lord found himself at any particular time. Even a mere 'hunting lodge' of which there were many in medieval England, could be palatial in luxury if not in scale. For although they might appear at first sight to be insubstantial places for the weathy to spend their time, yet one should not forget the outlay required to create the surrounding parks and to stock forests with animals for the chase, to employ a permanent staff of huntsmen and others to manage the game, to keep and train falcons, hunting dogs and all the paraphernalia of the hunt, quite apart from the outlay on such luxury items as fishponds (*see* Fig. 1).

This investigation of palaces looks not only at the buildings, but also at the whole lifestyle of some of those who owned these pleasure domes between the time of Edward the Confessor (1042–66) and Henry VIII (1509–47). This opening chapter introduces two areas of analysis: first the élite and their lifestyle in relation to their buildings, and second the layout of the sites, topics which link the material in succeeding chapters.

The medieval palace had a variety of functions. It was the private luxury home of those members of the élite who chose such a lifestyle. It also had a pub-

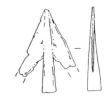
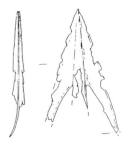

Fig. 1 A selection of hunting arrowheads found at Clarendon, Wiltshire. A number of these showed evidence of treatment with non-ferrous metal, presumably an extravagance to create an effect as they flew through the air. (*Drawings by Frances Rankine, Society of Antiquaries of London*)

lic face; the palace provided an impressive setting for audiences with foreign ambassadors and potentates and was a meeting place for kings, lords and bishops with their subjects, tenants or dependants. By its location and provision with chapels, the royal palace proclaimed the close links between rulers and God. The proclaimed link between ruler and the deity was true of ancient and medieval palaces, though it is perhaps less true of modern ones. Available resources, political circumstances and personality affected the degree of sophistication and extravagance with which a palace was built. These matters also affected the length and nature of its use. Thus, in the late fourteenth century Richard II was especially attached to the palace at Sheen (Surrey). When his wife died there, in his grief he had the entire palace razed to the ground (page 135). These unhappy events have their echo in more recent history. Osborne House in the Isle of Wight was the preferred residence of Albert and Victoria in the nineteenth century. After Albert died his belongings there were left untouched (and remain largely so) by the mourning queen, and when she herself died there in 1901 the building passed out of use as a royal residence, being put to various institutional purposes.

Residences proclaimed the status of individuals. Medieval kings, nobles and bishops enjoyed enormous incomes compared with most of their subjects. Amongst the greatest royal builders were Henry III (1216–72) and Henry VIII (1509–47), but every monarch who occupied the throne of England left a mark on the royal building stock. In large part the same point holds good for bishops and nobility. A great prelate, such as Henry of Blois (d. 1171), brother of King Stephen, built mightily in his diocese, at Winchester and at Bishop's Waltham (Hampshire) and elsewhere. He was also abbot of the wealthy monastery at Glastonbury (Somerset), which provided further income for building enterprises.

Economic boom and recession, as well as demographic ebb and flow, certainly affected the incomes of great families and the medieval Church, but those who lived in palaces were usually so wealthy that building programmes continued even in the bad times. Palace projects were not, therefore, restricted to the high Middle Ages of the twelfth and thirteenth centuries when profits from the cultivation of land (the basis of the medieval economy) were large in a period of economic and demographic growth. There is plenty of evidence of extravagant building works from the late fourteenth, fifteenth and early sixteenth centuries, a period when manorial incomes were low and the population relatively small. Windsor Castle was built after 1350, and great builder bishops such as Wykeham (d. 1404), Beaufort (d. 1447), Waynflete (d. 1486) and Wolsey (d. 1530), as well as magnates such as Ralph, Lord Cromwell (d. 1446), found the money for building projects. Such moneys as these might come from various sources: the profits of war, manorial income in a wealthy see, the profits of royal service or, in the sixteenth century, from the proceeds of the dissolution of the monasteries.

In addition to the magnificence of the buildings, the residences of the powerful were decorated both inside and out to the highest standards of contemporary building and furnishing practice. Royalty, nobility and the ecclesiastical hierarchy cross-fertilised one another's ideas of building fashion and appointment. Because of their fashionable nature, palace buildings were regularly modernised to comply with new ideals of comfort and taste. Study of the remains provides valuable insights into the aspirations of those who ruled the English state and Church in the Middle Ages. Information comes from three sources: documents, standing remains and the results of archaeological excavation. Each source has its unique role to play, for all are highly fragmentary, so medieval palaces can only be recreated, and palace life explored, by the reassembly of these disparate materials.

As a result of the many rebuildings (and demolitions), not only in the Middle Ages but also subsequently, what can be discovered of medieval palaces has to be gleaned from often shattered remains. The physical remains of royal palaces, such as Cheddar (Somerset) excavated by Philip Rahtz, or Clarendon (Wiltshire) excavated by Tancred Borenius and John Charlton, or of ecclesiastical palaces such as Wolvesey in Winchester (Hampshire) excavated by Martin Biddle, are highly significant in a study such as this.

Before Borenius and Charlton began work at the royal palace of Clarendon in 1933 little was known of the archaeology of English medieval palaces. Half a century later very much more is known, not only of the buildings and their decoration but also, through specialist analysis of the artefacts from the sites, about subjects such as diet and daily life, which are being illuminated through archaeology. In addition to the results of archaeological work, a mass of valuable documentary material still exists. The details of the building works of Henry III in particular, found in contemporary accounts, give us dazzling insights into an era from which almost all his domestic and residential buildings, with the exception of the great hall of Winchester castle, have disappeared. Although we have some knowledge of the buildings from documents, the location of the royal house at Guildford (Surrey), for example, is now not known with certainty. From other periods we have physical remains, such as the twelfth-century remains at the bishop's palace at Lincoln, but little documentation. Archaeology and documentary research each have a unique role to play: the long time-scale of archaeology has to be supplemented by the precise detail of documentation. No-one has ever excavated the bones of a camel from Henry I's menagerie at Woodstock, or of Henry III's elephant from the Tower of London. More importantly, not one wooden shingle from the hundreds of thousands known from documents to have been cut in the medieval forest has survived in the archaeological record of a medieval palace, although roof tiles abound. Documents and archaeology provide complementary insights.

Virtually nothing of the sumptuous contents of palaces or the rich clothing of their occupants has survived the centuries, although occasional detailed documentary accounts of such contents and apparel are extant. One such account is the inventory of Edward III's daughter, Joan, prepared in 1348 in advance of her journey to Spain for her proposed marriage to King Pedro of Castile. Sadly, Joan died of the Black Death in 1348 at Bordeaux en route to Spain, but the meticulous preparation for the important diplomatic coup of her marriage led to the recording of everything she was to take with her. This list provides a rare snapshot of the household goods from chamber and chapel to kitchen and stable. Sumptuous clothes in silk and fur, furniture such as a chair for her to sit on while being washed, wedding gifts including magnificent saddles, chapel furnishings and even pots, pans and herbs for the kitchen are listed for use in the stopping-over places along the road. The inventory, which is discussed in detail below (page 125), reminds us how medieval nobility travelled with equipment against all eventualities. The analogy of the residence as the tortoise shell and the slow procession of the carts of contents moving from place to place as the head and body of the tortoise is a good one. This tendency to take all requirements from place to place helps explain why comparatively little high-status evidence of contents is commonly found in archaeological investigation of important residences. Silver thread, perhaps from a discarded saddle, or a broken fourteenth-century wine glass hint at good living at Clarendon in the later Middle Ages. Shattered Italian glass recovered from archaeological levels in the wine cellar at Kings Langley (Hertfordshire) tells a similar tale, while a silver plate found in a midden at Shrewsbury (Shropshire) probably represents the hidden and unrecovered proceeds of theft from a royal party passing through the town (Neal 1971, 67–9; James and Robinson 1988, 193–5; Campbell 1988, 312–3). Occasionally an outstanding artefact has survived the years, such as the copper alloy jug bearing the arms of England and badges of King Richard II (1377–99) which was inexplicably rediscovered in the palace of the Ashanti King Prempeh at Kumasi (Ghana) in 1895 (Alexander and Binski 1987, 524) (*see* Fig. 2).

A central feature of élite lifestyle in any age is the potential for mobility regardless of cost. This was as true in the Middle Ages as it is today, although Europe and the Middle East were, with few exceptions, the limits of experience of medieval people. So the élite of medieval society was highly mobile, unless prevented by ill-health, old age or imprisonment. King John (1199–1216) was never in the same place for more than a month at any one time in the whole of his reign of seventeen and a half years. It is often said in jest, but with a grain of truth, that the great households moved on from one place to the next when the latrines began to smell. In the early days at least there were more profound reasons for moving from place to place, namely that the excess produce of manors could be consumed by the feudal lord and his household at the point of origin. This became less of an issue as the post-Conquest period moved towards a society working with money rather than exchange of goods. Mobility continued, and distinctions began to appear between royalty, who seem to have become less mobile, for political as well as economic and social reasons, as perhaps also did members of the nobility, and the higher clergy, who remained the most active group of all, ceaselessly conducting business within their dioceses and very often combining this with responsibilities in government as well. These trends are investigated below.

Analysis of places of birth of royal children – for this is the family about which most is known in all respects – gives some insight into this mobility, as do places of death and burial. Preparations for birth can be made, and a glance at the places of birth of a sample family of royal children is instructive. Of Edward III (1327–77) and his wife Philippa of Hainault's children, for example, two were born at each of the Tower of London, Windsor (Berkshire) and Woodstock (Oxfordshire) and one each at Antwerp, Clarendon (Wiltshire), Ghent, Hatfield (Hertfordshire), Langley (Buckinghamshire) and at Waltham (Essex). The Black Prince, Edward III's eldest son, had three children born respectively at Angoulême, at Bordeaux, and in the case of his illegitimate son Roger, at Clarendon.

Death and burial tell a similar story of mobility, as the places of death of William the Conqueror, his sons William Rufus and Henry I and his grandson Stephen show. The Conqueror himself died in 1089 at Rouen and was buried at Caen; William Rufus died in 1100 in the New Forest (Hampshire) and was buried at Winchester. However, medieval burial customs may weaken burial as evidence of mobility during a king's lifetime. Henry I died in 1135 on the Continent, as his father had done, and the intention was that his remains should be buried in England. However, as in the case of his father, there were problems with putrefaction of the corpse which interfered with these arrangements. In the case of the Conqueror attempts to force the body into a stone coffin led to such an unbearable stench that the funeral service had to be cut short (Douglas 1964, 362–3). Henry's body is said to have exploded and was abandoned overboard during the Channel crossing, although the heart was saved for interment at the king's great abbey at Reading (Berkshire). Stephen (d. 1154) similarly chose to be buried at his own monastic foundation at Faversham (Kent), beside his wife. The mobility which resulted in the scattered deaths of the kings can be plainly seen in the lives of prelates and nobles, for example in the itinerary of Bishop Swinfield both in his Hereford diocese and visit to London in 1289–90, or in that of Elizabeth, Countess of Warwick, in 1420–1 when she travelled in her 'chariott' from Berkeley (Gloucestershire) to Walthamstow (north east London), thence to the Midlands. Details of her stops for snacks of bread and white wine, or for more substantial meals, and overnight, are all carefully documented (Ross 1951, 81ff). Clearly, age affected people's ability to be mobile so that Edward III, who was very active in his younger days, moved about very little in his later years (pages 127 and 167).

Royalty, nobility and prelates enjoyed a range of residences, by no means all of which were palatial in scale; besides palaces there were castles, manor houses and small hunting lodges scattered across the country. Accommodation at examples of all these various residences is treated here. Different activities demanded different sized residences, quite apart from changes in the popularity of different residences whose fortunes rose and fell according to the character of individual kings, bishops and nobles in the Middle Ages as now. Receiving embassies or taking counsel from the magnates required space and so could take place in comparatively few venues. Private hunting parties needed much less accommodation (*see* Fig. 3). The Norman kings, for example, enjoyed hunting and the widespread geographical locations of their hunting lodges and other residences throughout the country reflect this interest. Rural residences usually doubled as manorial centres for the collection of dues. There was a permanent staff, and archaeology may perhaps tell more about the lifestyle of this group than of the élite occupants. In that curious thirteenth-century list of places and their associations possibly written down by a royal official in his cups, Woodstock is recalled as a manor rather than for its palatial accommodation, and the reference to Charing, memorable to the writer for its prostitutes, may be a reference to the royal manor on the outskirts of London where Edward I built palatial accommodation for his falcons, rather than to Charing in Kent where the Archbishop of Canterbury had a palace (Rothwell 1975, 881ff).

Fig. 3 A series of plans of great halls to show their relative sizes. Palaces usually had more than one hall. The size of the structures and their development provide insights into the scale of activities envisaged at different times. Long and narrow halls of the romanesque period developed into more spacious early gothic halls. Later medieval halls such as Windsor and Eltham were less grand. Key: a) Westminster; b) Wolvesey east hall; c) Lincoln, east hall; d) Clarendon; e) Winchester Castle hall; f) Canterbury, Archbishop's hall; g) Windsor; h) Eltham; i) Hampton Court. (*Drawings by Alex Turner*)

a)

b)

f)

)

g)

d)

h)

e)

i)

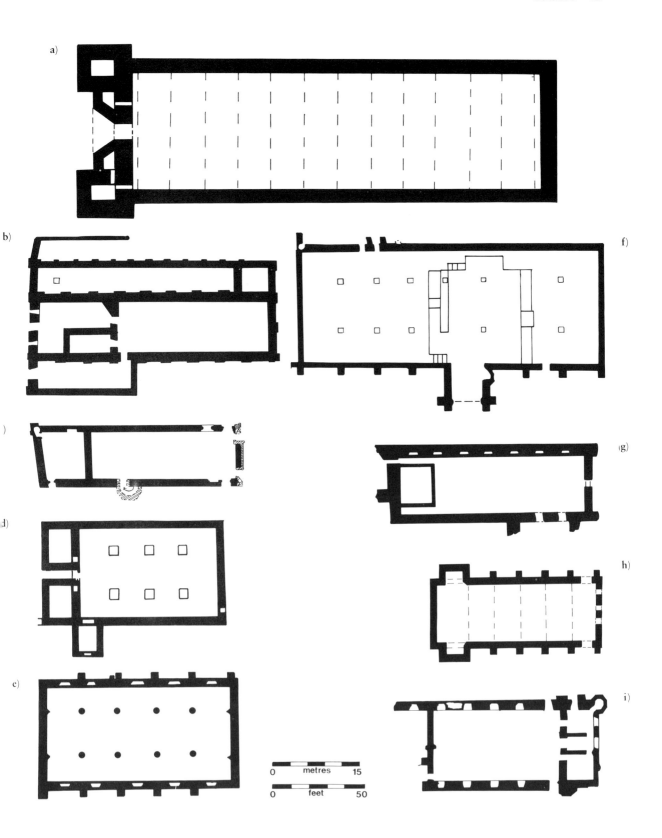

| 0 | metres | 15 |

| 0 | feet | 50 |

Compared with their predecessors, the Yorkist and the Tudor monarchs tended to reside in the Thames valley and within easy reach of London. This perceived necessity may have contributed to the ease with which Richard III, whose power base lay in the north, was disposed of by the Tudors. Of the eighty-six residences (not including their 150 or so castles) which at one time or another belonged to the kings of medieval England, fewer than ten remained in royal hands when Henry VII seized power in 1485 and these were mostly in and around London, with only Woodstock and Clarendon in anything like distant locations. This helps explain not only the reasons why royalty stayed near to London, but also the Tudors' reputation for acquisition of residences, such as Hampton Court (Surrey) and Knole (Kent), for by the death of Henry VIII in 1547 the number was greater than it had ever been (page 164).

The sites of episcopal residences, of which there were some 150 in all, were much more settled in the long term, although as we have seen, the bishops were perhaps the most mobile sector of the élite. A bishop had a major residence at his see, usually with a second important residence nearby, a collection of manors, and a London palace, often referred to as an 'inn'. Large or well-endowed dioceses such as Winchester, Worcester and Lincoln each had around seventeen residences. Rochester at the other extreme relied largely on two, although being close to London the bishop had much less need of stopping-over places, which the more provincial or larger sees needed (Barley 1986, 81–3). The houses of the nobility are much more difficult to categorise, and await detailed study as a group. Castles, manors, a London residence and perhaps a house in a provincial town might form the predictable mixture which a wealthy noble might have enjoyed. Where inheritance brought scattered landed possessions into the ownership of an individual noble, conveniently located manors were kept in readiness for the lord's visit in the same way as members of the royal household used residences in a scatter of locations on their lands.

The second area of analysis of the medieval palace is the matter of site and layout. Few palaces were built on virgin sites in the middle ages and so constraints of size of site and structures already in place informed building programmes. Thus Westminster palace was sandwiched between the abbey and the river, the position perhaps reflecting the availability of space at Westminster when, at an uncertain date before the Conquest, the royal residence was apparently removed from within the walls of London to be established beside the abbey (page 29). At Clarendon (*see* Fig. 4) there was room for the buildings to multiply and sprawl across the hillside. However, documentary references to an 'old hall' and the crowding of the major buildings along the edge of a steep slope from the late twelfth and thirteenth centuries onwards, indicate that there were a number of phases to the site, and that the existence of earlier buildings dictated the choice of position of later ones. At Henry VIII's Nonsuch (Surrey), on the other hand, a village which previously occupied the site, parish church and all, was cleared in advance of building works. But Nonsuch, as its names suggests, was the exception rather than the rule.

Francis Bacon, that Tudor polymath, provides a convenient definition of a palace from the generation which followed Henry VIII. Although Bacon's overall concept might be said to be Renaissance rather than medieval as he had in mind such creations as Philip II's Escorial palace in Spain, begun in 1557, his

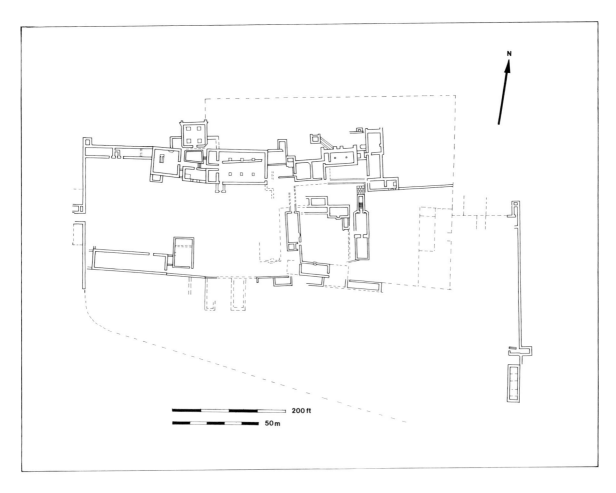

definition provides a useful starting point. The palace, he tells us, should have two elements within a single structure: a banquet side for feasts and triumphs, and a household side for dwelling. The banquet side should contain the major reception hall, with associated retiring rooms; the household side chambers (including a summer and winter parlour), chapel, kitchen, butteries, pantries, and cellar (Bacon 1900, 110–112). These are the elements to be found in various combinations in lay and ecclesiastical medieval palaces.

The most striking difference between the ideal palace of Bacon's day, Nonsuch for example, and the palaces of England from the period of the Normans and Plantagenets, is that the earlier palaces consisted of various separate structures, which might be said to have grown organically. In the earlier period buildings were separate groups connected by pentices; from around 1500 they were gathered up into major blocks containing many rooms, as found at Hampton Court (Surrey). In pre-Renaissance palaces in England the courtyards were asymmetrical. Thus Clarendon (*see* Fig. 4) and Westminster presented a somewhat higgledy-piggledy appearance of buildings roughly aligned round courtyards in contrast to Bacon's more formal vision. The contemporary nomenclature of the Middle Ages, 'the king's houses', sums up very well the difference between the medieval layout and that of the mid-sixteenth century, as at Nonsuch, which had symmetrical courtyards surrounded by blocks of several stories (*see* Fig. 5).

One element not mentioned specifically by Bacon is guest accommodation. Major royal centres required space for consultation with magnates, those 'natural counsellors' on whom the king depended for advice and administrative support. The great men might have expected to be accommodated in a style befitting their status, but it is not immediately apparent how this was achieved before the appearance of guest and retainer accommodation in the later middle ages and in the Tudor period, added for example in a special courtyard at Knole by Henry VIII, and to be seen at the palace at Bishop's Waltham (Hampshire) where a galleried wing or block in the style of a medieval inn survives. Certain nobles had their own rooms at royal palaces, such as the chamber of Hugh de Nevill at Clarendon from the early thirteenth century, although this may have been a reflection of de Nevill's administrative significance rather than an indication of his role as a counsellor (page 62). On the whole magnates and their retainers must have either stayed locally, no problem in towns, or in temporary accommodation, as used on campaigns or, and this seems less likely, on the floor of the great hall. When Becket came to Clarendon in 1164 to oppose the Constitutions of Clarendon, proposed by the king to limit papal power, the prelate stayed at Old Sarum, and crossed the river by the bridge which still bears his name to appear at the palace.

It is noteworthy that Francis Bacon makes no reference to fortifications to defend the palace. On the whole, fortification of royal residences in medieval England was deemed unnecessary. The monarch relied on the authority of the Crown to defend himself and his family. If that authority were challenged then he could withdraw to a castle. However, residences frequently changed hands between royalty, magnates and, to a lesser extent, the ecclesiastical hierarchy and this process brought various fortified manors into royal hands. These had been fortified by subjects who thought it wise to take precautions to defend themselves, as at Eltham (Kent). In unsettled times and in particular in the immediate aftermath of the Norman Conquest, during the anarchy of Stephen's reign and in periods of upheaval in the thirteenth, fourteenth and fifteenth centuries, measures were taken by nobles and higher clergy to fortify their residences. Certain of these people, for example marcher lords and the bishops of Durham, had specific military responsibilities to defend the realm and so had more reason to fortify. The castle-palace could perhaps be said to be derived from military and security considerations, as at the Tower of London or at Goodrich or Chepstow in the Welsh marches. Changes in style of living, and a more relaxed attitude to security, contributed new elements to castle-palaces. Palatial accommodation on just one or two floors appeared in castle baileys: an additional chapel and great hall within the bailey at the Tower, Richard II's beautiful small palace beside the old keep and the even older Roman walls at Portchester (Hampshire), the 'gloriet' accommodation ranges at Corfe Castle (Dorset) and Leeds Castle (Kent) of the thirteenth century.

A final element not referred to by Bacon is the prison, a feature of rural locations but not so obvious at urban sites. The prison was a stock feature of many manors. Prisoners were gathered to await the dispensation of justice, particu-

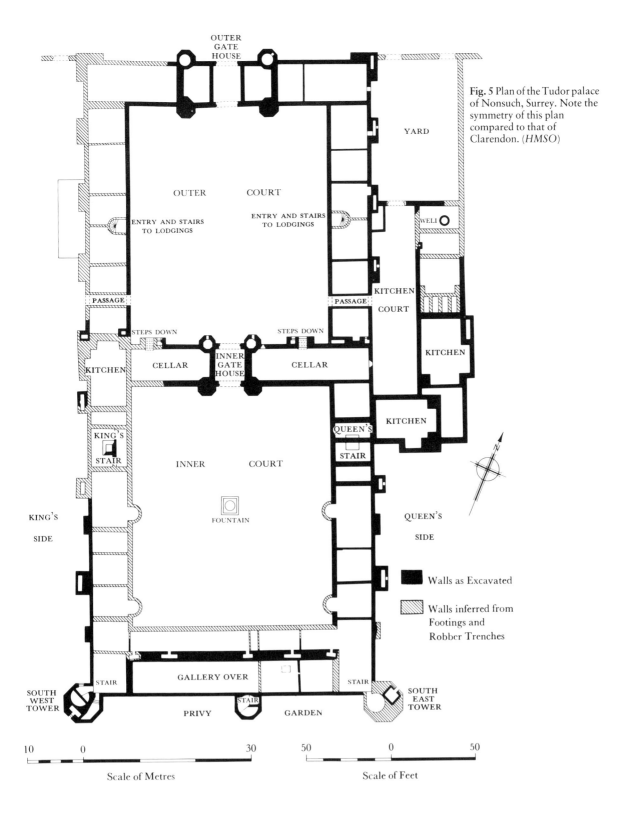

Fig. 5 Plan of the Tudor palace of Nonsuch, Surrey. Note the symmetry of this plan compared to that of Clarendon. (*HMSO*)

larly in the forest residences during the Norman and Angevin eras when forest offenders were numerous and harshly dealt with. However, prisons other than in castles have proved elusive in the archaeological record, and at the royal manor of Havering (Essex) there is no record of a prison until 1465 (McIntosh 1986, 67), although documents elsewhere refer to prisons much earlier, and it would therefore be surprising if there had been no prison at Havering before the late fifteenth century, as profits of justice were a major element in royal and manorial finance.

The entrance to great buildings was always symbolic and significant, at least from Roman times onwards, and became increasingly so in the later Middle Ages. With the improvement of artillery in the fourteenth century and subsequently, full-scale artillery defences became prohibitively expensive. Builders provided several-stage entrance towers in fashionable brick, to impress as much as to defend. Remarkable survivals are to be seen from the late fifteenth century at Bishop Waynflete's residence at Esher (Surrey) and at Layer Marney (Essex), and although still impressive enough the entrance towers at Hampton Court have now lost their upper stages. In concert with palace entrances, ceremonial façades were always important, especially on major religious buildings where the bonds of Church and state might be displayed. So the Norman kings wore their crowns on major ecclesiastical festivals, and the now-vanished westworks of Winchester Cathedral have been suggested by Martin Biddle as a possible platform for such crown-wearings before the people. The northern entrance of Westminster Abbey, designed for the monarch's use and modelled on that of Amiens Cathedral, facing the city of London and adjacent to the palace, is as impressive as any in England from the Gothic era. At Wells (Somerset) the combination of a spacious episcopal palace and superb western cathedral façade was designed to bolster the image of the bishop.

Explicit links between Church and state were expressed in royal palaces in various ways. Proximity to a monastery was important for leading palaces. In France the association between royal palace and the abbey of St Denis, which became a royal mausoleum, was fundamental. At Edinburgh the palace and abbey share the name Holyrood, and also in Scotland the abbey of Scone, where the kings of Scotland were 'set upon the stone' and acclaimed king, lay adjacent to the royal city of Perth, although divided from the city by the river Tay. In England, as already shown, Edward the Confessor's abbey, rebuilt by Henry III and his successors in the thirteenth and fourteenth centuries, and the palace lay adjacent outside the walls of the city.

Royal residences had a multiplicity of chapels where members of the royal family, household and servants might worship. By the thirteenth century separate chapels for the king, the queen, religious orders serving them and others on the site were a regular feature of major residences. The higher the status of the user, the higher the status of the chapel, as at St Stephen's chapel at Westminster, remodelled in the late thirteenth century on the recently built royal chapel of La Sainte Chapelle in France. The great chapels were on two levels, including a chapel for the royal family and a chapel for the household. This meant in practice a gallery and separate entrance for the family, as now seen at Hampton Court, although it could mean an upper chapel and an undercroft, as in St Stephen's chapel. Private devotions were as important as communal worship:

kings and queens attended their own personal chapels in their apartments, as well as appearing at public services. Compared with royalty and the church-men, the nobility tend to have created fewer chapels at their residences. With the chapels of royalty and nobility, the dedications, decor and the religious enthusiasms they signal, are as yet poorly understood, and blithe references to 'favourite' saints and biblical events used in dedications, wall paintings and painted glass windows obscure this lack of understanding.

In common with developments in domestic architecture in general in the period from 1050 to 1550, palaces became increasingly subdivided with more small and private chambers. The chapel arrangements described above under-line this trend. Separate suites for the queen, for royal children, and for senior courtiers increase from the twelfth century. Particular buildings were provided for particular purposes. When Henry II decided to create private accommoda-tion for his mistress Rosamund Clifford near the palace of Woodstock, the building which materialised was designed along Moorish or Sicilian lines with interconnecting pools. It is mere speculation to suggest that the king might have had in mind an embryonic eastern harem, but if he had he would not have been the only western medieval ruler to enjoy such an arrangement. The ex-traordinary Hohenstaufen emperor Frederick II (d. 1250) combined eastern and western cultures to an unprecedented degree in his court in Sicily, where he not only did have a harem, but also kept his official records in Arabic, Latin and German. When Henry VI became mentally ill while at Clarendon in 1453, a special kitchen may have been provided, built of brick adjacent to his suite, where meals could be prepared for him. However, the community based on the great hall began to disperse to smaller rooms to eat and to socialise as the Middle Ages progressed, although halls continued to provide general sleeping accommodation (page 171).

Sanitary arrangements and water supply improved little in our period. King and peasant alike relied on well-water or, provided their means permitted, could enjoy wine or beer, cider or perry to drink. Sanitary arrangements centred on the earth privy, or the garderobe tower with a chute into a moat or down a hillside. Disposal of food remains and other rubbish, in the period be-fore the ravages of plague focused men's minds on hygiene after 1350, was usu-ally in pits in the immediate vicinity of the kitchens, as at Clarendon. But here discoveries of kitchen refuse in a variety of different places across the site may indicate that opportunities to reorder the site included relocation of kitchens.

This study is devoted to the period from Edward the Confessor (1042–66) to the Reformation age, and ends with the death of Henry VIII in 1547. It has been persuasively argued that the Viking raids stifled the development of Romanesque architecture in England *c.* 1000. Although the reign of the Danish King Canute (1016–35) restored calm, his architectural inspiration was from overseas, for example from the palace of Conrad II at Goslar (Germany), which was begun in 1025. Thus there seems to have been a clear break in the development of English Romanesque after the tenth century. This gives heightened significance to the reign of Edward the Confessor when the rapid development of English architecture began again, and was carried on after the Conquest of 1066. This renewed flowering of English architecture grew from

Fig. 6 Edward the Confessor's palace at Westminster, as depicted in the Bayeux Tapestry. It was shown so close to the abbey that a ladder could join the two structures. The man on the ladder symbolises the completion of the abbey by placing a weather cock on the roof

continental and not from English roots (Gem 1975, *passim*). Edward the Confessor's work at Westminster, a palace to which he was obviously attached, set that Thames-side residence on the road to becoming the focus for the government of England for over 950 years. Although better known now as the home of parliament, the Palace of Westminster remains a premier royal possession today. Thus, for example, the parliamentarians who use the Palace of Westminster are not allowed personalised notepaper, for they are allowed the use of Westminster Palace only by the grace and favour of the monarch.

No standing remains of pre-Conquest palaces survive in England, although the Bayeux tapestry gives a picture of what the palace of Edward the Confessor (1042–66) at Westminster might have been like (*see* Fig. 6). However, there are legacies of Norman palaces, for example the castle-palace at the Tower of London and William Rufus's great hall at Westminster. Fragmentary remains of palaces throughout the remainder of the Middle Ages are still to be found, often scattered through the countryside: a small section of wall of Henry I's hall at Dunstable (Bedfordshire) survives as part of a barn, and part of the water system laid down by Henry II for Rosamund at Everswell (Oxfordshire) can be found in the park at Blenheim. The ruins of Clarendon lie overgrown in a Wiltshire wood, but other palaces have entirely disappeared, such as the Black Prince's palace at Kennington now recorded only in a street name, although excavations did much to elucidate the site before it was built over (Dawson 1976). The palace at Kings Langley was lost until excavations in 1962 revealed some remains: it was not until workers on a major building programme accidentally stumbled across the site in 1970 that more of the palace was discovered (Neal 1971, 31).

Remains of bishops' residences can be found, for example at Amberley (Sussex) in the Chichester diocese, and ruins of the Archbishop of York's palace at Southwell (Nottinghamshire). No gazetteer which identifies standing remains and sites of medieval episcopal residences has been compiled. Surviving elements of some medieval bishops' palaces have been put to new uses: the archbishop's former palace at Canterbury is in part used by a boys' school, and the ruins of his palace at Mayfield (Sussex) have been partially restored as a convent. The episcopal and later royal palace at Eltham in south east

London is the headquarters of the Army Education Corps. Almost all the remains of London residences of medieval royalty, higher clergy and nobility have long since been swept away, but again portions occasionally survive, such as the superb chapel of the medieval bishops of Ely at St Etheldreda's Ely Place, or the gable end and fine rose window of the bishop of Winchester's formerly huge palace at Southwark, which was later converted into the 'Clink' jail (*see* Fig. 7). Not infrequently bishops' palaces still survive on or adjacent to their medieval sites, as at Lambeth (London) and Wolvesey (Winchester).

Fig. 7 The surviving gable end of the great hall of Winchester House, Southwark, the Bishop of Winchester's London residence on the south side of the Thames. The high rose window was designed to gather light from above the roofs of adjacent buildings. (*Photograph John Steane*)

At the end of the period with which we are concerned, the reign of Henry VIII (1509–47) ushered in Renaissance palace styles at Hampton Court and Nonsuch as well as elsewhere. The former survives remarkably intact, but Nonsuch has almost entirely vanished, as has the once huge brick palace at Otford (Kent), amongst many others. It was the Reformation in concert with the acquisitive nature of Henry VIII, whose father had inherited such a depleted palace stock, which changed the face of the medieval Church. As head of the Church, Henry VIII had power over bishops and their possessions which his predecessors (such as Henry III, who struggled for four years to prevent Bishop Ralegh establishing himself at Winchester, page 88) constrained by papal power would have envied. The Tudor king exercised this power to the full. The bishops' residences were often palatial and, unlike many royal and noble buildings, had remained in the care of a single institution over several centuries. They therefore form a dominant group of palaces throughout the Middle Ages. Thus, although the reign of the Confessor is a useful starting point and the Reformation a useful end point for this investigation, the period has a unity in the fragmentary nature of the evidence and the knowledge of history and architecture and archaeology which is necessary to recreate the world of medieval palaces.

Chapter II
Traditions and Normans (1042–1154)

The topic of palaces and palace life before the Norman Conquest is a large one, and no more than an outline sketch is possible here. Francis Bacon alludes to one of the many palaces mentioned in the Bible, that of King Ahasuerus (i.e. Xerxes I of Persia, 486–465 BC), in the Book of Esther. In his palace of Shushan the king, enthroned, entertained foreign dignitaries and his own servants at a great feast amidst the splendour of gold and silver tableware and brightly coloured wall hangings which offset the patterned marble floor. Further tables were set in the palace gardens. Such a scene might readily find a parallel in medieval England, except that possiblities of entertaining outside in England were somewhat limited by inclement weather, although even today royal garden parties remain a feature of the summer social programme, allowing for the entertainment of large numbers of people.

The term 'palace' is derived from the Palatine Hill where the Emperor Augustus had his grand dwelling, and which came to be an area noted for its great houses. In the Roman empire the term palace came to have a meaning which transcended mere buildings, for the palace in this sense was wherever the emperor and his household were. Their very presence converted the surroundings into a palace. This general meaning carries through into the Middle Ages to bind together disparate types of places where kings, nobles and bishops happened to be: some of these residences retained the title 'palace' even when not in use. The palaces of Rome were mirrored elsewhere in the empire, a notable example being the first-century Roman palace at Fishbourne (Sussex). The reasons why one of the largest palaces outside Rome, perhaps excepting only the palace of Diocletian at Split, should have been built on the south coast of England, remain obscure. Excavations have shown the exceptional extent of Fishbourne palace, but there is little documentary evidence to help unravel the mystery. The style and decoration of Fishbourne, courtyards with open walkways surrounded by airy audience chambers with mosaic floors and so on, was essentially Mediterranean in concept, transplanted to England (Cunliffe 1971, 151). With the help of documents linked with standing remains and below-ground archaeology we can speak with much more certainty about palaces of England which were created after the Roman and Saxon eras. The link with Fishbourne is that much of the inspiration for medieval palaces in England was also Mediterranean or Continental in origin and, as at Fishbourne, not always well suited to the English climate (page 172).

In the wreck of the western empire following the barbarian invasions which culminated in the sack of Rome in 410, the popes continued the Roman tradition of palaces, first in Ravenna and then once more in Rome. As the popes led, the bishops followed. Administrative responsibility, formerly in the hands of imperial officials, now fell to churchmen. The comparative stability of the

Church and the inalienability of its lands provided a solid foundation of settled residences and steady income built up over many centuries providing sufficient wealth to create palaces throughout western Christendom. By the ninth century the papal palace enclave of St John Lateran in Rome had developed into a small town, from which the popes ran the western Church, seeing themselves as the legitimate heirs and successors of the Roman emperors (*see* Fig. 8). It was here, in Rome, on Christmas day 800 that Pope Leo III (795–816) recreated the western empire with the coronation of Charlemagne as Emperor. The significance of these events for the historians of palaces is that the pope had the substance of the agreement with Charlemagne enshrined in the decor of his palace: mosaics depicted St Peter handing a standard to Charlemagne and a *pallium* (papal cloak) to the pope. This element of documentation, even propaganda, is a continuing feature of palace decor. In the great hall of Winchester castle in 1522 Henry VIII welcomed Charles V, the Holy Roman Emperor. On entering the building the visitors saw King Arthur's round table hanging on the wall (*see* Fig. 69). The bearded monarch depicted as Arthur on the table was none other than Henry himself. The frail Tudor dynasty drew strongly on the long-established Arthurian legend to bolster its image with the visiting emperor.

As Rome declined Constantinople became the greatest Christian city, resplendent with palaces which dazzled visitors from northern Europe, In the late tenth century Liudprand of Cremona was despatched from Italy as an ambassador to Constantinople. He observed that in contrast to western bishops, those in the east were not stately prelates possessed of palaces and great admin-

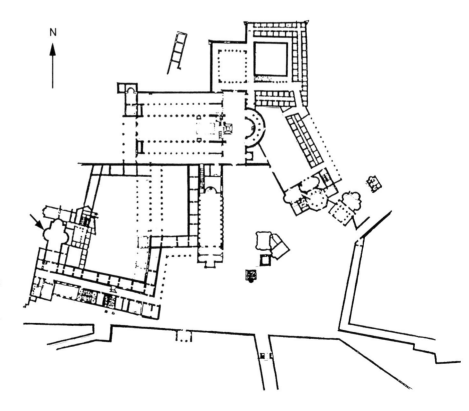

Fig. 8 Plan of the palace complex of St John Lateran in Rome, showing the basilica and domestic accommodation including the great banqueting hall or triclinium (arrowed) added in the eighth century. Across the Tiber, outside the ancient city, the Vatican palace developed subsequently out of the late fifteenth-century Belvedere pleasure villa.

istrative powers. In the east, bishops had little by way of luxuries, few servants and lived humbly (Mango 1980, 49). Nonetheless, in Constantinople Liudprand saw a most impressive display of imperial status. Protocol was of the utmost importance and a spectacular display of machines enhanced the emperor's dignity. The bright flash of insight which Liudprand provides into a great palace of the post-Roman era is quite splendid. The palace itself was called 'Fresh Breeze' and was of 'remarkable size and beauty'. Before the emperor's seat there was a tree whose branches were filled with birds, both tree and birds being made of gilded bronze. The birds had different songs according to their species. The throne itself was 'so marvellously fashioned that at one moment it seemed a low structure, and at another it rose high into the air. It was of immense size and was guarded by lions, made either of bronze or wood covered over with gold, who beat the ground with their tails and gave a dreadful roar with open mouth and quivering tongue'. As Liudprand entered the emperor's presence, supported by two eunuchs, the birds began to cry out and the lions to roar. The ambassador had fortunately discovered in advance about these potentially disturbing creatures, and so was not afraid. Lying face down to make obeisance, he lifted his head to find that the throne, which had formerly been moderately elevated, had disappeared up to the ceiling rendering the emperor (now in different clothes) too distant for polite conversation, so an intermediary was introduced to carry messages. Liudprand speculates, with western practicality, that the device used to raise the throne was similar to that used in the west 'for raising the timbers of a wine press' (Wright 1930, 207–8). Perhaps the noise of the winding gear was drowned by the singing birds and roaring lions. Liudprand was clearly impressed by this eastern magic which he describes as 'marvellous and unheard of'. The extravagant mechanical gadgetry seen by Liudprand, together with mosaics inside and fountains outside were aspects of conspicuous consumption which characterised palaces from antiquity onwards. Mechanical gadgets seem to have had eastern origins, and when they did appear in western Europe in Artois around 1300, the inspiration came from an Arabic text (page 94).

Mosaics, such as those in Rome, were less common although not unknown north of the Alps: fine examples have been discovered in sixth and seventh-century contexts at a bishop's palace in Geneva, and in episcopal residences in the south of France. It is possible to argue that the floor tiles of medieval Europe are a degeneration of the mosaicist's art, which can be traced directly from Rome. Wall painting was a familiar feature of the decoration of northern palaces, and reference to it is found in abundance in the records of medieval English palaces. From Roman times onwards statuary was significant to remind visitors of the dignity of palace dwellers. Thus the links with the Roman empire as inherited by Charlemagne were illustrated for all to see at his palace at Aachen by a statue of a wolf. Towards 1400 Richard II had a series of statues of monarchs sculpted to adorn his refurbished Westminster Hall (*see* Fig. 9). Like the wolf at Aachen, these statues of thirteen of his predecessors, presumably going back to the Confessor, emphasised the antiquity of his line and so the legitimacy of his royal authority (Alexander and Binski 1987, 515).

As the Middle Ages progressed, various European influences can be detected in English palaces. Roman influence, either direct or through romanised

Fig. 9 Statues of kings from the Richard II series in Westminster Hall, carved in Chilmark stone from Wiltshire. (*HMSO*)

Mediterranean countries, and eastern influence, whether Byzantine or Arabic and filtered through Spain, both contributed to the development of medieval English palaces. A third influence in northern Europe came from the Germanic peoples. The Germanic tradition bred the great hall, not found in southern Europe or the east. William Rufus's great hall at Westminster, as perhaps the largest hall of the time in Europe and the largest medieval hall built in England, is particularly important, combining the role of administrative centre and ceremonial and communal hall throughout the Middle Ages (page 35). There were not only differences in the structures that were central to the élite of the Germanic peoples, but also in the uses to which they were put in general and in detail. The high table in the great hall which separated the warrior élite from others even in the communal hall was a feature of northern rather than southern European palace life. At the table, Germanic peoples sat, where Romans and Byzantines had reclined. Influence of one kind and another did not just flow northwards in Europe. The barbarian invasions and the power of the Germanic peoples had their effect on southern Europe. Already by the time of Liudprand of Cremona's visit to Constantinople, old southern European ways were giving way to new northern ones. Liudprand noted that for the important Christmas feast at the 'palace of the nineteen couches' the Emperor of Constantinople and his guests unusually reclined in the old manner rather than sitting at the table which was then common practice even in Constantinople (Wright 1930, 209).

Unlike France, where the Capetian dynasty, established in 987, survived in unbroken male succession until 1328, England was dogged by unsettled succession, invasion and civil war for several generations before the Normans imposed their rule in 1066. Indeed after the Conquest no eldest son actually succeeded his father on the throne until Henry III succeeded John in 1216. Uncertainty in the decades before 1066, and especially the Viking raids, *c.* 1000, took their toll of the development of English architecture. Although the Danish King Canute (1016–35) did much to restore order, and strengthened the Germanic influence on English building, the break between Saxon and Norman building in England, and the traditions on which they drew, are nevertheless more strikingly contrasted and make a clear break with the past by the mid-eleventh century (pages 21–2).

Although there are no standing structures left, palace life was already well established in England before the Conquest of 1066. Winchester, Westminster and Gloucester boasted Saxon royal palaces, known from documentary sources. Nor should it be thought that pre-Conquest courts were necessarily poor affairs, for when William the Conqueror revisited Normandy to enjoy celebratory feasts in the aftermath of the Conquest of England, those who had stayed behind in the duchy were astonished at the gold and silver tableware, the fine metalwork and at the embroidery which had been captured in England and which was being used for ostentatious display at banquets (Douglas 1964, 209).

The royal treasury was at Winchester from the tenth century but Edward the Confessor particularly favoured Westminster. The origins of the palace at Westminster remain obscure: claims that it was begun by Canute, whose son Harold was buried there, remain unproven (Lethaby 1906, 131). Edward the Confessor built the abbey, which probably replaced an earlier church on the site. The existence of the new abbey church restricted the area available to the palace buildings to a strip of inhospitable and marshy land beside the river. The development of the palace outside the city to the west may have been a result of the abandonment of a site within the north-western Bassishaw area of the city of London. There may have been a dispute with the ever more powerful Londoners which drove the Saxon royal house out, but we do not know (Schofield 1984, 29–30). Archaeology has much to tell about the origins and development of Westminster palace, but to date the excavation history of this prime site has been unfortunate.

Excavation has, however, revealed much about two rural pre-Conquest palace sites, the massive structures of the court of the seventh-century kings of Northumbria at Yeavering, and the ninth-century Saxon palace at Cheddar (Somerset). Yeavering was within a defended enclosure, Cheddar was undefended. Philip Rahtz, the excavator of Cheddar, refers to the possibility of other Saxon palace sites identified from aerial photographs at Hatton Rock, near Stratford-upon-Avon (Warwickshire), at Atcham (Shropshire) and elsewhere (Rahtz 1979, 2). Other Saxon royal residences such as King Harold's with its over-hall at Bosham (Sussex), shown in the Bayeux tapestry (*see* Fig. 10), and another first floor hall at Calne (Wiltshire), which collapsed while the Witan was in session, hint at a variety of Saxon hall types, including ground floor and first floor halls. The Saxon kings had a residence at Woodstock, while the description of Clarendon as 'ancient demesne' in the Domesday Book (1086), suggests that this site also had belonged to the Normans' predecessors, although archaeology has yet to provide evidence of Saxon occupation on either site. Germanic and Nordic tradition led to the construction of Saxon domestic structures in wood, a tradition which began to give way after the Norman Conquest to stone buildings as Norman builders, influenced by their transition to France from Scandinavia, were more familiar with stone.

Fig. 10 Harold's over-hall at Bosham, Sussex shown in the Bayeux Tapestry. It appears as a rather cramped affair when compared to William's spacious residence, which is specifically referred to as a palace.

The victory at Hastings in October 1066 brought the old Saxon kingdom into the hands of the Normans. Symbolically, on Christmas day that year William was crowned king in Edward the Confessor's abbey church at Westminster. The new king was presented to the people both in English and French, but the ceremony nearly descended into chaos as a result. Mercenary troops surrounding the abbey, hearing and misunderstanding the shouts of acclamation, feared a riot and began to set fire to neighbouring buildings before calm was restored.

The king and the Norman lords of England, confronted by many threats both from within and without the kingdom, needed to establish themselves in their new lands. Their military power was displayed through the violent Conquest and subsequent harrying of the land, supported by the construction of castles, a new concept in England. Another creation was a hugely enlarged royal estate estimated to have amounted to a third of the whole country, which gave William his reputation for avarice. The conquerors wished to maintain continuity with the past: William I (1066–87) promised, for example, to rule according to the laws of Edward the Confessor, whose heir he claimed to be. The Anglo-Saxon church survived in many respects but was reorganised by the appointment of Norman bishops who initiated an unprecedented programme of cathedral building. The royal family, ecclesiastical and lay lords required residences commensurate with their newly acquired power. New men were rewarded for their service to the king with grants of land and important positions. From these beginnings post-Conquest palace life arose.

William the Conqueror did not capture London. Its citizens decided in December 1066 to allow him into their city after due deliberation. The acquiescence of London was crucial to William's survival as a monarch, as indeed it was to so many of his successors. The populous city constituted a continuing threat to William's small forces. The new king established a strongpoint in the south-east corner of the old Roman defences, probably at first a fortified bailey construction, maybe without a motte or mound. These makeshift defences gave way to that most famous Norman builder-bishop Gundulf's keep, the Tower of London, which is traditionally although uncertainly dated to 1078. Over the centuries the Tower was considerably extended, but the original White Tower, begun in the Conqueror's reign, remains the centrepiece (Allen Brown and Curnow 1984, 9).

The Tower served the dual function of providing an awesome military base, and palatial accommodation for the king and his family (*see* Fig. 11). Undoubtedly the Tower was amongst the largest structures of its kind in medieval Europe, a fine example of feudal, or even colonial, building on a grand scale. It may have derived from Carolingian palaces of the Frankish kings through the tenth century tower keep of the Norman dukes at Rouen (Allen Brown and Curnow 1984, 9). It would not be surprising if the Tower were larger than the long-demolished Rouen keep, as English cathedrals and abbeys outstripped in scale their models in Normandy. Even so the Tower was somewhat smaller than the remarkably similar castle at Colchester, which may also have been Gundulf's work.

Fig. 11 The formidable exterior of the White Tower at the Tower of London. (*Photograph John Steane*)

The White Tower was originally built mainly of Kentish ragstone rubble, with ashlar details of Caen stone (Allen Brown and Curnow 1984, 60). Caen stone had the dual advantages of being familiar to the Norman builders and was easily brought from France to the site by boat. Its rich creamy texture has deservedly earned its title 'the stone of kings'. The Romanesque arcading of the second floor exterior extravagantly distinguishes the upper palatial accommodation from the largely defensive lower floor. The suite included a hall, chamber, garderobes and chapel.

The apsidal chapel, dedicated to St John, which is constructed in two stages, still exists much as it did in the late eleventh century (*see* Fig. 12). The splendid Romanesque columns show a mixture of influences in their capitals. Parallels are well drawn with Westminster Abbey, begun by Edward the Confessor, and the same masons may have worked on both the abbey and the Tower. Just as the contemporary castle chapel at Winchester revealed characteristic Saxon long and short-work on its quoins (Biddle 1973, pl. xxiia), so Germanic influences are visible in the Tau-cross capitals in the Tower chapel, reminiscent of cross-Conquest continuity and of the continental influences, which had such a profound effect on English palaces throughout the Middle Ages and beyond.

Fig. 12 Chapel of St John, Tower of London. Note the 'St Anthony' or 'Tau-cross' capitals. (*Copyright English Heritage*)

Fig. 13 Castle Acre, Norfolk as it might have appeared in the 1080s, an enclosed but unfortified noble's residence. (*Drawing by Richard Warmington, Copyright English Heritage*)

The hall, which once rose to the roof of the building, has been truncated by the insertion of an additional floor at the level of the original encircling mural gallery. The impressively high hall must have had a central hearth from which the smoke rose through roof-louvres. Nothing is now known of the Norman interior decoration of the White Tower, but it would have been coloured, probably richly so. The exterior, already enriched by use of pale Caen stone, may well have been painted white in Norman times, as it was to be in the thirteenth century. The Tower provides an excellent example of the early combination of defence and grand accommodation for the Norman kings. The Normans' military background is well reflected in the great castle-palace of the Tower.

Not all Norman lords lived in castles with halls integrated into the upper part of the structure, nor were all upper-floor halls found in castles. At Castle Acre, the Norfolk home of William de Warenne, Earl of Surrey (d. 1088), the earliest post-Conquest great hall was at ground level. The manor was not heavily defended, having only a slight bank round it (*see* Fig. 13). The building was no mean structure but was of palatial dimensions with a broad and impressive entrance, as excavation has revealed. Castle Acre was subsequently fortified on a grand scale. Similarly at Richmond in Yorkshire Alan the Red of Penthièvre, a close associate of the Conqueror, was probably the originator of the stone buildings still to be seen there. These include very substantial remains of a fine Romanesque hall, again built at ground level, separate from the stone keep and over a vaulted undercroft.

The Normans, as their Saxon predecessors had done, brought with them from the Continent new perspectives on royal living. Stone building has already been mentioned, but the Normans brought changes in scale as well as in building practice, with much larger structures than had hitherto been seen in England. The Norman great hall at Westminster, completed in 1099, is the sole survivor of its type from the eleventh century. Its dimensions, 240 ft in length by 67 ft 6 inches wide (73.2 m×20.6 m), made it the largest hall in England at this date, and probably the largest hall in Europe (Colvin 1963, 45). The only structures to rival it in ground plan must have been the naves of the cathedrals being erected at that period. It dwarfs the great Saxon halls at Yeavering and Cheddar (*see* Fig. 14). There is a significant discrepancy between the alignment of the east and west walls, which is possibly explained by the great hall having been constructed round a previous building, which may have remained *in situ* until the new work was completed. If this is so the former structures may have

Fig. 14 Plan of a) Westminster Hall compared to the Saxon royal halls at b) Yeavering in Northumberland and c) Cheddar in Somerset. (*Saxon halls after Brian Hope-Taylor and Philip Rahtz*)

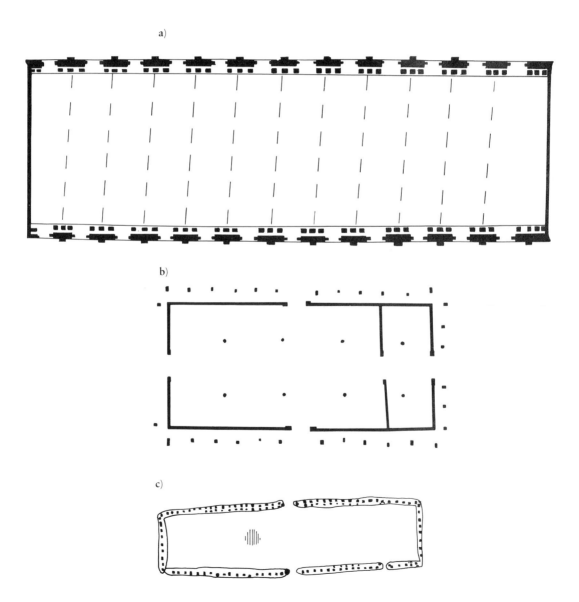

a)

b)

c)

been of similar ground area as the discrepancy is apparent from end to end of the hall, though more so towards the north end. The slightly boat-shaped ground plan of William Rufus's hall harked back to Viking and Saxon halls such as that at Cheddar; the plan at Westminster was possibly dictated by the building already in place on site (*see* Fig. 15); (Schofield 1984, 41). Hurried work was often the result of medieval royal building enthusiasms. William Rufus, in the matter of building, showed as much singlemindedness as his father had done in establishing control over England. In 1097 the Anglo-Saxon Chronicle complained that the harvest lay ungathered in counties owing to works at Westminster and the Tower, so heavy was the demand for building labour. Rufus probably completed both the hall at Westminster and the Tower. That both these great buildings have survived is a reminder that there were certain very positive elements in Rufus's generally ill-regarded reign.

Westminster Hall remained central to the administration of the government of England through many centuries, and has been the scene of many stirring events, such as the trial of Walter Raleigh in the seventeenth century. Perhaps Adam Smith came as close as anyone to visualising an original function of the hall. In *The Wealth of Nations* (1776) he paints a vivid picture of his perception of Westminster Hall as it might have been used in Rufus's day:

'Before the extension of commerce and manufacture in Europe, the hospitality of the rich and great, from the sovereign down to the smallest baron, exceeded everything which in the present times we can easily form a notion of. Westminster Hall was the dining-room of William Rufus and might frequently, perhaps, not be too large for his company.'

Fig. 15 A reconstruction drawing of the Westminster abbey and palace complex as it might have appeard in the late eleventh century. Rufus's hall dwarfs the buildings of the former Saxon palace, which are sited somewhat further from the abbey than the Bayeux Tapestry (Fig. 6) suggests. (*Drawing by Terry Ball and Richard Gem*)

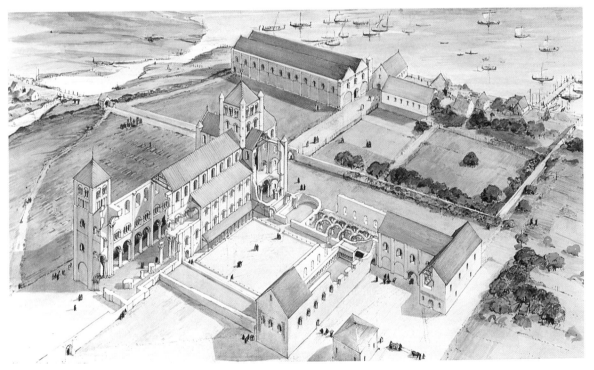

The surplus produced by an agricultural economy, as Smith explains, was used in medieval times to feed bountifully a multitude (of hundreds or thousands) not only of retainers and dependants, but also for the distribution of alms (as food or money) to paupers. In the consumption of the surplus victuals in 'rustic hospitality', his surmises are amply borne out by evidence from the reigns of Henry III and Edward I later in the Middle Ages (pages 169–70). Smith himself had seen such beneficence in highland chiefs in his lifetime. While no doubt an oversimplification, this acute observation by an eighteenth-century intellectual provides a bridge between the often sentimental idealisation of the Middle Ages by more recent writers, and the court of William Rufus itself where, amidst the return to long hair and tight clothes (seen by contemporaries as the outward signs of immorality), one contemporary observer remarked 'there was no unnatural vice which was not practised' (Barlow 1983, 99–103).

Little is known or can now be reconstructed of the interior decoration of the hall in its original form. The twelve bays, each with a window on the north and south side set in an arcaded gallery, have been established easily enough. The arcading supporting the roof may well have been of wood, analogous perhaps to the surviving vestiges of wooden pillars erected about 1138 by Henry of Blois at Farnham castle. There is plenty of contemporary evidence from ecclesiastical sites of Romanesque arcading of stone, although it is puzzling that no evidence of any such arcading has ever been recorded in any works on the floor of Westminster Hall, although Romanesque sculptured capitals from unknown locations within the hall are now to be seen on display in the Jewel Tower (Baines 1914, 4) (*see* Fig. 16). Within the wall passages (*see* Fig. 17) some indications of early paint schemes have been found. Red and blue colouring with black lines was discovered, which may be remnants of an interior

Fig. 16 Westminster Hall. Nineteenth-century drawing of a capital thought to be associated with Rufus's works. (*Brayley and Britton*)

Fig. 17 Westminster Hall. Detail of Romanesque wall passage arcades. (*Lethaby*)

decoration of bold and brilliant colours dating from the late eleventh century. Externally there were buttresses defining the bays and chequered stonework was set in place for decoration (*see* Fig. 17). The architecture of Rufus's day, durable though it clearly was, found little favour with a nineteenth-century observer who saw it as 'entirely uncommendable'. Such a judgement of a building which has truly stood the test of time seems harsh.

In the Middle Ages royal and ecclesiastical power went hand in hand. Medieval kings were pious men and a growth in the number of personal chapels from the eleventh century bears witness to private devotions. Edward the Confessor's love of religion was widely acknowledged in his own lifetime, and within a century of his death, partly due to miracles at his tomb, he was canonised in 1161 by Pope Alexander III. In 1163 at the translation of his body under the supervision of Archbishop Becket and in the presence of Henry II, the remains of the saint-king were found to be remarkably preserved, despite a century of burial. The warlike William the Conqueror was likewise a pious man, despite the violence displayed in his reign.

The religious basis of kingship was plainly apparent in the role of churchmen at the coronation. It was no accident that Edward the Confessor was crowned on Easter Day and the Conqueror on Christmas day, as Charlemagne had been, or that the most sumptuous state occasions and feasts in Norman England were the great crown-wearing ceremonies at royal and ecclesiastical centres at the major religious festivals of Christmas, Easter and Pentecost. These ceremonies coincided with gatherings of the great and influential. At Whitsun 1068, Queen Matilda was crowned at a major ceremony in Winchester. She was given an active role in the royal dominion (Douglas 1964, 249). This elevation of the queen was a change in the organisation of palace life after the Conquest, and may be associated with greater respect for the Church and so for institutions such as marriage in the eleventh century. The queens of England maintained this higher status throughout the Middle Ages. The contrast is striking with the unseemly coronation ceremony of the Saxon King Eadwy (955–59), in which the king retired to his chamber with two women in the midst of the ceremony, and had to be brought out again by senior churchmen. Similarly Eadwy's brother Edgar, a patron of the tenth-century reformation, misused a meeting with nuns who were forced to flee through monastic drains! Such distinctions between the Saxon and the Norman royal houses should not be drawn too firmly, for William the Conqueror's mother is said in one source to have been a court dancer found irresistible by the Conqueror's father, hence William's status and tag 'the Bastard'.

Despite such strong links and mutual dependence, particularly in the light of the eleventh-century reformation under Pope Gregory VII from 1073, Church and State entered a period of conflict and competition. In the immediate post-Conquest period, however, Norman kings rewarded their followers with rich sees taken from their Saxon predecessors. The establishment of Norman royal and ecclesiastical hegemony ushered in an unprecedented boom in building. Alongside the mighty cathedrals of Norman England, such as Winchester, Old Sarum and Durham, royal and ecclesiastical palaces grew up to provide imposing and fashionable residences for the new masters of State and Church. Archbishops and bishops rivalled royalty and nobility in the standard of life they enjoyed.

In order to establish their power over State and Church and to view the lands they had gained and must now administer, Norman kings, nobles and prelates were indefatigable travellers. The restless mobility of the Norman kings is legendary. For example, in 1072 the Conqueror travelled to Scotland and brought King Malcolm to terms at Abernethy (Fife); he also toured his Norman possessions as well as spending time at hunting lodges and elsewhere in England. This mobility required a variety of places in which to stay. The greatly extended royal demesne lands provided at once a spread of properties through the land, while the demesne estates surrounding these properties provided produce to supply the travellers' needs.

Riding from place to place required considerable strength and stamina, which these kings possessed in abundance in the prime of life. It was less uncomfortable to go from place to place on horseback than to travel in unsprung wagons or 'chariots'. Familiarity with horses and skill in the saddle encouraged sports which involved riding. The Norman kings are quite rightly associated with hunting. Brill in Buckinghamshire had been built by Edward the Confessor as a base from which to hunt in Bernwood forest. Other hunting lodges such as Brigstock (Northamptonshire), Cheddar (Somerset) and Woodstock (Oxfordshire), inherited from the Saxons, also provided respite from the cares of state, and remind us that hunting was a popular pastime in pre-Conquest England. These sites together with Alveston (Gloucestershire), Brampton (Cambridgeshire), Clarendon, Dunstable (Bedfordshire), King's Cliffe (Northamptonshire), Kinver (Staffordshire) and Odiham (Hampshire) were undefended sites under the Normans, and the widespread locations of these places indicate the increased scope of Norman demesne lands and forests.

It goes without saying that travelling on horseback, campaigning and hunting in similar manner, involved risks to life and limb. Therefore it is no surprise that the Conqueror himself died as a result of a riding accident, while his sons Rufus and Henry I both met their ends while involved in hunting expeditions. The Conqueror, by then a corpulent man, was fatally injured by the saddle of his horse, which stumbled in the ruins of Mantes in 1087. The news that the king lay dying spread quickly, and apart from those members of his family whom he had imprisoned and key officials such as Lanfranc, on duty in England and in any case very elderly, the court gathered. Many magnates were already on hand, taking part in the savage campaign in progress at the time.

The unexpected death of the king is a timely reminder of the value to courtiers of being at the king's side, however difficult and uncomfortable medieval travel might have been. However, William's eldest son, Robert, was in prison. William Rufus was given his father's sword, sceptre and crown, and departed to make sure of England, hearing en route of the king's death. Henry was bequeathed a substantial sum of money and left his father's deathbed to claim it. With the family and other senior men gone, the king was left in the hands of lesser men, who, Ordericus Vitalis tells us, behaved with great callousness towards him. They stole all the plate, linen and furniture they could carry. It is hinted they even robbed the corpse, leaving the remains of the great king 'almost naked on the floor of the cell' (Douglas 1964, 362). Thus the reign of William I, which had begun with a chaotic coronation, ended in a scene reminiscent of the marginalia of the Bayeux tapestry, which show bodies being stripped in the aftermath of the battle of Hastings.

The sum total of historical research over the years has revealed much circumstantial detail of the reigns of the Norman kings, as the account of the death of the Conqueror shows, to add to well known tales such as that of the sorry end of his son Rufus, whose remains were transported in a humble cart from the New Forest to Winchester for burial. The area of knowledge where much remains to be revealed is in the artefactual and architectural side of palace life and palace buildings at this period. Apart from the Tower, in any case incomplete at his death, the Norman buildings in which the burly King William I entertained in state in full regalia, accompanied by his diminutive wife (analysis of Matilda's bones reveal she was probably no more than four feet two inches tall), surrounded by his prelates and lords, are now lost to us. The site of the palace at Winchester, to the west of the present cathedral, originally built by the Saxons and extended in characteristic style by the Normans, is now only known in most general outline through the present topography of that area of the city, which may have been determined by the palace layout (Biddle 1973, 258). Part of a Norman column now embedded in an office wall is believed to be a remnant of the Norman palace, which was demolished in or about 1140.

The location of the royal palace at Gloucester is still less clear, although it is well known that it was in Gloucester at the Christmas gathering of king, court and counsellors in 1085 when 'deep discussion' took place and it was determined to embark on the compilation of the astonishingly detailed Domesday survey, completed in the following year. There had certainly been a hall at Gloucester in pre-Conquest days and this may have been the 'king's hall' later used by the Conqueror and his successors up to the early thirteenth century. This residence is generally believed to have been at Kingsholm in the royal manor of Barton to the north of the city (Colvin 1963, 43–4). The pre-Conquest form of the name and the distinction made in the documents between the king's hall and castle would seem to support this theory. There is clearly much to be discovered by future generations.

Henry I, who succeeded his brother William II in 1100, enjoyed a commendable reputation for his administrative efficiency from the moment of his coronation when he undertook to reform Rufus's unsatisfactory administrative practices. At least in theory, the court and household were to be informed a month in advance of the king's intentions for travel so that necessary arrangements could be made to feed and accommodate the royal party. The royal entourage was divided in the Middle Ages into permanent household (*domus*) and the extended household (*familia*). The size of the permanent royal household is difficult to determine, but seems to have been upwards of 100 people, perhaps 150, in the first half of the twelfth century (Given-Wilson 1986, 4–6). In view of later developments this was a small number.

Documentary evidence is a little more detailed from this time, providing insights into individual sites and their uses. We learn, for example, of a royal visit to Woodstock in 1110, in which year the park there was enclosed with a stone wall. One reason for this expenditure is not difficult to ascertain, for here in the park, we are told by William of Malmesbury, Henry had a collection of wild animals including lions, leopards, lynxes, camels and a porcupine sent to him by William of Montpelier (Marshall 1875, 21–3). Compared with the circumstantial detail of chronicles, administrative records are by their nature more prosaic, but are often at least as valuable. In particular the earliest financial, or pipe, roll survival of 1129–30 reveals a wide range of unfortified houses being used by the king. In addition to those half-dozen or so mentioned above (page 38), the royal residence at Aylesbury (Buckinghamshire) appears in the pipe roll. The pipe roll's tantalising information for just one year of the reign helps an understanding of the way the mobile court worked, fleshing out the administrative theory outlined above. Thus Henry moves round with his queen and household from Woodstock to Clarendon, amongst other places, in the wake of provisions sent ahead to await arrival. When at Clarendon he gives orders for the despatch elsewhere of venison, no doubt the product of the chase, and cheese (James and Robinson 1988, 4). That these rural residences were unfortified is an indication of the effective way in which the Normans had established peaceful rule in England. No doubt Henry I felt secure on his throne.

Like his predecessors, Henry moved round the country, not only enjoying the pleasures of the chase, but also transacting business as he went. For example, charters of his reign were dated at Brigstock (Northamptonshire), as they had been in Rufus's time, and at other residences away from London. Again, like his predecessors, Henry was much involved in Normandy, where he spent just under half of his thirty-five year reign. It is a further tribute to his organisational skill that matters in England went so smoothly for a king who was obliged to be absent so frequently. The rigours of the itinerary of a medieval king such as Henry I, and no doubt the added responsibility devolved on to officials, took their toll. The demise of Henry's chancellor, Arnulf, exemplifies this. During the Christmas court at Henry's favoured residence at Dunstable in 1122, Arnulf fell from his horse and suffered a painful death from his injuries. In the same year Henry was riding in the park at Woodstock accompanied by a retinue including Bishop Bloet of Lincoln. In the course of their ride the bishop suffered what appears to have been a stroke or heart attack and died on the spot. However, it was wise to attend royal gatherings, not only to support the king, but also to preserve position. In 1127 the long-running quarrel over precedence between the archbishops of Canterbury and York erupted at the Christmas court at Windsor. An unseemly affair took place in which Thurstan, the Archbishop of York, attempted to place the crown on the King's head to the detriment of Canterbury, and as a result York had his staff and crosier banished from the royal chapel.

Responsibilities in England, and after 1106 in Normandy as well, kept the king busily on the move and were very demanding of resources. Henry's reign is not noted for major royal residential building programmes. Such works which did occur in England at this time were carried through on their own behalf by the bishops, as will be shown below. A striking feature of Henry's domestic life, and a further contrast with that of his brother Rufus (who had none), is the number of children he fathered, twenty-four in all. Henry's offspring were by far the largest number of any ruler of England in the period which concerns us here. Of these two dozen children only three were legitimate issue, all by his first wife Maud (d. 1118), and one of these three died in infancy. Of the other two, Prince William would have inherited the crown but for his unexpected death, under the very eyes of his father, in the White Ship disaster during a stormy channel crossing in November 1120, a further reminder, if any were needed, of the hazards of medieval travel. It was claimed by contemporaries that the crew of the prince's ship had imbibed far too much before setting out. Although the widowed king married again in 1121, presumably to try for further male issue, none was forthcoming and his daughter Matilda remained his sole heir. On the matter of the illegitimate issue, nine sons and twelve daughters, although this must have arisen from Henry's tendency to promiscuity, the king's ceaseless travelling may have contributed to this unusual element of his reign. Certainly successors, especially King John, another notable traveller, enjoyed a similar reputation for womanising.

Ultimately, Henry was taken ill while hunting in Normandy in 1135 after flouting his doctors' advice to the contrary and eating lampreys. The combination of the lampreys and hunting was blamed for his death at Lyons-le-Forêt. It is just possible that the king paid the penalty of over-organisation, and his lampreys may have been ready too far in advance and so have poisoned him. The circumstances of the transportation of his remains across the Channel have been mentioned above: the body of Henry I joined the remains of his son William in the Channel.

Henry's sudden death brought to the throne Stephen, son of Henry's sister Adela. A legacy of the efficient reign of Henry I is a detailed description of the structure and function of his court, probably written by a senior official from Henry's time, no doubt to assist the new king who was unfamiliar with the sophisticated administrative systems of Norman England. This document gives an unrivalled insight into the royal household in the twelfth century. The basic officials who served the king were the chancellor, the most highly paid, responsible for the chancery (writing office) and royal chapel; stewards and master butler (food and drink); master chamberlain (chamber and finance) and constables (security and hunting). These arrangements reflect a broad range of tasks undertaken by household officials, a range which was to narrow considerably by 1300 (Given-Wilson 1986, 2). As it turned out Stephen had little opportunity to savour the finer points of administrative practice in his strife-torn reign. Indeed it is a monument to the effective organisation of the medieval government of England that despite anarchy, civil wars and usurpations, the civil service continued to function as well as it clearly did.

As a group the Norman kings were preoccupied at first with establishing their dynasty in England, then with the intractable problems of Normandy, under Henry I, and finally with civil war in Stephen's reign. After Rufus there seems to have been a decline in royal palace building. Throughout the first century of English feudalism, up to 1154, the higher clergy who had been rewarded with the sees of their Saxon predecessors served their Norman masters well in a wide variety of capacities. No less than the kings, and often on behalf of the Crown, the archbishops and bishops stand out as great builders in the Norman era. Amongst senior churchmen, certain individuals come into focus. Bishop Gundulf of Rochester's contribution to work on the Tower has already been mentioned (page 30). Gundulf was appointed to the see of Rochester in 1077 in the reign of William I. He outlived the Conqueror and the building of Rochester castle under his supervision during the reign of William Rufus epitomises the way in which the finest builders of the age served successive monarchs, so ensuring continuity. Interestingly, despite his experience of building on a grand scale at the Tower, Gundulf's work at Rochester is different in type and form. Instead of making a payment of £100 to be confirmed in his possessions at Rufus's accession, Gundulf undertook to provide a castle for the king at Rochester. By constructing a stone enclosure for £60 rather than a tower keep, Gundulf used his skills to the utmost, saving money for himself and providing the king with the defences he demanded (Allen Brown 1969, 8). These defences, notably, were first brought into play not against the English, but against insurgent Normans. These invaders, led by the Conqueror's eldest son Robert Curthose and by his half-brother Bishop Odo, sought to reunify England and Normandy by dispossessing Rufus.

Church and palace building often went hand in hand. William Giffard, made Bishop of Winchester in 1100 but not consecrated until 1107, is a prime example of a man who combined palace building with cathedral building in his diocese. Excavations at Winchester suggest that it was Giffard who re-established the great complex at Wolvesey, the former island site, which has been a principal residence of the bishops of Winchester for 1,000 years. Before becoming Bishop of Winchester, Giffard had been chancellor to William Rufus in the years 1093–4. It is therefore perhaps significant that Giffard's west range at Wolvesey alone rivalled Rufus's mighty Westminster Hall in the scale of its plan, although apparently there was no hall constructed in this west range. It has been argued that the Saxon hall was still in use when Giffard began work at Wolvesey. Indeed it is quite possible that the eastern range, uncertainly attributed at present to Henry of Blois, Giffard's successor, may also have been Giffard's work, his previous association with Westminster and the lack of a hall in the new west range supporting this argument (*see* Fig. 18). In the east range a mighty hall with a gallery was constructed. This hall was, in Martin Biddle's words, 'a true hall, a place of gathering, not merely for feeding and sleeping large numbers of retainers but for meeting and ceremonial'. The hall within the east range was 88 ft×29 ft (26.8 m×8.8 m) (Biddle 1986, 9).

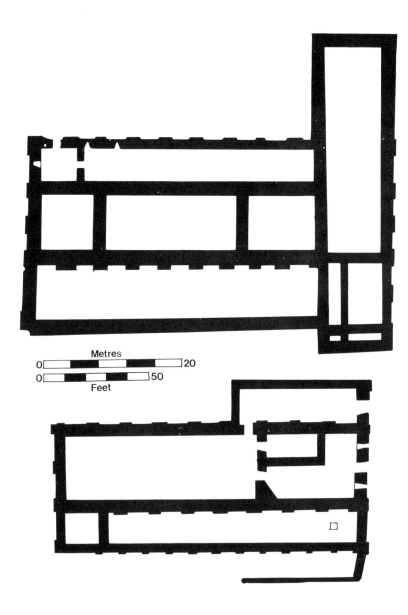

Fig. 18 Wolvesey. West and east ranges. (*After Biddle*)

As his predecessor, William Walkelin (1070–98) had done, Bishop Giffard made considerable contributions to the cathedral fabric at Winchester. From the early twelfth century comes the fine work on the tower and transepts, rebuilt after a collapse in 1107 (attributed by some to the presence within the cathedral of the body of the evil Rufus). The work on the cathedral is hailed as amongst the finest Romanesque ashlar work in the land, and its attribution to the great building era of this bishop's episcopate is a further demonstration of Giffard's energy and skill. At Southwark, then in the Winchester diocese, Giffard created a major residence for himself south of the Thames (Kingsford 1916–20, 57). This notion of a London residence was emulated by every other bishop in the land, and by many nobles besides. Winchester House, as it became known, was developed by subsequent bishops in its park of some seventy acres (28 ha.), and some ruins still survive (*see* Fig. 7). Recent excavations at Witney (Oxfordshire) have shown that the buildings on that manor of the bishops of Winchester date almost certainly in their original form from Giffard's episcopate (*see* Fig. 19).

A contemporary of Giffard's in the neighbouring diocese of Old Sarum was Roger of Caen. Bishop Roger's career mirrored that of Giffard. He had been a chief justiciar, treasurer and chancellor of England and was appointed to Old Sarum in 1102 although, like Giffard, he was not consecrated until 1107. He inherited a ruinous cathedral and set about the major task of rebuilding it and providing suitable accommodation for himself and his household. Until his equivocal part in the civil war led to his deprivation and his subsequent death in 1139 on the orders of King Stephen, Bishop Roger was a prodigious builder. As local materials were unfamiliar to him, he preferred to import stone from his native Caen for his builders. The cathedral plan also came from Caen, from the classic Romanesque Abbaye aux Dames.

With royal permission Bishop Roger rebuilt the castle at Old Sarum. The complex he extended there included two halls, one for his palace and one for the castle which he also occupied, as well as extensive ranges of other buildings. The hall within the castle was a simple structure without the buttery, pantry and kitchen accommodation which would be expected in a hall designed for entertainment. This may have been the business hall. The hall, with attendant suite of necessary rooms, was found at Old Sarum across the courtyard from the cathedral (HMSO 1922, 13). Although Roger's work at Old Sarum survives today only in plan, some impression of his building enthusiasm can be gained from a reconstruction drawing (*see* Fig. 20) based on the remains surviving at Sherborne where he built another castle, as he did also at Malmesbury and Devizes. Roger of Caen's exceptionally fine work matched that of Giffard at Winchester (*see* Fig. 22). William of Malmesbury was inspired to say of Roger's building that it appeared to be carved out of a single stone. This indi-

Fig. 19 The Romanesque ruins of Witney palace, Oxfordshire as they stood, largely intact, in the eighteenth century. (*Copyright Bodleian Library*)

Fig. 20 The bishop's palace at Old Sarum, Wiltshire as it might have appeared in the twelfth century. (*Drawing by Alan Sorrell. Copyright English Heritage*)

cates the improvements in stone building techniques which had occurred by the early twelfth century. The mason's craft had developed, partly through practice and partly through contacts with the greatest builders of that era, the Arabs, brought about by the crusades. For Bishop Roger's projects stones were cut at Caen, and transported by ship and cart to their destination.

While these works were in progress in the neighbouring diocese, Giffard was

succeeded in 1129 at Winchester by Henry of Blois, a grandson of the Conqueror, who had already been Abbot of Glastonbury since 1126. Henry's brother Stephen was to become king in 1135. After some preliminary work on the water supply, Henry of Blois concentrated his main efforts (if indeed they were his efforts and not Giffard's) at Wolvesey on the eastern range. The splendid hall created by Giffard and Henry of Blois with its two-storey chamber block has parallels in France at Rheims and Paris, but also more close at hand in Bishop Roger's ranges of buildings at Old Sarum, no doubt also derived from continental models. The courtyard surrounded by the buildings is found both in the episcopal arrangements at Old Sarum and at Wolvesey (*see* Fig. 22). Such courtyard arrangements perhaps provided a key to the layout at Wolvesey. On the other hand the monastic cloister provides a plan, and on the other hand the defensive and enclosed nature of the castle provides a further template. Wolvesey is perhaps an amalgam of both these ideas, for while the monastery is a general source from which the unfortified episcopal palace flowed, considerations of defence were important both to the Norman bishops of the Conquest era and also to their successors who experienced the twelfth-century civil war between Stephen and Matilda. The bishop's places at both Old Sarum and Wolvesey made concessions to defence, and both Roger of Caen and Henry of Blois were elsewhere noted castle builders.

Such great ecclesiastical statesmen ran the risk of appearing to rival the monarchs they served. Both Roger and Henry were disgraced in the turmoils of the mid-twelfth century civil war. Roger paid the debt with his life, while Henry, despite deserting his brother Stephen's cause, escaped retribution during his brother's lifetime. Winchester, on which Henry of Blois had lavished so much attention, was severely damaged in the campaigns of 1141. In the desperate struggle Henry of Blois, the patron of so much of the late Romanesque glory of the city, was himself the destroyer of much of his beloved city. This destruction included the slighting of the Norman royal palace to the west of the cathedral. The remains of the palace were used in the reconstruction of Wolvesey, symbolically representing the fact of Winchester's change of role from essentially a royal city to an ecclesiastical centre.

Henry of Blois left other palatial monuments behind him outside Winchester. At Bishop's Waltham, he began work on a palace in 1135, the year his brother became king, and lived to oversee a substantial reconstruction in the period after 1160 before his death in 1171. A first-floor hall with an undercroft, much altered subsequently, is still to be seen there. Henry of Blois was the instigator of work begun in about 1138 at Farnham (Surrey) where the hall has been cited as providing a significant stage in the move towards greater domesticity and away from military tendencies in architecture. However, more recent work such as that on the Warennes' place in Norfolk has shown that domestic, unfortified buildings were in existence from the earliest post-Conquest era (page 33). In Stephen's reign, while the king himself was racked by the problems of survival, it was great lords and prelates such as Henry of Blois who took the lead in palace building. This trend of magnate innovation in palace building is observable again in the reign of Richard II in the late fourteenth century, although Richard was a more active builder than Stephen, so far as we know.

In addition to major secular buildings, patronage of ecclesiastical buildings

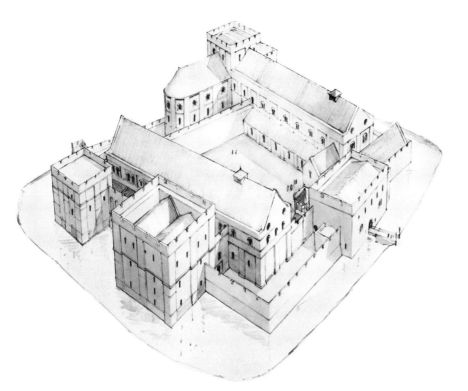

Fig. 22 Wolvesey palace in 1171. Compare the layout with that of Old Sarum, above. (*Drawing by Terry Ball. Copyright English Heritage*)

in Stephen's reign included many monastic foundations, perhaps to expiate the wrongs of the civil war. The Augustinian priory at Ivychurch (Wiltshire) was established by Stephen and supplied canons who took the services at the chapels in the nearby palace at Clarendon until they were displaced by the arrival of the friars in the first half of the thirteenth century. Stephen's abbey was at Faversham (Kent), where he was buried, although nothing now survives of that once great religious house. On a smaller scale he made a significant contribution to Westminster palace, the chapel dedicated to his namesake St Stephen. This chapel developed into a focus of royal worship, especially after 1292 when Edward I began to rebuild it (page 116ff.).

Chapter III

Early Plantagenet palaces (1154–1216)

The end of the civil war and the death of Stephen in 1154 brought Henry II (1154–89) to the throne. Henry married Eleanor of Aquitaine, described by one waspish chronicler as 'a woman richer in the endowments of her person than in those of her mind'. This marriage provided a crop of male heirs, to the considerable embarrassment of the royal house of France, for Eleanor's marriage to Louis VII had ended in divorce because of a lack of children. But her marriage to Henry II also ended unhappily with her imprisonment for over fifteen years.

The marriage to Eleanor made the king lord of substantial continental lands as well as of England, Wales and Ireland. Although we loosely term Henry II an emperor, which he was not, the scale of his landholdings was unprecedented for a medieval king of England. His continental lands were undoubtedly of more interest to him than those in Britain. His broad interests and experience, together with the indefatigable energy which he expended on visiting all parts of his possessions made him readily conversant with contemporary fashions of art and iconography. This knowledge, combined with the rich revenue from his lands, enabled Henry to initiate and carry through a thorough programme of enlargement and modernisation of his many residences, both in comfort and style.

Increased sophistication and comfort are features of the Henrican works. In particular the unfortified provincial residences at Clarendon and Woodstock were enlarged and embellished to become true palaces like the established castle palace of Winchester and the great palace at Westminster. A smaller hall was added at Westminster (*see* Fig. 23). This 'new' or 'lesser' hall was in keeping with the move towards increased comfort. The painting of the royal chambers at Winchester castle, notably with a representation of the eagle (Henry II) on the nest being attacked by its four eaglets (his sons Henry, Geoffrey, John and Richard), provides a glimpse of interior decor, a subject of which we know

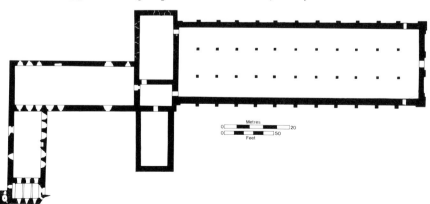

Fig. 23 Plan of Westminster palace at the time of Henry II, 1154–89. (*After Lethaby*)

Fig. 24 Fragments of historiated capitals excavated at Clarendon palace. They show a human torso on a feathered or scaly body and a feline head. It is not known whether they came from domestic or chapel accommodation. (*Drawing by Frances Rankine, Society of Antiquaries of London*)

very little at this period. This fierce scene of family discord, presumably from the king's own chamber, contrasts the increased comforts of living with the violence of the life of the English royal family at this date. Wars between Henry and his sons were waged the length and breadth of the Angevin dominions. There was an extended siege by the king of Kenilworth castle, held by his eldest son, the young Henry. The untimely death from dysentery of the heir to the throne in 1183, resulted from a siege by his father in southern France. Not long afterwards, in 1186, Geoffrey died of wounds sustained in a tournament.

Amongst the embellishments of royal palaces at this time was the increased use of historiated sculpture and of Purbeck 'marble', a shelly limestone which takes a high polish, for architectural detail (*see* Fig. 24). In the Hampshire section of the pipe roll for 1176 it is recorded that marble columns, no doubt hewn and prepared at a Dorset quarry, were taken to Clarendon. The inference from the appearance of the charges on the Hampshire section of the roll is that the stone was transported by sea from Dorset to Hampshire, perhaps to Southampton, and was then dragged overland to Clarendon, thus incidentally providing us with an insight into royal transport arrangements. More significantly the reference to the use of Purbeck in the 1170s points to an early introduction into royal buildings of this black stone, so much a feature of Early English architecture when it was used so strikingly to contrast with creamy limestone (*see* Fig. 25). If it is so that the period of architectural style known as Early English can be pinpointed to William of Sens's rebuilding of the chancel of Canterbury cathedral from 1174, then this royal use is very early indeed, or alternatively may be seen as a royal continuation in the use of Purbeck pioneered by Henry of Blois (page 52).

Decorative detail such as sculptured capitals, the use of contrasting colours of stone and the emergence of identifiable scenes of wall painting within buildings is matched by an improved environment without. The attention paid to

Fig. 25 Fragment of a Purbeck marble column excavated at Clarendon but now lost. (*Photograph by John Charlton, Society of Antiquaries of London*)

gardens at Arundel, Winchester and Marlborough where turfs were laid and buildings landscaped in, perhaps indicates a royal interest in the relaxation which a garden could provide. Such lawn projects may also have eased the task of garden maintenance for those who administered the royal buildings for a busy king such as Henry II. An apparent growth of interest in gardens may in addition reflect the most clement climatic period in medieval England, which prevailed in the two and a half centuries after the Conquest.

Additional external features to improve and vary diet are apparent in the time of Henry II, such as dovecotes at Nottingham and elsewhere. Fishponds were increasingly common at royal residences as the reign progressed. Little at present is known about their twelfth-century development apart from the occasional reference to expenditure, such as that on the new vivary or fishpond made at Feckenham (Worcestershire) in 1168–9, and to others at Eye (Suffolk) and at Newcastle-under-Lyme (Staffordshire). They were clearly going concerns by the time the documentation recorded them in detail from the early thirteenth century (Steane 1988, 40). Apart from kings, wealthy churchmen like the bishops of Winchester also invested in such capital intensive luxuries as fishponds and more particularly deer parks (Roberts 1986, 1988).

If the variety of meat and fish was increasing in the twelfth century, provision was also made for the production of wine and unfermented verjuice (from green or unripe grapes) encouraged by the temperate climate at that time. Vines were commonly grown in England, for example at the Little Park by Windsor. Windsor, Winchester and other royal vineyards produced quantities of wine, although it is not clear to what extent vineyard products went for wine or for verjuice. Despite English production, the greatest quantity of wine came from abroad. Imports grew in volume and range, enhanced greatly by contributions from continental areas under English control.

Castles remained prime items for royal expenditure in the post-civil war decades, although Henry contributed only one new castle, Orford, to the royal stock. Unfortified residences came a fair second and in 1176–7 outstripped even castles in attracting royal investment (Colvin 1963, 81). Reasons for widespread expenditure no doubt included Henry's enormous energy coupled with his notorious indecision about by what route, when and to what destination the royal household would proceed. If it was uncertain when the king would arrive, royal servants must have been at pains to keep both castles and other residences in readiness. Henry's rages are legendary and contemporaries apparently thought it quite unexceptional that the king should writhe on the ground in furious rage or angrily sit biting floor rushes.

Henry II enacted business as he travelled round the country. The continuous upheavals of the administration caused great uncertainty and much resentment amongst his officials, who no doubt contributed to this king's reputation for being disorganised and indecisive. However, this reputation is belied by the knowledge that business meetings, unlike other elements of the royal itinerary, had to be organised well in advance and summonses sent out to those who should attend.

In 1164 a royal council was summoned to Clarendon, to which palace the nearest town at that time was Old Sarum. The 1164 council produced the Constitutions of Clarendon. This meeting was attended by fourteen leading churchmen, including Archbishop Becket, and many lay magnates. Thomas of Bosham, a member of Becket's household, was highly impressed with what he called 'the nobility' of the site at Clarendon. The meetings which produced the Constitutions (1164) and the Assize of Clarendon (1166), the latter produced 'with the assent of all his barons', must have taken place in the great hall of the palace, and must have involved considerable numbers of people. The east gable, which still stands amidst the ruins of the hall, contains the remains of a twelfth-century corbel-springer of the north arcade of the hall (*see* Fig. 26). Excavation of the hall in 1933–4 showed that it was certainly not the first structure on the site it occupies. Documents from the thirteenth century refer to a so-far unidentified building known as the 'old hall' which suggests that at Clarendon, as elsewhere, there were two halls on the site at the same time.

Where those attending the conferences with the king stayed while at Clarendon or elsewhere remains a mystery. Large retinues must have accompanied lords and churchmen when they attended council with the king. The halls and other buildings on the site would have provided sleeping areas for some. Others must either have stayed in Old Sarum some miles away or have camped out in Clarendon Park. The survival of Clarendon in its rural setting provides a unique opportunity for the archaeological investigation of the layout and phasing of the site as a whole, and so alone has the potential to throw light on details such as accommodation, building provision and catering arrangements across a complete royal palace site over the whole Middle Ages.

Thomas Becket maintained an establishment in keeping with his position as archbishop. Henry II entrusted the young Henry, his eldest son, to the archbishop's household for a time. The close personal links between the king and

Fig. 26 Clarendon. East gable of the great hall showing the northern arcade *tas de charge*, which includes 'the stone of kings' of Caen stone. (*Photograph by John Charlton, Society of Antiquaries of London*)

the archbishop, while they remained friends, spilled over into collaboration over building projects. Becket is credited with a rapidly accomplished campaign of works at Westminster in 1163, just a year before relations became strained at their Clarendon encounter. Becket shared the episcopal bench with contemporaries who were greater builders than he. Notable amongst these was King Stephen's brother Henry of Blois, who has already been mentioned for his works before 1154 when he fled abroad at Henry II's accession (page 46). The greatest standing monument to Bishop Henry's later years, after he returned from exile in 1158, is the church of the Hospital of St Cross, Winchester. This fine building has many innovative features, but was only partly completed when the great old bishop died in 1171, the year after the murder of Becket. At first sight it may appear odd that the closest parallel with St Cross is Darlington Church in County Durham, which carries the transitional features of Romanesque firmly into Gothic (Charlton 1954, 225).

The answer is in a sense a simple one. The builder at Darlington was Bishop Pudsey, or Puiset, who held the see of Durham from 1153–95. His uncle was Henry of Blois and it seems very likely that work by Henry of Blois influenced his nephew. Pudsey was one of the greatest builders, after the eleventh-century construction of the cathedral, ever to hold the see of Durham. The remains of the bishop's palace at Bishop Auckland contain significant elements attributed to Pudsey. Bishop Auckland palace and Darlington are amongst the earliest examples in the country of a Gothic programme, as opposed to elements of Gothic such as the ribbed vaults of Durham cathedral. The detail of the great hall at Bishop Auckland is of Frosterley 'marble', the northen equivalent of Purbeck, which was used so early to ornament St Cross (Charlton 1954, 222). At St Cross the Purbeck piers, which proved insufficient to take the strain of the roof, have been replaced (Kusaba 1983, chapter III). At Bishop Auckland the use of Frosterley stone for ornament and less fissile stone to bear the structural weight, has contributed to the survival of the hall much as it was built. At the bishop's castle at Durham, Pudsey contributed a stone great hall with a basement, and rebuilt in stone the north range, which had previously been timber framed (Charlton 1954, 262–3).

Meanwhile the king was not idle. At Woodstock and adjacent Everswell Henry II had a clear pupose in his building programme. This purpose was to provide accommodation for his household, and also to house his mistress, Rosamund Clifford, nearby but discreetly separate. The remains of Woodstock are now lost to us: the main buildings were unwillingly landscaped away by Sir John Vanbrugh in the early eighteenth century (*see* Fig. 27). Capability Brown later drowned the remainder in the ornamental lake. All this work was for the gardens of Blenheim palace, the noble successor of the royal palace and manor, and a further reminder of how secular palaces passed from hand to hand. Ruins of Woodstock appear on the skyline in a print of 1699 and Vanbrugh repeatedly procrastinated over his instructions to demolish them. But the Duchess of Marlborough, the wife of the new owner of the property, repeatedly and persistently requested that the remains be levelled and this was eventually done. Maybe the reputation of Woodstock as the residence of the mistress Rosamund Clifford fitted ill with eighteenth-century ideals of morality. On the other hand, it can be argued that England alone of the countries of

northern Europe never entirely abandoned the Gothic style, and that the Gothic revival was not so much a renaissance of Gothic as an Indian summer. If so, the enthusiasm of Vanbrugh for the preservation of medieval Woodstock was an element in the survival of English Gothic.

However that may be, Woodstock is lost. From what we know of it, this was a leading palace under Henry II. Here, in 1163, a great ceremony took place in which King Malcolm of Scotland, Welsh princes and other nobles paid homage to the king. In 1178 it was at Woodstock that Henry affectionately knighted his son Geoffrey. There were two complexes of buildings apart from the settlement which developed into New Woodstock, a new town which grew up at the entrance of the forest. The first group of buildings were those of the palace itself. These were the structures levelled by Vanbrugh and recorded in the print of 1699. Although there are no surviving remains, we are fortunate in the survival of the antiquarian John Aubrey's account of his visit to Woodstock in 1672. A good deal was standing then, as the print shows, and Aubrey gives some account of what he calls the 'mannor-house' where he saw an ancient window, and the chapel which still retained red and blue coloured wall paintings. Tantalisingly he does not give details of the subjects of these paintings. He also describes features of the hall, where the pillars and the 'semi-circular' arcading were still intact. It is not clear from his description, for he was apparently unable to tell from what he saw, whether the hall was divided down the centre by a single row of columns, or aisled. Aubrey could have been so much more informative, but only with hindsight do we know that having survived for half a millenium all the evidence would disappear within barely half a century after his visit.

Secondly there was an adjacent, but separate group of buildings at Everswell. It is Everswell which is of particular interest in the reign of Henry II since it was the home of his mistress Rosamund Clifford in the 1170s. The story of the young Rosamund, who was perhaps only seventeen when the middle-

aged king fell in love with her, has caught the romantic imagination of successive generations. In fact the affair was probably rather short, not more than
three years, lasting from about 1170–73, when Rosamund died and was
buried at the nunnery at Godstow, until her remains were subsequently unceremo-
niously removed. Various chronicles tell us (although it must be admitted
that such accounts are highly dubious) that the king created a maze at
Woodstock where only he could find Rosamund. But his queen, Eleanor of
Aquitaine, following a silken thread hanging from the mistress's dress, dis-
coveed her husband and Rosamund in the midst of the maze, with dire results
which were, according to the usual version of the tale, that Eleanor was imprisoned for the remaining sixteen years of her husband's reign. It is, however, uncertain that the imprisonment had anything to do with the queen's attitude to
Rosamund, for she may already have been in prison before the affair began
(Eyton 1878, vii). The lack of surviving structures at Woodstock cannot reveal
to us whether a maze existed there in the 1170s.

With or without a maze, the layout at Everswell was highly unusual in
England as far as can be discerned from the limited extant materials for its history and architecture. A sketch plan of the ruins which seems to show a
gatehouse and other buildings was made by the indefatigable John Aubrey.
The drawing also shows what appears to be a series of three interconnected
pools fed by the Everswell spring (*see* Fig. 28). There has been much speculation about the origin of these pools. Norman connections with Sicily have
been cited, for example La Zisa at Palermo (Colvin 1963, 1015). Princess
Joanna, Henry's daughter, was married to the King of Sicily in 1176. Certainly
shady pools such as those of Rosamund's bower were a feature of southern
European palaces and can still be seen at the Moorish Alhambra palace in
Spain. Artistic links have been traced between England and Spain at this
period, and these were no doubt strengthened by the marriage in 1169 of

Fig. 28 Everswell,
Oxfordshire. Sketch of the
interconnecting pools and
other remnants of Henry II's
unique Sicilian-style
residence. (*Drawing by C.J.
Bond after John Aubrey*)

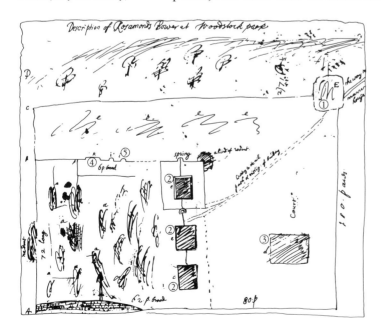

Ruins at Rosamund's Well
John Aubrey's sketch plan

① "Ruines of a noble gatehouse or
   Tower of Entrance"

② "Three Baths in trayne"

③ "a pond in the Court"

④ "seems to have been a seat in the wall
   about 2 yards long"

⑤ "Two niches, one very much ruined"

Fig. 29 Everswell. The surviving pool today, now called Rosamund's Well and from which spring water is bottled and sold. (*Photograph C.J. Bond*)

another of Henry's daughters, Princess Eleanor, to the King of Castile, immediately before the Rosamund interlude. How appropriate pools were in northern Europe, even in a comparatively temperate era, is a moot point. A remnant of the water courses of Everswell can still be seen at 'Rosamond's Well' at Woodstock (*see* Fig. 29).

Another avenue of research has suggested a link between the palace pools at Everswell and the romance of Tristan and Isolde, which was popular in the twelfth century. In this story the water ran directly through Isolde's chambers and Tristan communicated with her by floating messages down stream. Although the extant remains at Everswell are so scant, fragmentary remains of a fine polished Purbeck marble fountain of late eleventh-century date were recverted by excavation at Westminster. This fountain perhaps stood at the end of Westminster Hall, near to the entrance of the privy palace, has been excavated and can be reconstructed (*see* Fig. 30) (Colvin 1963, 1015; DAMBH 1975, 10).

The romance of Everswell was the prelude to the unhappy last sixteen years of Henry II's reign when the king's domestic life was so unsatisfactory, and he was engaged in fruitless civil wars with his sons. However, some of the greatest expenditure on domestic building took place in the mid-1170s.

When Henry II died in 1189 he bequeathed his great assemblage of lands on both sides of the Channel to his son Richard, who had been trained as an administrator in Aquitaine by Queen Eleanor. Richard's experience in France and his involvement as a crusader suggested that he would take less of an interest in England than his father had done. This as it turned out, proved to be the case. For much of his reign Richard I was away from England. Nevertheless royal buildings required maintenance in his absence, a further reminder of the effectiveness of the English medieval civil service. However, when Richard was in England he used residences just as his predecessors had done. A detailed account for rebuilding the royal hunting lodge in Kinver Forest has survived from

Fig. 30 Purbeck fountain at Westminster. (*Reconstructed by B.K. Davison. Drawing by Terry Ball. Copyright English Heritage*)

Richard's reign. This reveals the constituent parts of a timber-built complex. The buildings were standard types: a hall with adjacent buttery and pantry, a kitchen and a chamber. In common with the fashion by the late twelfth century, there was a vivarium for bream and possibly for pike. In addition, as was frequently the case in forest manors such as Kinver and Clarendon, there was a gaol for the holding of forest offenders awaiting the rounds of the justices. The gaol was enclosed by a palisade five metres high, and was defended by a gateway with a brattice. The total cost of the rebuilding works was £24 18s 9d. Such works, like the visits of the king to England, were rare in his eleven-year reign.

The story of the great reputation of King Richard as a crusader is too well known to need retelling here, except insofar as it passed into legend and provided an inspiration for decorative schemes in the palaces of his nephew Henry III half a century later (page 82). It was indicative of Richard's nervousness about his reputation in England that he chose to go through a second coronation at Winchester in 1194 during an interlude in bouts of crusading. His marriage to Berengaria of Navarre in 1191 resulted in no known effects in English palaces.

If there is little to report on royal palace building in the late twelfth century, a glimpse of what might have been afoot in the royal gardens survives from this

period. Before 1200 Richard's foster brother, Alexander of Neckam, compiled
a treatise on the natural world which lists seventy-seven English garden plants,
including what seems at first sight a disproportionate number of exotics. Recent research seems to show that the inclusion of the pomegranate, date-palm,
lemon and orange, far from invalidating the list, serve to remind the reader first
that the climate in England in the half-century following 1150 was as warm as
it has ever been in the historic period, and second that medieval gardeners may
well have protected such exotic plants over the winter, or even that palms
might have been half hardy in the south of the country during such a temperate
era (Harvey 1981, 66–7).

As for Richard the Lionheart himself, his most enduring legacy was the ransom incurred after he was captured while returning from crusade. This was not
only a huge drain on national resources, but also contributed to the insolvency
of the crown during his brother John's reign, and thus, indirectly, to the loss of
the English lands in France in the early years of the thirteenth century. Fatally
wounded while skirmishing in France in 1199, Richard was laid to rest and his
remains, like his father's, committed to the care of the nuns at Fontevrault in
Anjou. He was the last English king to be buried in France.

Richard's younger brother John reigned for seventeen and a half years. he
was continually on the move from place to place. The breathless pace of his
reign was exceptional even for highly mobile medieval monarchs. He inherited
twenty-three residences from his brother Richard and extended this to thirty by
both fair means and foul. If John was a failure as a ruler, it was certainly not
as a result of inactivity. The Abbot of Coggeshall said of John that he reigned
with '*satis labor*' although whether this means he did enough work, or had
enough difficulty, remains debatable. Scattered across England are a number of
buildings now called King John's house or King John's palace. It may be significant that other medieval kings' names have not been applied in this way and in
view of his great mobility John must have visited many places, but even so,
many of the buildings graced by his name were certainly not his creations and
some were not visited by him, as far as can be told from records.

Many of John's problems arose from his exceptionally itinerant life style. On
the credit side he was seen by many whose fathers and grandfathers had never
seen a king. Although he did his best to act as judge in many local disputes, his
good intentions were often regarded by barons as endless meddling and inter-
ference, making him unpopular with them. Also on the debit side, the administration found difficulty in keeping up with him, which they resented. He was a
great eater, as his interest in the insertion of new large kitchen fireplaces bears
witness; one, at Marlborough castle, and another at Ludgershall (Wiltshire),
for example, were designed to enable the cooks to roast two oxen at the same
time (Colvin 1963, 80). At Clarendon the west kitchen with its multiple
hearths has long been called 'King John's kitchen', and bones of ox, pig,
domestic fowl and mallard found in the ditch which once divided the kitchen
from the great hall may be fragments of his feasts (James and Robinson 1988,
8, 166).

If feasting was to John's taste, fasting was not: as Hilda Johnstone put it,
'given a king who in the end gorged himself to death on peaches and new ale'
(1929, 153). John was prepared to give much in alms to atone for his failure to

fast. For example, after enjoying two meat meals on successive Fridays, he gave food to a hundred poor on each occasion, and when he misbehaved in a similar fashion on Good Friday, he fed a thousand poor. In one year alone what records we have refer to 3,500 people enjoying bounty in this way. Courtiers repaid their debts to the Almighty at lesser rates of meal-provision for the poor. Hawking and hunting by the king on saints' days had to be paid for, as in 1212 when on Holy Innocents Day (28th December), perhaps while working off the Christmas feast, he caught seven cranes and fed fifty poor for each of them (*ibid*). A more fierce side to hunting is revealed in the rich rewards given in 1210 by John to huntsmen in royal forests who had killed a wolf near Clarendon and two others at Gillingham (Dorset), the scale of the rewards, fifteen shillings, perhaps reflecting the rarity of wolves in the southern forests by this date (James and Robinson 1988, 8).

John was not the first or last monarch to resort to usurping properties from his subjects. His widespread travelling enabled him to see many places which took his fancy, for example Bishop Jocelyn of Wells's manor at Cheddar, which the king acquired for a time. During his brief tenure John left his mark on the buildings there with works on the hall (*see* Fig. 31). Places such as Cheddar and Writtle (Essex), normally described as 'hunting lodges', should not be underestimated in terms of the scale of the buildings. The hall area at 'King John's hunting lodge' at Writtle, excavated by Philip Rahtz, when compared for size

Fig. 31 Cheddar Palace as it might have looked in the reign of King John. (*Drawing by Alan Sorrell. Reproduced by permission of the Axbridge Archaeological and Local History Society*)

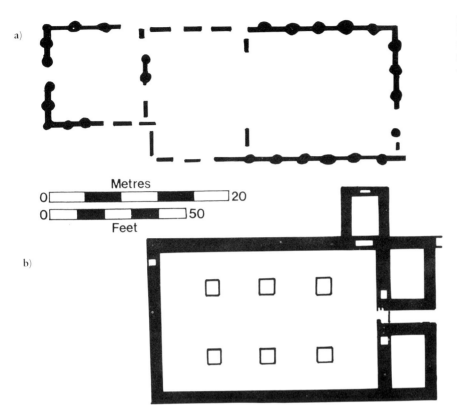

Fig. 32 The hall and chamber block at a) Writtle and b) Clarendon great hall drawn to the same scale. (*Writtle after Philip Rahtz*)

Metres
0 ⌷ 20
0 ⌷ 50
Feet

with a hall such as that at Clarendon, more usually referred to as the great hall of a palace, does not appear so very much smaller (*see* Fig. 32). Undoubtedly wooden structures such as those at Writtle and at Cheddar were less durable than stone, but the scale of the buildings was impressive nonetheless. Where he had no residence of his own John stayed with lords and bishops, who often went to considerable lengths to ensure the king's stay was comfortable. In 1208–9 Peter des Roches, Bishop of Winchester, welcomed him to his palatial manor at Witney (Oxfordshire), where the records tell us a new garderobe was especially made for the occasion. The fine ashlar work of this garderobe has been revealed in recent years by excavation (*see* Fig. 33) (Durham nd, 5). Documents also reveal the purchase of wash basins or bowls for the king at Witney in the same year, and a bath tub (*cuve balneala*) was made there in 1211–12 for the king's use. These were welcome comforts for this itinerant king.

John's long journeys through the realm brought him into contact with many of his magnates, with whom he stayed. He made himself unpopular with certain lay magnates by lusting after their wives. John's first marriage ended in divorce, though not for this reason. Royal affairs with non-noble women were acceptable within limits, but a king who took the wives of his lords against their will was not to be tolerated happily. Magna Carta brought John to account for many grievances in 1215. Although he was forced to give up certain manors and residences, nonetheless on his death in 1216 he was able to bequeath some thirty houses to his son Henry III.

Fig. 33 Remains of ashlar
garderobes at Witney palace,
Oxfordshire, probably those
made for King John in
1208–9. This is part of
substantial below-ground
remains which are under
excavation and now
constitute the only remains of
this once great country
residence. (*Photograph Brian
Durham. Copyright Oxford
Archaeological Unit*)

Recent research has suggested that building developments in episcopal palaces, and in particular a spate of sumptuous halls erected between about 1180 and 1220, may have had a profound influence on royal building. The work of the bishops does not, however, begin to produce parallels in John's reign but in the minority of his son Henry. Current knowledge seems to suggest that episcopal palace building draws ahead of royal building in the time of John, although Henry III rapidly redressed the balance after he came of age in 1227.

The introduction of new styles and heightened extravagance in buildings has recently been credited, so far as palace building is concerned, to William de Vere, Bishop of Hereford (1186–98). De Vere had been a member of the court of Henry II, before he was appointed to Hereford where he created a new clerestoried hall at his palace (*see* Fig. 34). This hall is now seen as the precursor of a fashion for magnificent halls in palaces at Lincoln, Exeter, Canterbury and elsewhere (Blair 1987, 63). Thus the Hereford hall, formerly considered a rural throw-back echoing an archaic Saxon hall-type, is reinterpreted as creating a new fashion in the late twelfth century.

If Hereford was the first in this new tradition, other work followed shortly afterwards or was in progress simultaneously. At Lincoln, Robert de Chesney (1148–66) had comparatively recently provided a new hall, a large-scale undertaking and very much in the tradition of the work of bishops such as Giffard and Blois at Winchester and Pudsey at Durham. The existence of the remains of de Chesney's east hall beside its successor, built by Hugh of Avalon (1186–1200) and Hugh of Wells (1209–35), provides an opportunity to compare the old and the new style on one site (*see* Fig. 35). By 1163 Bishop Robert had begun work on his residence, built on land obtained at great expense from Henry II. Chesney created an east hall before 1166, consisting primarily of a Romanesque upper and lower hall. Excavations in 1968–72 showed that the construction of the east end of this block had necessitated the quarrying away of natural bedrock to accommodate the building demanded by the bishop. A survey of 1647 gives the dimensions of this structure as some 30 ft by 114 ft, (9 m × 34.7 m), perhaps including a later chamber block to the south added by 1200. Substantial remains stand today (Ambrose 1980, 7).

De Chesney's east hall was, as it transpired, much less magnificent and spacious than Hugh of Avalon's west hall, begun in about 1186. As de Vere at Hereford in the same period was associated with the court, so Hugh of Avalon enjoyed particular royal favour under Henry II. The king's enthusiasm for St Hugh's Carthusian order was one manifestation of this support, and Henry's practical contributions to palace building at Lincoln another. Forty trees from royal Sherwood forest were promptly provided to form the great roof timbers of the Lincoln hall. These were supplied under the supervision of that doughty

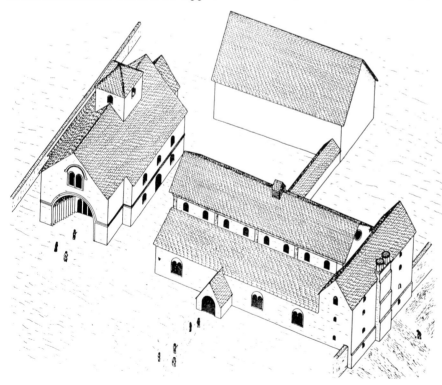

Fig. 34 Hereford. Reconstruction of the bishop's palace complex in the twelfth century. As elsewhere, the palace and cathedral complex dominated the part of the city in which it lay. (*Reconstruction by John Blair*)

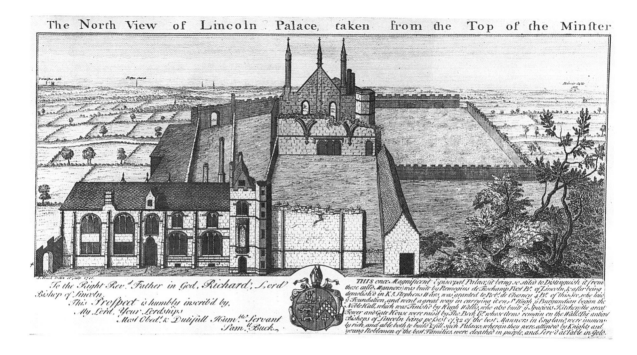

The North View of Lincoln Palace, taken from the Top of the Minster

*To the Right Rev.ᵈ Father in God, Richard; Lord
Bishop of Lincoln.
This Prospect is humbly inscrib'd by,
My Lord, Your Lordships
Most Obed.ᵗ & Dutifull Hum.ᵇˡᵉ Servant
Sam.ˡ Buck.*

royal official Hugh de Nevill, whose associations with royal building works, and especially with works involving provision of forest timber, were commemorated from John's reign onwards in the so-called de Nevill chamber at Clarendon. The apparent paradox of support both for the austerity of the Carthusians and for the extravagant palaces of the bishop can be explained by the king's devotion to God's work in expiation of the murder of Becket in 1170. Contemporaries, however, pointed to another link between Henry II and St Hugh, in the form of wild speculation that the bishop was an illegitimate son of the monarch, which does not seem to have been the case (Given-Wilson and Curteis 1984, 9) (page 174). St Hugh died in 1200, long before the west hall was completed, but the work was brought to a triumphant conclusion by Bishop Hugh of Wells soon after 1224.

The functions of the west and east halls at Lincoln are uncertain. They may have been an administrative and domestic hall or, as found at Wells and Winchester, a personal hall for the bishop and a great or audience hall. Alternatively, as was found at Sir John Fastolf's fifteenth-century castle at Caister, they may have developed into a summer and winter hall (Ambrose 1980, 2; Girouard 1978, 60). The new hall at Lincoln was twice as wide as the west hall and 90 ft (27.5 m) long. There were four bays supported by six pillars, and a free-standing hearth lay towards the north end. The detail of the building was of the highest quality. Clusters of Purbeck columns, matching those of the cathedral, supported the roof, as they still do in the great hall of Winchester castle, begun after Lincoln but completed more rapidly (page 65). The transportation of Purbeck stone from the south coast to Lincoln must have been a most expensive undertaking.

Today, even in their ruined state, the buildings of de Chesney and of Hugh of Avalon at Lincoln retain much of their medieval grandeur. Visiting them on a hot summer's day, the sun makes little impression on the dark, cool undercroft of the earlier hall, while the shadows of the truncated transoms and mullions of the windows of the later west hall give a good impression of how the new hall must have been comparatively well lit by windows compared to the solid, dark and narrow old hall. The terrace, below the presently very ruinous remains of the kitchen to the south of the west hall, has a vineyard planted on it, in an imaginative evocation of the Middle Ages.

Most notable in scale of this group of architecturally innovative great halls was the great aisled hall at the archbishop's palace at Canterbury, built by Hubert Walter and Stephen Langton between 1200 and 1220. With eight bays, this was the largest hall in England after Westminster. It was demolished in the 1650s, but fragmentary remains have subsequently been noted or recovered, so that it is now possible to produce an impressive reconstruction drawing (*see* Fig. 36). Some idea of the interior can be pieced together. The observant eighteenth-century writer Gostling, walking in the garden created inside the ruins after its demolition, noted a revetment wall constructed out of building materials: 'this was the upper end of the hall, and along it runs a terrace, raised on fragments without number, of the Petworth [Purbeck] marble, once the ornaments of the great hall but now laid on one another, like billets on a wood stack, the ends of which were visible till some years ago, when a tenant of this

Fig. 36 Reconstruction of the archbishop's hall at Canterbury, remains of which are still to be seen embedded in more modern structures. (*Drawing by John Bowen. Reproduced by permission of the Canterbury Archaeological Trust*)

house raised a turfed slope of earth against them, to give the garden a better appearance' (Gostling rp. 1825, 142) (*see* Fig. 37). Recently a large shaft-ring has been recovered in excavation. This early thirteenth-century use of Purbeck provides a useful bridge between the 'marble' columns from Henry II's reign at Clarendon, and the increasingly subtle use of Purbeck, for example in the bishop's hall at Lincoln and in Henry III's great building projects of the mid-thirteenth century (page 83). The archbishop's hall had a raised and stepped dais at the east end. The early floor levels revealed in excavation were of clay laid on crushed chalk. Later it is thought this hall must have been tiled and some evidence of this was found but, as at Clarendon, finds of tiles in the hall itself were comparatively few (Tatton-Brown 1982, 230–232).

By the time this spate of halls, which was apparently begun by de Vere with imitations and developments elsewhere amongst the households of the ecclesiastical hierarchy of England, was coming to a climax, Henry II's sons Richard and John were both dead and his grandson Henry III (1216–72) was on the throne. In this reign the splendours of Gothic, foreshadowed in the episcopal works described here, reached their apogee.

Chapter IV

Henry III: champion of Gothic (1216–1272)

When King John died in 1216, his son Henry was a minor aged nine and William the Marshal ruled in the young king's place in the early part of the reign. Not surprisingly in view of his young age, there was no hint at his accession that Henry III was to prove such a great patron of art and architecture, who improved the royal buildings in quantity and quality far beyond anything achieved by his predecessors. The sum in excess of £30,000 estimated to have been spent by Henry III on his residences was double the expenditure of his father. However, since Henry reigned more than three times as long as his father, father and son may have had more of a common interest in buildings than might appear at first glance (*see* Fig. 38).

Peter des Roches, Bishop of Winchester 1205–38, in common with so many medieval prelates was a man of many skills, 'by turns warrior, military engineer, builder, financial agent, statesman and diplomatist' (DNB). He also had various illegitimate children, at least one of whom, Peter des Rivaux, became in turn a key royal administrator. Des Roches knew King John well and had welcomed him to various of his residences (page 59). The revenues of the Winchester see provided the bishop with ample funds to pursue building schemes. The pipe rolls of the bishop give useful information on aspects of this work in various locations. For example, in 1210–11 the bishop was purchasing boards for making windows for the 'painted room' (*camera depicta*) at Marwell, no doubt decorated with mural paintings although the nature of the subjects is lost to us. Much work was involved, for Luke the painter worked there for over six months (Holt 1964, 13). With so much varied experience Bishop Peter was an obvious choice to be appointed young Henry III's personal guardian. This appointment gave the bishop a significant role in Henry's minority. Des Roches was a keen builder, and it is this skill in particular with which he inspired the king. Thus throughout his reign Henry took an increasing interest in the royal buildings inherited from his father.

The king's guardian found himself in the happy position of having royal funds at his disposal which, provided he performed certain specific tasks, could be used at his pleasure. A major task which he undertook was to construct or reconstruct the great hall of Winchester castle. This was done between 1222 and 1235. The hall we see today consists essentially of work from des Roches's tenure of the see, carried out under the supervision of Elias de Dereham, and is the finest hall of its date to be seen in England (page 67). The combination of builder-bishop and royal favour was much to the benefit of the Winchester palaces. Henry spent eighteen Christmases during his long reign at Winchester. By his death in 1238, des Roches had not only completed the great hall at the

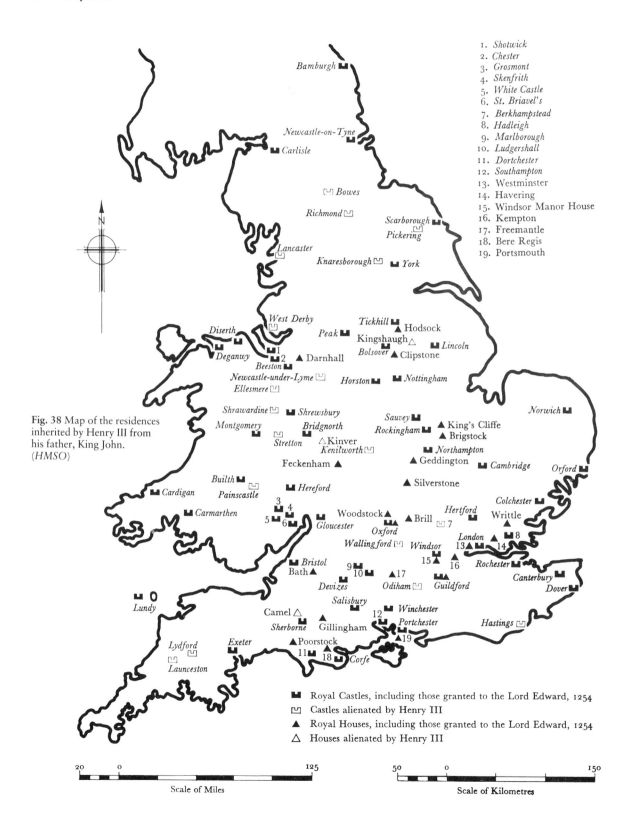

Fig. 38 Map of the residences inherited by Henry III from his father, King John. *(HMSO)*

castle, but was also almost certainly the author of the remodelling of the east hall at Wolvesey to bring it into line with contemporary architectural thinking. This was achieved by the insertion of an arcade between the hall and the western gallery, and by the sub-division of that gallery to give the arrangement of buttery, central passage and pantry. This produced the fashionable screens area which is to be seen in work of the same period in the bishop's palace at Lincoln, at Clarendon and elsewhere. Royal and ecclesiastical builders advanced in step at this time. This cross-fertilisation led for example to the copying in 1242 by Henry III into his chapel at Windsor of representations of Old and New Testament scenes from the chapel at Wolvesey (Biddle 1986, 15).

The removal of the Salisbury see from Old Sarum to New Sarum by Bishop Richard Poore in 1220 provided a rare opportunity for building a thirteenth-century cathedral and palace together in unified style. Poore's episcopate was dominated by his building activities and there is much left to be seen today, notably his great cathedral so famous for its unified programme of Early English style, which distinguishes it from the disparate elements of such a programme as seen in the chancel of Canterbury cathedral, or a fragmentary Purbeck pillar from a royal site (page 49). Parts of his palace remain as well. A clue to the scale of the palace comes from the surviving vaulted basement from *c.* 1221, divided down the middle with columns to give additional width to the whole building. Bishop Jocelyn, a near contemporary of Poore's, was at work at Wells from *c.* 1206–40, building a palace with the hall, solar, and parallel gallery, and garderobe raised on vaulted undercrofts. Much of his fine structure is still to be seen.

Compared with most medieval kings, Henry III was a refined and cultured man, but very busy with matters of state. Although he took a particular interest in architecture, art and sculpture, an able team of practitioners was needed to give the king's wishes concrete form. Most notable amongst these men was Elias de Dereham (d. 1245). During Henry's minority Elias worked with two of the great builder-bishops of the thirteenth century, Jocelyn of Wells and Poore of Salisbury (Thompson 1941, 5–7). By 1220 Elias had an exceptional reputation for architecture amongst senior churchmen, being consulted that year by Archbishop Langton (himself a major palace builder at Canterbury and at Lambeth) on the translation of the remains of St Thomas Becket from the crypt to a new site behind the high altar. Subsequently Elias oversaw the winching into position of the great roof timbers of Winchester castle hall, and the provision of the remarkable king's chapel at Clarendon (Colvin 1963, 100; James and Robinson 1988, 9, 15–16). What is so significant for the student of palaces about Elias de Dereham is that his busy career spanned the great royal and ecclesiastical building projects of the first half of the thirteenth century. He provides one of those so often elusive links between the achievements of contemporary kings and bishops. The proportions of the body of the great hall at the bishop's palace at Wells and those of the castle hall at Winchester are sufficiently similar to be a remarkable illustration of this cross-fertilisation (*see* Fig. 39).

Henry III was the greatest palace builder in England in the Gothic style. His piety led to the addition of eighteen new chapels at royal sites in his reign. He enhanced existing buildings with new wall paintings, painted ceilings, stained

Fig. 39 Plan of a) Winchester castle great hall and the great hall at b) Wells, Somerset, built by Bishop Jocelyn. Elias de Dereham was employed on both projects and the remarkable match of the plans may be a reflection of this. (*Drawing by Alex Turner*)

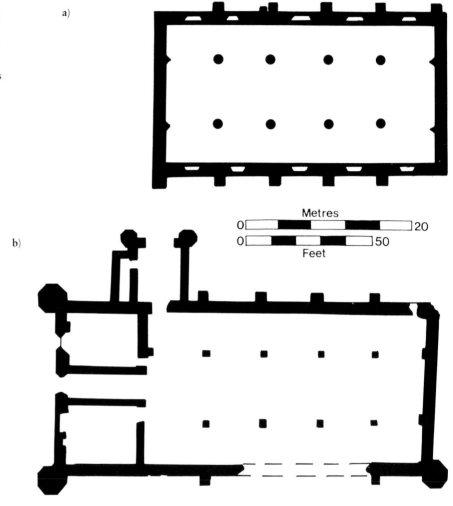

and painted glass for the windows, and on occasions coloured glass was set in wall decorations. Novelties such as ceramic floor tiles set in circular patterns date from his reign. Gilded stone and metalwork were commonly found glittering in royal houses and churches, and at Clarendon it has been shown that the rich blue of painted plaster almost certainly from his reign, was derived from crushed lapis lazuli from Afghanistan (James and Robinson 1988, 253). His queen, Eleanor of Provence, whom Henry married in 1236, shared her husband's enthusiasm for building and interior design. Together they made a supreme effort to place England, which lay on the edge of the medieval world, in the mainstream of European art and architecture. In addition, the necessity of providing proper accommodation at all royal residences for the queen, who was used to living in comparative luxury in southern France, led to much work on suites of buildings for her personal use and for her household. The hand of Eleanor's mother, a daughter of the sophisticated Count of Savoy may be detected in these improvements. Provençals and Savoyards became influential at Henry and Eleanor's court, to the annoyance of the barons of England whose sense of position in English society was offended. A residence, later known as the Savoy palace, in the Strand was given to the queen's brother, Peter of Savoy, who left it to a Savoyard hospice from which the queen bought it back. Having repossessed it the queen gave it to her son Edmund of Lancaster, thereby ensuring a descent through the duchy of Lancaster to John of Gaunt (Powicke 1962, 249–50n) (page 128). Lucrative offices also went to the Savoyards and Provençals, which was perhaps even more wounding to the pride and pocket of the English barons.

Some of the foreigners no doubt performed their tasks honestly and diligently, taking their example from Eleanor herself, but where they were corrupt and rapacious the English were fiercely critical. Amongst those who had criticism heaped upon them was Peter de Aquablanca, a fat Savoyard with a carbuncle on his nose, whose unpleasant physical appearance was a problem in itself. This man was foisted on the canons of Hereford in 1240 by Henry III, who thereafter tried to have Peter advanced to more lucrative sees such as Durham. Attempts to impose Aquablanca elsewhere failed, not least because of his performance, or lack of it, at Hereford, which he rarely visited, choosing to live abroad, although he ensured the profits of the bishopric were diverted overseas to further his enterprises there. Matthew Paris, who opposed Henry III in his writing, was not a chronicler to mince his words and wrote that the memory of Aquablanca 'exhales a foul and sulphurous stench' (Moorman 1955, 167). Aquablanca left Hereford diocese in disarray, and his successors, such as the Kentish Bishop Swinfield, found ample work to be done in his long episcopate later in the century (page 101ff.).

It is no surprise to find that from this period of royal enthusiasm for architecture, art and iconography, the records are in some respects the best we have from the entire Middle Ages. Almost daily instructions were issued by the king and queen detailing work to be done at residences throughout the country. These instructions are preserved in the Liberate rolls of the chancery where, despite the translation into the language of officialdom, the impatient personality of the king comes through. For example in 1227, almost as soon as the king came of age, repairs to a wine cellar were ordered by him to be performed 'immediately on sight of these letters' (James and Robinson 1988, 28). The king and queen were the initiators of many building schemes and the documents read as their personal verbal commands, committed to parchment in the chancery. Their tastes and enthusiasms are clearly seen in the surviving written records. All kinds of precise information are found in these records, including matters relating to the construction and reconstruction of buildings, details of interior decoration, schemes of wall painting, window decoration, sculpture, furnishings and flooring.

In the matter of floor tiles the queen may have taken a particular interest. It was formerly thought that it was Eleanor who was personally responsible for the introduction into England of ceramic floor tiles. This is no longer tenable, for the sudden appearance and growth in usage of this type of tile in England is noted in the late twelfth century and is now associated with the rebuilding of Canterbury cathedral from 1174. In the thirteenth century royal palaces and other royal works led the way, in particular in the period after 1236, which

leaves open the possibility that the queen was in some way associated with the development of tiled floors in royal buildings (*see* Figs. 40 and 41). Ceramic tiles were then, as now, more associated with the sunny climates of southern Europe than with the colder north, and it is noteworthy that the thirteenth century was one of the warmest during the Middle Ages.

The influence of the queen noted here was one element in a much broader trend in medieval building and decoration in England. From the Conquest onwards art and architecture in England were inspired largely by French and Italian models in both secular and religious work. These influences arose from political and economic ties and are epitomised by English Romanesque and Gothic.

Recent work has begun to open up some previously unexplored avenues which link palace works and ecclesiastical buildings in the thirteenth century in general. An interesting case has been made for grouping work from the early thirteenth century into what is labelled 'southern-English Gothic *c.* 1215–40'. These buildings include Archbishop Langton's work at Lambeth palace and his hall at Canterbury, Bishop Jocelyn's hall at Wells, Winchester castle hall and Clarendon, as well as at various cathedrals in the region, notably Salisbury, Chichester, Rochester and others. Qualities of spaciousness in the lightweight structures are associated with restraint and even austerity (Jansen 1985, 95–7, 97–8n). This unadorned work is contrasted with the more highly decorated work at Lincoln, both in the cathedral and in the bishop's palace. Continental influence is noted in analysis of work by Bishop des Roches, while new men who emerge after John's reign, such as Archbishop Langton and his protégé Richard Poore, successively at Chichester and at Salisbury, are identified with buildings in specific locations. Thus the debate about what was 'new' or 'old' in style in the late twelfth and thirteenth centuries continues with the research into Hereford, referred to above, and that into southern Gothic mentioned here. There is clearly much more work to be done on this significant period of English architecture, the transition from what is called in England 'Norman' to 'Early English'.

Naturally enough the royal household did not wish to stay in residences which were surrounded by scaffolding and filled with workmen. From his minority Henry was used to an itinerant lifestyle, as a glance at the locations of the Christmas courts in the 1220s shows. Christmas was spent in 1220 at Marlborough, in 1221 at Oxford, in 1222 at Winchester (no doubt at Wolvesey as the castle hall would have been embryonic, and 'where Bishop Peter . . . supplied all necessaries in a splendid manner'), in 1223 at Oxford once more,

Fig. 40 Ceramic floor tiles from Clarendon decorated with various animals, real and imaginary, and motifs appropriate for a hunting base in the forest. (*Trustees of the British Museum*)

Fig. 41 The royal coat of arms on a floor tile at Westminster Abbey, where a rich series of hunting scenes, Bible stories and other designs are still to be seen in the Chapter House. (*Copyright English Heritage*)

in 1224 at Northampton and in 1225 at Westminster. The king, like his father, (and in common with the younger magnates) developed a taste for mobility. Particular feasts were enjoyed at particular places, for example the feasts of Edward the Confessor on 5 January and 13 October at Westminster if possible, with swift moves afterwards. Such mobility, especially in the depths of winter, had its dangers and probably contributed to the illness of the king in 1226 when, after Christmas at Winchester, the court moved off to Marlborough where the king's life was despaired of. Mobility enabled the king to avoid major building works at his own palaces while facilitating the enjoyment of the amenities of various of his own and other men's residences. Examples include Christmas at Winchester in 1222 and at London in 1231, where the king spent the festival with the archbishop and justiciar, Hubert de Burgh, who provided the feast.

Henry was a great francophile and in particular admired Louis IX (1226–70). The story that Henry admired Louis's Sainte Chapelle in Paris so much that he said he would have liked to have carried it off in a cart to England may be apocryphal, but indicates the relationship of these two kings. Henry's visit to France in 1254, when he saw the famous royal chapel, reputedly gave him ideas for the decoration of Westminster Abbey, and may have been where he saw for the first time stonework and plasterwork finished with a fine coat of gypsum. Louis and Henry were married to two sisters, daughters of the Count

Raymond of Provence, who had four daughters in all. The other two daughters were in turn married to the two kings' younger brothers. Such prestigious marriage alliances revealed a wealth of diplomatic skill to balance Count Raymond's better known tag 'the poet count'.

The barons' war of 1258–65, while a widely-based baronial rebellion against Henry, was fuelled by personal animosities, for example Simon de Montfort's long held grudge against the king who had failed to provide a dowry when his sister married Simon. The increasing proportion of national revenue which Henry and Eleanor poured into their building works was a further reason for their unpopularity. It was to King Louis that Henry turned in his hour of need and his brother-in-law responded with military support.

Henry III used the French model of the royal monastery at St Denis, north of Paris, for his own rebuilding of the abbey at Westminster, although stamping his work with English motifs. Major works were begun on Edward the Confessor's abbey and the adjacent palace. Until Henry III's time the kings of England had been buried in a variety of places, including the nunnery of Fontevrault in Anjou, but no longer since John's reign in English hands. Despite this fact, John's heart was sent to Fontevrault, although his other remains were laid to rest at Worcester. The heart-burial was no doubt a pledge of continuing claims to former Angevin lands in France. The treaty of Paris of 1259, sealed with Louis IX while Henry was hard-pressed in the barons' war, established the position of the English king as a liege vassal of the king of France. Arguably, thereafter, the position of the kings of England with regard to lands in France was weaker. The deep admiration for and trust in Louis IX displayed by Henry III accounts both for his ready acquiescence in the vassalage agreement (which was to turn so sour in the fourteenth century) and also for the English king's emulation of French models, illustrated in the rebuilding of the abbey church at Westminster which, though not completed until long after Henry's death, was to become the royal burial place in England in the time of Henry's son Edward I. This was a direct imitation of the French royal monastery and burial place at St Denis. When compared to the scale of building demanded in the major royal religious centre, refurbishment of the domestic accommodation in the palace of Westminster was an altogether more easy task, and Henry enlarged and embellished the buildings on a scale not seen before. Extravagant royal palace building and reconstruction programmes on the scale carried out by Henry III provided an inspiration for his contemporaries to build and refurbish on a grand scale also. Thus we see from the decades before 1250 archbishops at work on their great palace at Lambeth, across the river from Westminster. The crypt and chapel of this major archiepiscopal palace survive and are dated to *c.* 1225–45 (Schofield 1984, 64).

Henry III's favourite predecessor and his patron saint was Edward the Confessor, in whose honour he named his eldest son Edward. Further, Henry determined to make the saint-king's shrine at Westminster a place of pilgrimage. In the works associated with moving the shrine to the new abbey a piece of the robe in which the Confessor had been buried was recovered. The king saw to it that the fragment of this relic was saved and was sewn into the robe long used in coronation ceremonies, to provide a tangible link with the past. The tomb had previously been opened in the twelfth century, when Abbot Laurence found a sapphire finger ring, which became a holy relic. This sapphire is still to be seen in the upper cross of the Imperial State Crown, worn at the end of coronation ceremonies (*see* Fig. 42) (Holmes 1955, 5). For Henry III, as for the relic hunters of the twelfth century, Edward the Confessor remained a powerful symbol of English kingship, which subsequent leaders of Church and state wished to keep in the forefront of the growing national consciousness.

Henry favoured the palace of Westminster more than his ancestors had done and he made it perhaps the finest royal palace in Europe. The most remarkable feature of the palace was the king's main private room which became known as the 'Painted Chamber' in the early fourteenth century (*see* Fig. 43). Here he had his bed, carefully positioned so that he could see the altar in the adjacent chapel through a specially positioned window. The bed in the Middle Ages was

Fig. 42 Imperial State Crown. The sapphire in the topmost cross is said to have been recovered in the twelfth century from Edward the Confessor's tomb. The Black Prince's ruby can be seen at the bottom. This is said to have been worn by Henry V at Agincourt. (*HMSO*)

a highly prized possession and Henry's bed at Westminster was uniquely spectacular in keeping with his status. Green was a colour which especially appealed to this king, thus his bed had green painted posts studded with gold stars and green curtains. The curtains were decorative but also served to exlude the draughts, for the painted chamber was a large room 80 ft long by 26 ft wide and 31 ft high (24.4 m×7.9 m×9.4 m). The canopy over the bed, complete with a tabernacle, was probably reminiscent of the canopied tombs which were to appear in the rebuilt abbey church nearby. Apart from our knowledge of this bed we know little of the furnishings of this or other palaces. A glimpse is to be had in the Westminster Chronicle under 1255 where it is recorded that Henry III received from France a stone bath in the shape of a peacock 'covered all over with eyes like a real peacock, made of precious stones called pearls, gold, silver and sapphires'.

There is no doubt that the Painted Chamber contained one of the finest decorative schemes ever executed in England. Depiction of aspects of the life of Edward the Confessor was central to the overall conception. Most notable was a splendid account of the Confessor's coronation labelled '*Cest le Coronement de Seint Edeward*'. This scene was embellished with gold foliage on blue glass with copious enamel work. Considerable damage to the chamber resulted from a fire in February 1263, but the paintings were restored and maintained until eventually they were covered over. Fragments were rediscovered in the late eighteenth and nineteenth centuries. Below the dado the room was painted with dark green false curtains in Henry's reign. Above at this period were found didactic elements such as a *mappa mundi* and a Jesse tree, both devices well known at other Henrician palaces such as Clarendon. The scenes of Edward the Confessor (*see* Fig. 44) and the royal bed lay towards the north end of the room. What remained of the paintings was largely destroyed in the early nineteenth century through a combination of building works and the disastrous fire of 1834 (Colvin 1963, 495–9). The civil war between Henry III and the barons almost brought about the destruction of the Painted Chamber by opponents of the king who 'broke the doors and windows and scarcely withheld their hands from the burning of the whole palace'. The wooden ceiling of

Fig. 44 The head of Edward the Confessor recorded by Stothard in 1819 in the Painted Chamber. The text reads, in French, 'Pilgrim, take this ring . . . ' (*Society of Antiquaries of London*)

Fig. 45 The only known fragment of the ceiling *'paterae'* of the Painted Chamber. (*Trustees of Sir John Soane's Museum*)

Fig. 46 Two of the depictions of virtues/vices from the window splays of the Painted Chamber, recorded by Crocker in 1819 before their destruction. They were brightly painted with reds, blues, green and gold and were some 10ft high (3.05 m). *Left*: Largesse treads down Covetousness. Note in the border the arms of the Holy Roman Empire as well as of England. Henry III's brother, Richard, had been elected King of the Romans in 1257. *Right*: Cheerfulness treads down Anger. (*Ashmolean Museum*)

the Painted Chamber, as restored after the fire of 1263, was decorated with a rich and regular coloured pattern. A fragment of one of the panels survives in the Sir John Soane Museum in Lincoln's Inn Fields (*see* Fig. 45). The coloured record drawings made by Crocker and Stothard of the decorations as they could be discerned before the fire of 1834 give a most striking and vivid impression of the rich colour scheme of this most remarkable chamber (*see* Fig. 46). Other elements of the palace such as the queen's chambers and chapel also survived until the nineteenth century (*see* Fig. 47).

Fig. 47 Queen Eleanor's chambers and chapel at Westminster built in 1237–9 and now demolished, as they stood in 1809

The £10,000 spent by Henry on the palace of Westminster was surpassed only by the £15,000 spent on Windsor where, although much of the Windsor expenditure went on defensive works, Henry added fine accommodation and chapels, fragments of which survive today (*see* Fig. 48). Clarendon (£3,600) and Woodstock (£3,300) were equally favoured, followed by Havering (£2,000) and Guildford (£1,800). A further £2,500 was spent on other occasional residences, primarily Brill, Clipstone, Feckenham, Freemantle, Geddington and Silverstone. Evidence of the kind of use to which a residence might be put survives from 1247 (Colvin 1963, 120). In that year Woodstock was the scene of marriages arranged by the king for two young wards, the Earl of Lincoln and Richard de Burgh. These young men had been brought to the palace to be 'instructed in polite manners and accomplishments'. The Westminster chronicler sourly points out in that time of growing national consciousness that the brides were 'foreign women of low birth' and that the marriages were of 'ugly women to handsome men to bring about degeneracy by a spurious admixture of race'. Such xenophobia utterly fails to acknowledge that it was foreign marriages such as these which were a major force in improving the quality of life of the generally unsophisticated English nobility.

Fig. 48 Windsor. Detail of one of the west doors of Henry III's chapel. The highly ornate thirteenth-century ironwork is signed by the iron-worker 'Gilebertus' in three places. (*Reproduced by permission of the Dean and Canons of Windsor*)

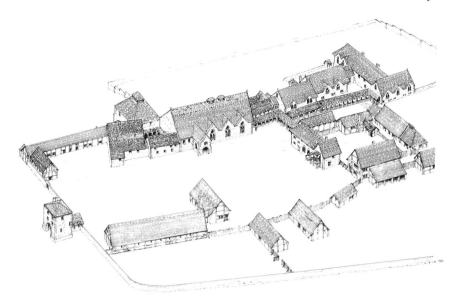

Fig. 49 Clarendon as it might have been towards the end of Henry III's reign. Reconstruction of the main ranges so far revealed by excavation looking north-east. From left to right can be seen the gatehouse and stables, kitchens, great hall and royal apartments. Behind the range lying north-south beside the great courtyard can be seen the wine cellar. (*Drawing Allan Adams. Society of Antiquaries*)

Clarendon was the major royal residence in Wiltshire in the thirteenth century and well exemplifies royal building works at a rural site in Henry's reign. In the thirteenth century the main structures were of flint rubble construction plastered over, and with ashlar quoins, the whole whitewashed over. The roofs were at first shingled, over 130,000 of these small wooden tiles being ordered for Clarendon between 1238 and 1252 from adjacent forests in Hampshire, Wiltshire and Dorset. In the course of the century shingles began to give way to roof tiles, some glazed, surmounted by glazed and decorated ridge tiles. There was in 1216 a great hall, kitchen, chapel, a suite for the king's use, a barrel-vaulted wine cellar and a variety of manorial buildings. The great hall was aligned east-west on the scarp of a slope which falls away steeply to the north. Here there was an artificial terrace. The king's chambers lay to the east of the hall and the kitchen's to the west (*see* Fig. 49).

In the course of the reign the buildings were extended and embellished. The main additions consisted of a new large kitchen 40 ft square (12.1 m), other buildings in the kitchen area and a suite of rooms for the queen. The wine cellar was doubled in size and a gatehouse added further to the west to increase the size of the enclosed area. These additions did not cost the £3,600 referred to above. Much of the expenditure was on improving and extending the buildings already present on the site. The Romanesque great hall 82 ft by 52 ft (25 m × 15.9 m) was remodelled in the Gothic style by the addition of larger reshaped windows which were glazed. In 1267 the four evangelists were depicted in the hall windows.

The king's chambers received much attention during Henry's reign. As at Westminster and elsewhere the king's principal chamber, an upper hall, was richly painted. Scenes from the life of St Margaret the Virgin and the four evangelists together with a series of heads of men and women were ordered in 1246, to be executed in 'exquisite colours'. The general scheme of decoration was based on green painted wainscot sprinkled with gold stars, no doubt with pictures above the dado as at Westminster. Similar paintings were executed at Havering in 1251. Green painted wainscot is documented in various locations

Fig. 50 Clarendon. Stars and
crescent made of lead and
originally gilded. (*Drawings
by Frances Rankine, Society
of Antiquaries of London*)

at Clarendon at this date so it was therefore not surprising that excavations in
the 1930s produced fragments of both light apple green and darker green plaster from the site. These finds are now stored in the British Museum. The green
demanded by the king must have been very much in keeping with the hues of
the surrounding forest. Eight-pointed lead stars and crescents which showed
traces of gilding when analysed in the laboratory were recovered from the area
of the king's chambers during excavations in the 1930s (*see* Fig. 50). These
stars may have been part of a decorative scheme of golden stars on a green
ground. Analysis of the pigments of other plaster fragments from Clarendon
has shown that a remarkable deep blue was achieved at Clarendon. Perhaps
stars were used against a blue ground to depict the night sky, as can be seen in
the Guardian Angels' chapel of similar date in Winchester cathedral. A striking wall decoration of stars and crescents against a blue background is seen in
an early thirteenth century manuscript illumination depicting cats hunting
mice (*see* Fig. 51).

During his pre-Christmas stay at Clarendon in 1247 Henry ordered a re-
placement chimneypiece, to be decorated with a wheel of fortune and a Jesse
tree. He issued careful instructions that the other paintings were to be screened
with canvas to prevent damage while the works were in progress. A wheel of
fortune was depicted at Winchester at the same period, and the remains of
another, surviving in Rochester cathedral, may well have been by painters of
the court school. Below the king's principal chamber were his lower chambers.
The main one of these was decorated with a frieze of heads of real and imaginary
kings and queens of England. This work, now lost, has been rightly hailed as
an important development in English portrait painting (Borenius and Charlton
1936, 60; James and Robinson 1988, 8ff).

Under the supervision of Elias de Dereham in about 1236 work was undertaken
on a further royal chamber block. This contained the king's chapel on the
upper floor. The lower floor was occupied at first by his wardrobe and, after
1251, by the Antioch chamber, the most celebrated room at Clarendon. The
chapel was in itself remarkable. We do not now know what scenes were depicted on the walls, the lower part of which were wainscoted. The windows
were glazed, and fragments of painted window glass recovered in excavation
closely resemble contemporary glass from Salisbury cathedral, which shared a
workforce with Clarendon at this time. This accounts for the similarity of

Fig. 51 A decorative scheme of stars and crescents akin to that which must have existed at Clarendon is depicted as a backdrop for this early thirteenth-century illustration of cats hunting. (*Bodleian Library, Oxford. MS Bodl. 764, fol. 51r*)

many architectural and decorative details. The most remarkable survival of the decorative scheme from this chapel is a circular tile pavement, composed of alternating bands of green and brown inlaid tiles which were fired in a kiln specially erected in the kitchen area of the site, some distance from the royal apartments, and now on display in the British Museum. Round the edge of the pavement ran a legend, some letters from which were found in the 1930s excavations, although what the text was is not now known. Floor tiles were still comparatively rare in secular buildings in England and a sophisticated floor such as this in an upper chamber again emphasises the high quality and innovative nature of royal works under Henry III. We know from excavations that there were in addition at least two other circular tiled floors laid at Clarendon (James and Robinson 1988, 143).

In 1251 orders were issued by the king for work to begin on converting the old wardrobe room beneath the chapel into an audience chamber by the demolition of interior walls and the addition of a scheme of paintings of 'the story of Antioch and the duel of King Richard'. At the back of Henry's mind may have been a desire to celebrate the passing of some fifty years since his uncle Richard's death, or sixty years since the third crusade in which Richard took part. The request was somewhat unhistorical if Henry had an association between Richard and Antioch in mind, as Acre was the scene of his uncle's triumph in 1191. Alternatively he may have wanted two series of paintings, one of the misdeeds of King Antiochus (as was depicted in the painted chamber at Westminster) and another of Richard duelling with Saladin (*see* Fig. 52). The paintings were to be placed above the familiar gold spangled green wainscot. The decorative scheme was supplemented in the following year by the addition of a tiled floor, fragments of which were found in place in the 1930s (*see* Fig. 53).

Queen Eleanor's rooms, to the east of the Antioch chamber, consisted of hall and chamber and a chapel constructed within a decade of her marriage to Henry III in 1236. The decorations included a window containing a depiction of Mary with the Holy Child bearing a ribbon which read '*Ave Maria*' and additionally an earthly queen and child, presumably Eleanor herself and Prince Edward. Tiled floors, one of which was still in place in the 1930s and is now

Fig. 52 Highest quality floor tiles depicting Richard the Lionheart and Saladin in combat. They were recovered from the site of Chertsey Abbey but are now believed to have been made for a royal palace, perhaps Westminster. (*Trustees of the British Museum*)

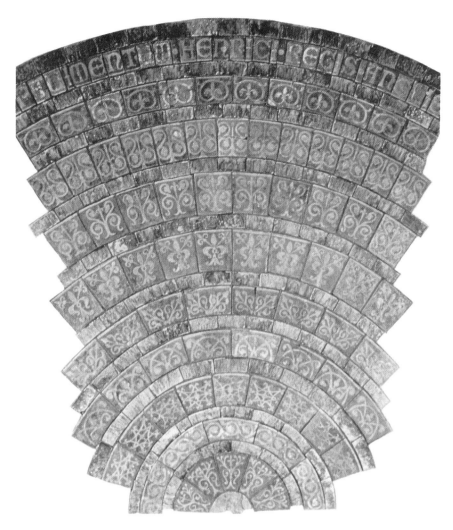

Fig. 53 A reconstructed segment of the circular pavement believed to have come from the king's chapel at Clarendon. Remains of at least two other such pavements have been found at the site. (*Trustees of the British Museum*)

on display in the British Museum, added to the scheme and in 1251 a remarkable fireplace sculpted with representations of the months of the year and flanked by double marble columns was inserted in the queen's hall. The remains of a similar fireplace were identified by Stothard in the nineteenth century in the rubble used to block a window at Westminster palace. from the remains he was able to reconstruct the whole sequence. A series of painted roundels showing similar scenes adorns the roof of Salisbury cathedral, and may bear some relationship to the lost sculpture from Clarendon. Remains of richly painted plaster, certain fragments of which represented human hands, drapery and architectural features, were recovered from the area of the queen's apartments at Clarendon by excavation (James and Robinson 1988, 18, 252).

Ashlarwork, tiles and metal artefacts are much more durable in the archaeological record than ephemeral features of the palace environment such as gardens. It seems clear that royal gardens were primarily the responsibility of queens in the Middle Ages and there is plenty of evidence to support this view

(Colvin 1986, 9). Beyond the queen's apartments at Clarendon we hear of gardens, as well as elsewhere at that site and at all palaces. However, despite the lack of physical remains there is no doubt that gardens were very popular with both Henry and Eleanor. The queen may well have been the innovator in this respect as activities appear to increase significantly after marriage in 1236. The white *rosa alba*, which was the emblem of Queen Eleanor, was incorporated into the great seal by Edward I in his mother's honour. It was a popular hedge rose, and the tribute in the seal may have been a practical reminder of the queen's interest in gardens as well as the symbolic use of her emblem by her son (McLean 1981, 165).

Towards 1250 the appointment of royal gardeners were specified in the records for the first time, including at least one with a provençal name, which reinforces the view that the queen took a lead. Fathers and sons inherited positions in the royal gardens in the course of the long reign of Henry and Eleanor. From Henry's death in 1272 to her own death in 1291, the dowager queen maintained this interest, especially in her garden at King's Langley (Hertfordshire (Neal 1971, 32). At Gloucester, by special request of the queen, access was gained to the large garden of Lanthony Priory so that the queen and her household could walk there. The point of access was across a specially constructed bridge from the castle into the priory grounds beyond (Harvey 1981, 74ff.).

Gardens were maintained, remodelled or established at all the major royal residences. They display a number of characteristics of layout and content; references to gardens below chamber windows were a striking feature. The significance of lawns, or herbers, was alluded to in contemporary treatises. Lawns were created at all the major residences. One with a bench for royal use below a whitewashed wall was created at Clarendon in 1250. Much turfing was carried out at royal residences and a reference to rolling the lawns at Westminster survives from 1259. Whether the lawns were always of grass or were sometimes of camomile is unknown. Pools were featured on occasion, particularly at Everswell (Woodstock) where Rosamund Clifford lived in Henry II's time. References to a large pool at Everswell and a smaller one with a bench beside it are found from the thirteenth century. A pool was dug at Windsor in 1262, and turfing carried out. Other garden features include an iron trellis put up in the garden at Woodstock in 1239 and a marble cloister erected within a garden at Guildford in 1256. Many of these gardens were small and intimate, in the angles of buildings. But there were also more extensive gardens, replete with vines and orchards. The orchard of a hundred pear trees at Everswell must have been a magnificent sight in bloom. Pear trees, no doubt for perry, and vines are commonly found in the records in the mid-thirteenth century, and less often cherry trees feature, but more detail of particular fruits and flowers survives from the Edwardian period (pages 94–6). Royalty such as Henry III and Queen Eleanor were not content to spend money on their palaces and gardens without making good use of the pleasure domes they created. The carefully and richly appointed material environment of palace buildings and gardens, which derived from the personal wishes of the king and queen, provided a setting for a lifestyle in keeping with the extravagant buildings which are known from this period. The fundamental necessities of life, food and drink, were anything but basic at palaces in the mid-thirteenth century. Food and wine were consumed in increasing quantities by the royal family, household and guests until the baronial revolt of 1258 interrupted royal expenditure.

Ensuring adequate supplies for royal feasts was a major undertaking, and here again the royal couple took a personal interest and the officials saw to it that the requests were carried out. In the matter of provision of food for feasts as in politics, in periods of harmony the king and the magnates helped one another out. However, there were times when the king could take advantage of his magnates' resources for his own ends, with or without permission. Preparations for the Christmas feast of 1244, which Henry enjoyed at Wallingford, as the guest of his brother Richard, exemplify this interplay. The brothers had reason to wish to impress on this occasion, as the king's beautiful mother-in-law Beatrice was present as was Richard's bride, Sanchia. On 2nd September the king had 300 pigs sent from the manors of the Bishop of Winchester to be fattened in Clarendon forest, and a further 300 were sent to Chute forest. The date of 2nd September is significant, for it suggests that the king was making a grab for resources of the wealthy bishopric in advance of the new bishop gaining possession, after a four-year dispute with the king, just a week later on 10th September. Two months later, in early November, supplementary orders were issued for the herds of pigs to be rounded up and driven by stages to the Thames valley (James and Robinson 1988, 30). Henry, it appears, made a generous contribution to the feast on this occasion with the support, willing or unwilling, of the Bishop of Winchester.

After Christmas, as was his custom, the king returned to Westminster for the feast of the Confessor (5th January). Here he 'especially displayed the magnificence of his own palace' before accompanying the Countess of Provence in great style to the coast. Although the scale of this Christmas feast is hinted at by the supplies of pork, it probably paled into insignificance in comparison to the wedding feast which Richard and Sanchia had enjoyed in November 1243. Even the normally voluble Matthew Paris was lost for words, describing the feast as 'stupendous' and declaring that to describe the 'thirty-thousand dishes for the diners' prepared in the royal kitchens would be boring for his readers (Roche 1966, 96).

The supply of the 600 pigs described above was only one aspect of food production for a Christmas feast in the mid-thirteenth century. Some of the orders issued in advance of Christmas in 1236 and in 1240 provided a fuller picture. In 1236, when Christmas was to be spent at Marlborough, the provisions included forty pounds of dates, six frails of figs, four boxes of pressed grapes and five or six packets of good ginger, for ginger and balsam mixed were considered by Henry to be good promoters of appetite and digestion.

In 1240 the king ordered officials throughout the realm to supply what seems to be an amazing amount of flesh, fowl and fish. The meat consisted of five bulls, eighty porkers, fifty-eight boars, forty roe deer, 1,500 lambs, 200 kids, 1,000 hares and 500 rabbits. The poultry and birds requested were 7,000 hens, 1,100 partridges, 312 pheasants, 100 peacocks, twenty swans from Cambridgeshire and Huntingdonshire, ten from Buckinghamshire and Bedfordshire and as many as possible from the lands of the Bishop of Winchester and of the late Earl of Surrey, together with twenty herons and bitterns and, if possible, in excess of fifty cranes. Finally orders were placed for 300 shad, 120 salmon (to be turned into 300 pies and the remainder salted), thirty lampreys and an unspecified amount of herring. As well as relying on imports of fish and markets, Henry III considerably increased the number and scope of royal fishponds to provide fish for the royal table. Research shows the way in which the produce of the fishponds was used by the king. When the court was at Westminster the Northamptonshire fishponds at Brigstock, King's Cliffe and Silverstone were used; when at Windsor, Winchester, Clarendon or Woodstock the fish was transported from the Marlborough ponds, with all this provision implies in terms of transport, keeping the fish fresh and so on (Steane 1988, 49–50).

It is noteworthy that the quantities of different kinds of quarry ordered differ from year to year and feast to feast. This was partly a function of the time of year. For example, the traditional killing of the pig for Christmas is the most popular representation for December in medieval calendars. It will be observed that there were many fewer pigs ordered in 1240 than the 600 in 1244. Compared with the eighty bucks ordered from the parks of Clarendon, Chute, Melksham and Devizes towards the feast to celebrate Edward the Confessor's day in 1271, there was comparatively little venison required in 1240. The sheer scale of the requirements for royal feasts such as these must have meant periods of intense activity for many different officials throughout the royal estates, from the huntsmen (whose positions, like those of some royal gardeners, were becoming hereditary in the thirteenth century), warreners and falconers who had to collect the cranes and other birds, to the fishermen and keepers of the royal vivaria. It is not surprising the king needed aids to digestion!

Food was washed down with quantities of wine, and there is ample evidence of a variety of wines being sent to royal palaces during Henry and Eleanor's rule. The growth of wine consignments to Clarendon makes this point well. In 1227 two tuns of wine were earmarked in the port of Southampton for Clarendon and in 1228 there were nine. By 1236 the number had increased to four ordered on 10th December, with a supplementary order for a further ten to be sent 'with speed' on the following day. A further four were demanded in the following week. In 1239 the number rose to twenty-six and in 1240 to forty-six (*see* Fig. 54). Numbers peaked at double this level before civil war summarily halted the flow in 1258. By then the already substantial ashlar-lined and barrel-vaulted wine cellar, originally carved out of the chalk hilltop during Henry II's reign, had been extended in 1252 to double its former size.

The types of wine sent to Clarendon and royal residences elsewhere were largely French in origin, from Anjou and Gascony. In addition there are records of English wines arriving at Clarendon at this time: mulberry and raspberry, for example, together with what may have been a kind of iron-tonic wine described in the records as *ferrati*, and presented to the king by the Prior of Ogbourne St George (Wiltshire) (Harvey 1948, 99).

Who consumed all this food and drink? Under normal circumstances the answer must be that it was the royal family and their attendant household. Alms-giving in various forms must account for much of the rest. In one particular respect Henry III's reign differed from that of his predecessors with regard to alms-giving. A new avenue for the generosity of this pious king was to sup-

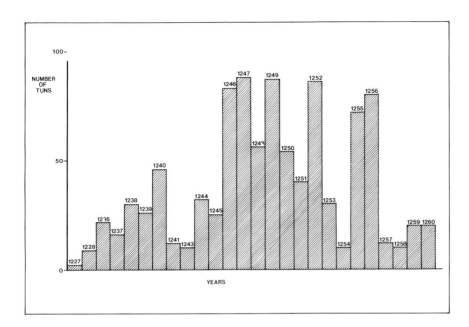

Fig. 54 Chart showing the wine deliveries to Clarendon for certain years in Henry III's reign. It reveals the interruption to the supply caused by the civil war of 1258. (*Drawn by Alex Turner*)

port the friars who appeared in England in the early 1220s and who practised poverty in their daily lives. Not only did Henry encourage the Franciscans and Dominicans through sponsorship of their houses, he also fed considerable numbers of friars on a daily basis, as for example the accounts for 1259–60 show. At Westminster on All Saints day (1st November) in 1259 no fewer than 390, as opposed to the usual 100 or so, joined his household to eat; 220 joined his meal with Archbishop Boniface at Canterbury, and the surprisingly large number of 150 travelled to France and were fed daily during a royal visit to the saintly King Louis IX. On the vigil of St Edward the enormous number of 5,016 friars is recorded as having been fed! (Johnstone 1929, 155).

Normal practice was to distribute to paupers large quantities of leftovers from royal meals. The poor gathered at the gates of royal residences in London and elsewhere to receive this bounty and the king expected to feed 500 a day (an annual total of 182,000 meals) as he revealed in a letter of 1242. A further 100 were fed on behalf of the queen and the royal children daily. Perhaps the highest figure recorded for a single occasion was the 10,000 for whom food was ordered to commemorate the soul of Eadgyth, Edward the Confessor's wife. What was provided is not stated but the expenses roll dutifully records the sum of £41 13s 4d, otherwise 10,000 pennies, spent on food for the poor. Occasional clues are given on where this phenomenal alms-giving was carried out. This was not mere dole at the gate, for instructions appear for example to 'feed in the great hall at Westminster as many as it will hold' and feed as many poor 'as can get into the hall' in the upper bailey at Windsor (Johnstone 1929, 156). This kind of charity may explain why the remains of feasts are not found in palace middens in the quantities in which the food appears in the written re-cord. There was little that could not be reused one way and another, and dis-posal of remains to the poor must have helped clear the kitchens and keep the palaces, if not the surrounding settlements, clear of refuse.

However, some bones have been found in palace refuse pits, although we have comparatively little evidence from excavation at present. What has been recovered gives some support to the picture given by the documents. Although undated, remains of ox, sheep and pig predominate in the Clarendon assemblage. Red deer bones can be seen on site in the photographic records of the 1930s excavations there. Bird bones of domestic fowl, goose, golden plover and either heron or bittern were recovered. Some oyster shells were found, together with a disproportionately high number of whelk shells. No doubt further investigations, aimed to extend our knowledge of environmental evidence from this medieval palace site, would enhance the limited material currently to hand. Nothing is so far known from evidence of seeds and pollen at Clarendon.

Feasting was not a prerogative of kings alone. Lords and bishops entertained in great style and the excellent records of the bishopric of Winchester give us some insights into this activity. In the first year of his episcopate, 1244–5, William Ralegh feasted at Christmas and Easter, although the most notable feast that year was to celebrate St Edmund's day on 20th November, just two months after Ralegh had gained access to his see from Henry III after the dispute and four-year delay mentioned earlier. The resources of the bishopric manors in Hampshire, Berkshire, Buckinghamshire, Wiltshire and Surrey were mobilised to bring supplies to Wolvesey palace in Winchester (*see* Fig. 55). The manors supplied ceramic wares in great quantities. Three hundred dishes and the same number of bowls came from Ecchinswell on the Hampshire/Berkshire border, together with sixty tablecloths. A further 280 dishes, 250 bowls, seventy-five saucers and forty platters were made and sent from Highclere. Further dishes and bowls arrived from Bishop's Waltham and East Meon specifically for this occasion, and 2,000 dishes sent from Wargrave about the same time may well have been for the 'feast of St Edmund'.

So far as meat was concerned, it is apparent that the king had taken all the swine, which acounts for the lack of a single reference to pigs or pork here, and may in part account for the rich variety of meats chosen by the new bishop. Venison was hunted on the bishop's orders in the park at Farnham and at Bishop's Waltham. Brawn came from West Wycombe (Buckinghamshire) in a specially hired cart with six peacocks and 'widfowl', the latter a commodity supplied in unspecified numbers from most of the manors. A wide selection of named birds were provided. Pheasant were caught by the episcopal falconers at Farnham and Highclere (a single bird); thirty-three partridge also came from Highclere, and the same numbers from East Woodhay and Ashmansworth, while eighteen came from Ecchinswell and a man and his boy were paid for catching others at Bishop's Sutton. Hens and chickens were supplied from Fareham (eighty-two hens), Bishopstoke (122 chickens) and Twyford (120 chickens) with further poultry from Downton (Wiltshire) and from Hambledon. Six woodcock, a single mallard and a plover came from Highclere. Fish came primarily from the bishop's vivarium at Alresford in the form of fifty pike, other fish came from Bishop's Waltham. Five tuns of wine were brought in for the occasion from Portsmouth, transported by boat to Fareham and carted thence to Wolvesey. The new bishop clearly wanted to make his mark in the diocese and country alike. Undeniably this was a special occasion, refer-

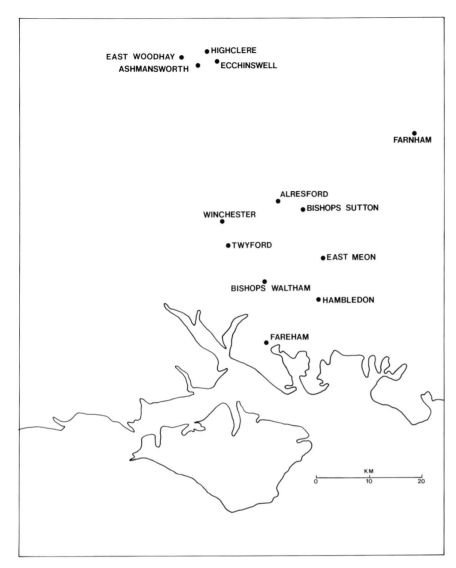

Fig. 55 Map showing certain bishopric manors which supplied William Ralegh's feast on St Edmund's day (20th November) 1244, soon after this bishop had gained access to his see. (*Information supplied by Edward Roberts. Map drawn by Alex Turner*)

red to as the 'feast of St Edmund', not an ordinary feast (*festum*) or banquet (*convivium*) for which no such special arrangements are recorded. Such a feast signalled the wealth of a see like Winchester, although the standard of living of most bishops was exceptionally high wherever they presided over a diocese (Roberts, 1989).

Of the entertainments which accompanied the feasting and royal and episcopal daily life, again we know little. In Henry III's time family life predominated and entertainments were perhaps more restrained than at other times in the Middle Ages. On one occasion early in his reign his guardians produced a bevy of bare-breasted dancers at court for the young king, but Henry was embarrassed and waved them away. Musical entertainment seems to have been preferred, for payments to the king's harper and his family were regular and generous. The wife of the king's fiddler received a fur trimmed cloak in

1240, and we hear of minstrels or players. The ecclesiastical hierarchy also enjoyed musical entertainment. Even the most severe of all thirteenth-century clergy, Bishop Robert Grosseteste (who died at Buckden palace in 1253), while implacably opposing the employment of minstrels by his clergy, kept a harper himself, no doubt following a biblical precedent (Poole 1958, 605). A substantial payment was made to Henry of Avranches 'the king's versifier' (Harvey 1948, 100–1). The king and queen no doubt enjoyed reading from his beautiful 'great book of Romances' embellished with silver hasps. Stories from the book formed the basis of various pictorial schemes in the best appointed residences in the land, where both secular and religious wall paintings were to be found.

Henry had already begun to assemble a menagerie at the Tower by the time he was married in 1236. The Holy Roman Emperor, Frederick II, born and bred in Sicily, probably provided the impetus for this. Frederick took pride in his own menagerie, which was enhanced in 1236 by the gift from the Sultan of Egypt of a giraffe, the first seen in Europe. The previous year the emperor had presented Henry with three leopards, which were in time joined by a camel. A polar bear was sent from Norway. The most exotic acquisition, an elephant, arrived in 1255. This was said to have been the first elephant seen in England, and was a gift from Louis IX of France. Sadly the great beast pined and within three years was dead.

After the barons' war had been fought and won by Henry's forces and Simon de Montfort, the baronial leader, was dead, Henry III and Eleanor were able to restore the style of life they had enjoyed before 1258. In the last few years of the reign before Henry died in 1272 expenditure on buildings and supplies of wine and other luxuries soared once more. The most remarkable survival of this indian summer of Henry's reign is the so-called Cosmati Pavement in Westminster Abbey (WA, 1989) (*see* Fig. 56). This was created, as its inscription reveals, in 1268 by Petrus Ordericus, a mosaic worker, at the instigation of Henry III. It is the finest example of such a pavement north of the Alps. The materials are porphyry, marbles and glass tesserae set in Purbeck 'marble' with a centre piece of rare onyx, possibly from Iran or Egypt. The creation and fortunate survival of this pavement in Henry's Westminster Abbey gives an insight into this great patron of art and architecture's world picture. Henry's successors and their queens in the middle ages and the early Tudor period are said to have made use of the pavement in the private annointing ceremony during their coronations. Although the inscription is now partly worn away, sufficient has been recovered to allow the following modern translation:

'If the reader prudently considers all that is set down, he will find here the end of the *primum mobile*. [Defined by Grosseteste (d. 1253) as 'The cause of unity, order and permanence in the way of nature'.] The field lives three years; add dogs and horses and men, stags and ravens, eagles, huge sea-serpents, the world: whatever follows triples the years of the foregoing. The sphere shows the archetype, this globe shows the macrocosm.'

Fig. 56 Henry III's remarkable Cosmati Pavement composed of exotic stones at Westminster Abbey, as depicted by Ackermann in 1812. (*By courtesy of the Dean and Chapter of Westminster*)

Within five years of this work the old king was dead, and perhaps the same mosaicists turned their skills to the production not only of Henry's tomb but also one for the remains of Edward the Confessor. This was necessary not only because the shrine of the Confessor was to be a centrepiece of the rebuilt abbey, but also because Henry, in an extraordinary final act of piety, had his own mortal remains buried in the very coffin formerly occupied by Saint Edward.

Chapter V

Early Edwardian palaces (1272–1327)

The Lord Edward was away on crusade when his father, Henry III, died in 1272 and he did not return home until 1274. In the course of his travels he learnt much about contemporary building styles in Europe and beyond. In particular his experience in Savoy clearly impressed him, as his employment of Savoyard clerks of works, notably in his Welsh castles, testifies. From the point of view of this study of palaces, however, more significant than the fortification of the Welsh castles was his encouragement of a court style in architecture, developing Henry III's enthusiasm for large scale schemes of wall painting and for French styles.

Edward I was an active warrior king, a role he combined with considerable activity as a builder of note. It is currently thought that the major series of wall paintings of biblical scenes commissioned at Westminster palace was in keeping with Edward's martial interests. Above the dado of the Painted Chamber was a series of 'warlike paintings from the Bible. . . .painted with wonderful skill and explained by a complete series of texts beautifully written in French'. So exquisite were these decorations that a visitor from Ireland to Westminster in 1323 described the Painted Chamber as one of the wonders of the world (Binski 1986, 1, 6). More obviously French in its influences was St Stephen's chapel at Westminster which was sponsored by the king in the 1290s. The chapel was largely destroyed in the disastrous fire at Westminster in 1834, although fragments of the original decoration survive in the British Museum.

Despite the king's absence at the beginning of his reign, building works, repairs and maintenance continued. As a survey of Clarendon carried out in 1272 or 1273 shows, buildings deteriorated rapidly. No doubt John Russell, who was assuming responsibility for the manor, had an interest in demonstrating the failures of his predecessor. 'And thus it is seen' concluded the report 'that Stephen de Eddeworth left the said manor in bad condition, and John Russell received it in that state'. There is much of the flavour of a modern surveyor's report in this account of Clarendon, in which the defects are emphasised and the strengths passed over without comment.

The roofs, gutterings and drainpipes in particular required attention, and there had been a fire in one of the queen's chambers. Elizabeth Eames, who led excavations to rescue the tiled floor from one of these chambers in the 1950s, discovered evidence of burning and an area of broken tiles where a blazing beam from the upper storey had apparently crashed down in this or a later fire (Eames 1988, 144–5). The roof of the great hall needed reshingling and the buttresses on the north of the building were in need of repair. Windows in the buttery and pantry required attention.

A clear distinction in function can be detected in this survey between the kitchen of the king and the kitchen in which food was prepared for the household. We cannot be sure which was which, although it seems likely that the original kitchen had continued in use at least since John's reign for the king's service. Such antiquity could explain the necessity recorded on this occasion for it to be reroofed. It is significant that the king was furnished with a separate kitchen at this stage, perhaps an element in the increasing demand for privacy which became a feature of building works in many contexts in the later Middle Ages. At Clarendon, the newer kitchen dating from 1244 was found to be in good repair in 1273.

Certainly from Henry III's reign adequate accommodation was needed for the queens of England, who had for a long time brought foreign sophistication to the court of England (pages 69–70). There is no doubt that Henry and his son Edward were devoted to their respective queens, who were both spirited and innovative royal patrons. Edward I had married Eleanor of Castile, in Spain, in 1254. He was just under fifteen, and his bride perhaps nine years old. When she came to England in 1255 she lived at Windsor for some time. The first of the sixteen (the number is uncertain, but not less than thirteen) children she bore Edward was Eleanor, born in 1264. With the king increasingly busy in national and international politics, the queen was provided with a variety of manors where she could enjoy family life away from the cares of state. The strenuous life led by the king was unsuitable either for his often pregnant wife, or for the delicate health of small children. These manors were in addition to her dower of Grantham, Stamford and the castles of Tickhill and Peak (Powicke 1962, 118).

In 1276 Eleanor was given the manor of King's Langley, where in 1278 a substantial building programme was initiated, which is referred to in the documents as 'a new start'. In the same year the ninth royal child, Mary, was born. Of these nine John, Henry, Isabel and Berengaria had already died. Alfonso (b. 1273) was the only surviving male heir. Work at Kings Langley included special accommodation for Alfonso, no doubt part of an attempt to ensure the survival of the precious little prince. But these precautions were barely complete when Alfonso died in 1284. Fortunately, also in 1284, the king was rewarded with another male heir, Edward of Carnarvon, who survived to maturity as Edward II. By 1284 the works at King's Langley were largely complete, and the mass of building materials, which included Reigate stone, timber, ironwork, plaster and floor tiles were all in place. Tiling was carried out in the queen's cloister and in her great and middle chamber. A number of fragmentary tiles were recovered in the excavations in 1970, which are comparable with types found at Westminster, and could be of this date (Neal 1971, 32, 67).

Another residence put at the disposal of the queen was the beautiful Leeds Castle in Kent, which came to the crown in 1278. It is no coincidence that the 'gloriet' at Leeds dates from the Castilian Queen Eleanor's days. The term 'gloriet', a Spanish term to denote a pavilion at the intersection of four quarters of a Moorish garden, was applied to the extensions of the castle at Leeds carried out between 1278 and 1290. As John Harvey has observed, Queen Eleanor's gloriet predates by a few years the much more intricate work with the same name carried out by Count Robert of Artois at Hesdin in northern France before 1302. At Hesdin the Arabic influence was taken up in earnest with a series of water-engines and fountains (designed in part to give visitors a surprise soaking). There were also other machines, including a talking owl, and machines which showered the unwary not only with water, but also with soot and flour. All these were drawn from an early thirteenth-century Arabic book of mechanical devices (Harvey 1981, 105–6). Such mechanical devices were not new, as Liudprand of Cremona had discovered in ninth-century Byzantium, and were always intended to impress credulous visitors and so enhance the reputation of the ruler whose property they were (pages 26–7). Perhaps in deference to the English climate, the water soaking machines were omitted, as were other extravagant machines so far as is known. Even at its wealthiest in the Middle Ages the English court did not choose such forms of conspicuous consumption to improve their standing at home and abroad. Mechanical clocks from Edward III's reign are the earliest examples of such gadgetry in England (pages 115–6).

The use of the name 'gloriet' at Leeds is significant, as is the Spanish and Arabic influence. Everswell at Woodstock, from a century earlier, was a gloriet in principle and had Arabic and Mediterranean associations (pages 54–5). At Corfe Castle (Dorset), King John's exquisitely appointed domestic accommodation block of the early thirteenth century, which survives as a ruin, later became known as a gloriet (Colvin 1963, 617). Perhaps it was Queen Eleanor who took an interest in internal plumbing at Leeds, for her executors in 1292 referred to the provision of one hundred Reigate stones which were required for paving 'the king's bath' at Leeds. References to a bath at the queen's manor at Langley also survive, reinforcing this speculation about her insistence on high standards of domestic comfort.

There is no doubt that Edward I was very devoted to Eleanor, and her patent interest in the appointment of royal houses may have contributed to this. There were also other reasons: the couple had married young and had effectively grown up together, producing perhaps sixteen children in the course of their marriage of over thirty-five years (page 93). Even for the royal family raising children to adulthood was problematical, so the king and queen suffered the bitter experience of seeing three of their four sons die in childhood: John aged five, Henry aged seven and Alfonso aged eleven. Their youngest son, Edward of Carnarvon survived to reign as Edward II, but his life was also cut short by his murder at the age of forty-three (page 108). Only one of their children, Margaret, lived to be fifty, having been received into the nunnery at Amesbury at the age of only five. When Eleanor died, still under forty-five, at Lincoln in 1290 Edward was grief-stricken, a grief expressed in the creation of the remarkable series of 'Eleanor crosses' along the route her body was taken to London for burial (*see* Fig. 57). After Eleanor's death, Leeds Castle, amongst other property formerly in her possession, passed to the new queen, Margaret, in her dowry in 1299. Though much restored now, the proportions of the buildings in their moated setting, give a good impression of their medieval beauty.

One of the shared interests of Edward I and Queen Eleanor was their gardens, an interest Edward had inherited from his father, Henry III, and which he and Eleanor passed down to Edward II. Indeed Edward II's relish of the heavier aspects of gardening such as digging and hedging were amongst the attributes considered by contemporaries to have been unkingly. In the matter of gardens and gardening, in contrast to their son, Edward I and Eleanor appear to have found a proper balance which attracted no criticism. With gardens, as with

Fig. 57 Eleanor Cross at Hardingstone, Northamptonshire. (*Photgraph John Steane*)

palaces (though not, of course, with castles), the emphasis in Edward I's reign moved away from the country places, such as Clarendon and Woodstock, towards residences in London and its immediate hinterland. The gardens at Westminster and the Tower were especially favoured and plenty of colour and variety was established in these London gardens at this time. Lawns were laid

(9,000 turfs on one occasion at the Tower), and a herber (lawn) perhaps of half an acre, on one estimate, at Westminster. Trees bought included 500 willows, and grafts of pear trees (one variety costing 3s 6d for each tree). Many vines were provided; 600 stocks were bought for 6s on one occasion in 1275. What seems to have been a palm was also purchased, as were quinces, peach trees and gooseberry bushes. If the entry of the palm in the records is correct (although it may have been a yew), it adds to the picture of especially warm weather in the twelfth and thirteenth century, already implied by Neckam's list of garden plants compiled three generations earlier. Flowers purchased for Edward and Eleanor's gardens included numerous lily bulbs, peony roots and roses, these last costing 2s 6d for 500 (Harvey 1981, 82) (page 57).

Edward I did not entirely neglect sites away from London. While Chester was in use as a base for military activity lawns were turfed and apple and pear trees bought in 1287. The castles in Wales, such as Conway, enjoyed some landscaping within their heavily defended precincts (Harvey 1981, 84). At Rhuddlan a garden including a small fishpond was fenced off for Queen Eleanor's use. This may have been at her special request, as she took an interest in the landscaping of her house at King's Langley, where the garden was re-positioned closer to the apartments, and a considerable area of vines was laid out (Neal 1971, 32, 118).

Edward took much pleasure in hawking as well as hunting. No fewer than fifty-three keepers of hunting animals and birds are accounted for in the 1280s of whom the majority looked after birds, the others having responsibilities as huntsmen and keepers of various types of hunting dogs (Prestwich 1988, 161). Royal mews were built for him at Charing Cross, together with accommodation for the falconers and for the royal hunting dogs. A dovecote was created to supply meat for the falcons and a 'house' for the cranes at which the gerfalcons were flown. The turfed garden at the mews had as its centrepiece a lead birdbath adorned with a metal falcon (Colvin 1963, 551; Fig. 58). The water supply to the fountain terminated in brass spouts in the form of leopards' heads, not inconceivably modelled on the leopard added by Edward to the menagerie his father had established at the Tower. This creature was a gift to King Edward from the Great Khan, who had been visited by English ambassadors hopeful of a crusading alliance against Islam. It is ironical that this crusading king should have been especially devoted to falconry, a sport imported from Islam. Edward maintained a detailed interest in his individual gerfalcons and is known on one occasion to have offered up a wax model of a favourite falcon at a shrine in an attempt to ensure the recovery of the ailing bird. On Ash Wednesday 1284 a surprising reference to general alms given on behalf of his gerfalcons is found (Taylor 1976, 106). On another occasion he complimented his falconers who sent him the heads of crane taken during a hawking expedition from which the king was absent. In recent years a replica medieval garden, with a falcon and leopards' head fountain in the middle, has been recreated on the south side of the thirteenth-century great hall of Winchester castle (*see* Fig. 58).

His indoor pursuits included chess. In 1300 he owned an ebony chess set and also one made of crystal and jasper. His interest may have been encouraged by his brother-in-law Alfonso of Castile's famous manual on the game. Edward's second wife, Margaret of France, was also a chess enthusiast, possessing two

Fig. 58 Replica of the Charing Cross fountain with leopards' head spouts, surmounted by a falcon, recently installed at Winchester. (*Photograph Alex Turner*)

chess sets valued highly at £40 each. Otherwise Edward enjoyed dice and listening to a harpist or minstrels. In the 1280s four minstrels and two trumpeters are found on the payroll. For special occasions what amounted to massed bands were required: 125 minstrels at Christmas 1288, 100 at the knighting of Edward of Carnarvon. Further entertainment came from acrobats and the aptly named Matilda Makejoy (Prestwich 1980, 24, 38; 1988, 117). An energetic king such as Edward I needed respite from affairs of state and his residences provided the requisite retreats. He relied heavily on his ministers of state, and while he did not, as other kings had, lavish gifts on them, he allowed his officers to acquire wealth in the course of their duties.

One such official was his chancellor, Robert Burnell, Bishop of Bath and Wells (1275–92). Edward I would have liked to have seen Burnell elevated to the archiepiscopal see at Canterbury, but this was not to be: Burnell's illegitimate offspring were an insurmountable problem. A contemporary annalist wrote on this subject: 'By means of his vast treasure he married off his relatives – I won't say daughters – to English noblemen. He acquired much property and many manors which he left to his nephews – or sons'. His inordinate wealth was derived partly from the diversion of the profits of his office, but his greatest assets were his manors, of which he amassed eighty-two, some belonging to his see, others obtained elsewhere. This figure contrasts strikingly with the fifty manors of the wealthiest bishopric, Winchester, and the archbishopric of Canterbury's thirty-four. A glimpse of Burnell's character is given in the Dunstable annals where it is written: 'He was pleasant in conversation with people, but was considered extremely slippery' (*lubricus*).

Chancellor Burnell provided himself at Acton Burnell with a crenellated private country house, in the style of a castle, and not part of his diocesan property (*see* Fig. 59). However, it is fair to suggest that the location of Acton Burnell towards Wales, encouraged the chancellor to opt for castle style, with a first floor hall, rather than for a more conventional residential design with a ground floor hall as he had built at Wells (Ralegh Radford 1961, 94–103; West 1981, 91–2). His enjoyment of royal support made the added expense of fortification unwise as well as unncessary. The wall walk is not reached easily or quickly, strenghthening the view that the crenellations were embellishments rather than practical defensive measures. Robert Burnell entertained the king at Acton for six weeks in late 1283. It was this visit which witnessed the formulation of the Statute of Acton Burnell. Building works, assisted by grants of timber from the king (which suggest flooring and the creation of the parallel roofs) continued in the mid-1280s, and were doubtless complete by the chancellor's death in 1292 (West 1981, 87, 90). Here we have an example of a stone country house appointed to meet the occasional needs of a wealthy churchman who held significant power in the state. The brief flowering of architecture at Acton Burnell did not long outlast Robert Burnell himself. The buildings passed to his nephew and then the latter's son, both of whom were dead by 1315. The evidence suggests that the residence was in decay by 1350.

In its heyday in the late thirteenth century Acton Burnell was particularly well endowed as befitted a country residence of such a wealthy chancellor-

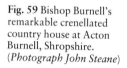

Fig. 59 Bishop Burnell's remarkable crenellated country house at Acton Burnell, Shropshire. (*Photograph John Steane*)

bishop. In addition to the standard layout of a hall, chamber and chapel, there were further chambers and audience areas. In the attics were small rooms for clerks and secretaries. Below them the bishop had his own chambers, bedroom and garderobe. Below the bishop's own accommodation lay a fine first floor hall. On the same level as the hall was an outer chamber where those of rank seeking audience with the chancellor could wait in comparative comfort. On the ground floor was the constable's quarters, the whole being a fine rectangular building with towers at the corners (Ralegh Radford 1961, 103). Acton Burnell was a private residence where Chancellor Burnell could escape some of the pressures of office, despite provision of audience areas. A combination of the isolated location and the fine building works has resulted in the survival of substantial remains today, although as recently as 1914 the north-western tower collapsed in a storm, and the remains have subsequently disappeared.

What we now see raises as many questions as it solves. We know that many more buildings once stood at Acton Burnell than now stand there. Apart from the 'castle' and the parish church, remains of a great aisled barn are also to be seen. But there was no doubt an earlier great hall and many other structures once stood but are now lost (West 1981, 91). Where, for example, was Robert Burnell's own household accommodated, and where did the royal family and entourage stay for that long period in 1283? Much remains to be explained about the phasing and total plan of Acton Burnell, whose ruins invite a wider consideration of the appropriate accommodation for a mobile monarchy and great households.

A second royal official who built magnificently at the same time was Bishop Thomas Bek, who sometime held the offices of lord treasurer and keeper of the great seal. Bishop Thomas held the see of St David's from 1280–93, and is usually credited with the transformation of the accommodation in the diocese, especially that at Llawhaden, from his own personal wealth. Whether his wealth derived from private sources or from the profits of office is not clear. What is known is that this bishop intended to realise a long cherished wish to establish a separate archbishopric in Wales, a wish which was frustrated. The grand buildings apparently established to support the proposed archbishopric remain as a testament to this fond hope. Llawhaden has a more public face than Acton Burnell, arising from the large scale of the work. At St David's an eastern range of true colonial proportions was created, probably by Thomas Bek, or by his successor David Martin (1296–1328). A chamber, fireplace and garderobe are found in the octagonal tower next to the chapel. The bishop's private suite at Llawhaden lay at the east end of the great hall. A western range was later added by Bishop Henry de Gower in the first years of Edward III's reign, to complete the 'new close' referred to in 1334. The buildings at St David's are remarkable for their scale and the relatively good state of preservation in which we find them today. But even in such a far-flung diocese, where travellers must have arrived weary from long journeys, there was, it seems, no guest accommodation at this date.

Bishops with provincial sees maintained establishments in and around London for use when they attended state occasions and fulfilled other duties in the capital. These palaces, often modestly termed 'inns', were generally well appointed and provided a fruitful quarry of fine buildings for the royal family of the day to draw on. One such fine building at Eltham, south east of London, belonged to Anthony Bek (d. 1311), Bishop of Durham and Patriarch of Jerusalem, Thomas's younger brother and also a noted builder-bishop. At Eltham there was a manorial complex sufficient for Henry III, whose lavish Christmas feasts have already been mentioned, to spend Christmas in 1270. Eltham was much enlarged, beautified and strongly fortified in the late thirteenth and early fourteenth centuries by Anthony Bek. Contemporaries marvelled at these building works where a considerable fortified episcopal palace was created. Much of Bek's work has now disappeared but it seems clear that he created the main moated enclosure, within which foundations of some domestic ranges, and octagonal tower works of this time survive, echoing the larger octagonal towers created by his brother in Wales (Strong 1958, 12).

Both brothers enjoyed the support of Edward I: perhaps they brought a particular flavour of opulence to the episcopal positions they held. Certainly Edward I made a special effort to be at York on 9th January 1284 when, at Bishop Anthony's own expense, the remains of St William were raised to prominence in a new shrine. Thomas Bek had given the remains of St Hugh of Lincoln a similar relocation also at his own expense (Taylor 1976, 100n). It is not unreasonable to ask what the Bishop of Durham was doing at York Minster, and the Bishop of St David's at Lincoln Cathedral leading these auspicious activities? The answers tell us much about these men and their background. They both came from a Norman family which had been given lands in Lincolnshire by William the Conqueror, and had prospered in the county thereafter. These local connections explain the association of Thomas with the translation of St Hugh's remains. The activities of Anthony at York are more surprising and help towards an understanding of his character. From the beginning of his episcopate he was in dispute with the Archbishop of York in an attempt to make Durham independent of the archbishop's powers, and reminiscent of his brother Thomas's dealings from Wales with the Archbishop of Canterbury. Failing to get satisfaction in his demands, Anthony Bek bypassed the Archbishop of York altogether by persuading his pseudo-archbishop brother Thomas to perform the necessary rites. It was but a small step to interfere further at York by involving himself in the relocation of the bones of St William. Although this might seem arrogant, contemporaries had no doubt about Anthony Bek's holiness – for example, he alone was considered sufficiently saintly to touch the bones of the revered saint.

Notwithstanding the good relations which brought Edward I to join the celebrations at York, the king and the Bishop of Durham fell out subsequently when the bishop supported the rebellious barons during the crisis of 1297. Anthony Bek's castle-building activities, notably the creation of his drum-towered castle at Somerton (Lincolnshire) and his fortification not only of Eltham, but also of Bishop Auckland were no doubt further reasons for royal suspicions of his over-mighty tendencies. Anthony Bek was notorious for his ostentation as well as for his arrogance, on one occasion buying cloth at huge expense because it was said that the cloth was too expensive even for the Bishop of Durham, and then having it cut up for horse cloths (DNB). He was an enthusiastic falconer, as he demonstrated by playing with his falcons during an interview in Rome with Pope Boniface VIII, surprisingly an act which was much to the taste of that ebullient pontiff. Despite the loss of favour with Edward I, Bek bequeathed Eltham to Edward II, who refurbished the accommodation, walled around the moat, and gave it to Isabella his queen. Edward III's younger brother John was born at the queen's new manor in 1316, and so took its name. Eltham palace remained in royal hands for the remainder of the middle ages, and was very much a favourite residence of fourteenth- and fifteenth-century kings (pages 144–6).

As the greatest royal patron of castle-building, Edward I could hardly fail to notice the way in which his contemporaries followed his lead. Roger Bigod's great fortified castle-palace at Chepstow, with its halls and private tower for Earl Roger himself, contained some striking features. These included pantry and buttery accommodation for the great hall built over the equivalent rooms of the lesser hall. The functions of the great and lesser hall are not entirely distinguishable, but may have been intended to separate groups of different status within the castle. Alternatively, if a parallel with the fifteenth-century castle at Caister is possible, the halls may have been for summer and winter use. In Bigod's castle the earl's accommodation included Marten's Tower, which had a first floor hall, second floor chambers and a fine-quality chapel. There is no doubt that this accommodation was for Roger himself (Platt 1982, 60–1). Fifteenth-century lordly towers were, ostensibly at least, to be reserved for royal visitors (pages 147–8). Earl Roger was sufficiently powerful, and maybe on sufficiently bad terms with the king, to reserve the best defended area of his castle for his own use. Here was a leading magnate who knew Edward I all too well.

Possession of such a palatial castle signals the confidence with which the earl defied the king in public during the 1296 parliament at Salisbury. The famous exchange with Edward occurred when Earl Roger refused to serve in Gascony. 'By God, O Earl, either you go or hang' said the king. 'By the same oath, O King, I shall neither go nor hang' replied the earl defiantly, and he did not go or hang. Gilbert de Clare's Caerphilly and Aymer de Valence's Goodrich are other striking examples of great palatial castles of this era. In common with Bishop Auckland, these were marcher residences, on which to an extent the king relied for defence of the realm. Edward I probably did not like the power of men such as Anthony Bek and Roger Bigod, but he was astute enough to realise the contribution they made to national defence.

The study of structural remains provides only a partial view of the way in which individual kings, lords and bishops used their buildings at any one time. The survival of much of the household roll of Richard de Swinfield, Bishop of Hereford (1282–1317) for part of the years 1289 and 1290 gives us detailed day-to-day information on where he stayed and how he was provided for, which is needed to reveal the way in which the bishop's own residences (and wardships) were used and how he made use of the hospitality of others. The bishop probably hailed from Kent, and we see links with his kinsmen and property in that county at several points in the accounts. The roll provides many illuminating insights into the rigours, and rewards, of episcopal life towards 1300.

Perhaps the most surprising revelation is how little Swinfield apparently actually visited Hereford, where his cathedral lay, for the portion of the roll which survives, between late September 1289 and July 1290, is virtually devoid of such references. We do know he visited Hereford on the occasion of the Palm Sunday procession, but of other visits, if any, we know nothing. We are not, however, given the impression of a man who was uninterested in his episcopal duties and religious obligations. Feast days and days of abstinence are strictly observed; visitation of parishes is rigorously carried out. The household is well regulated: organisation is good, the striped uniforms of the household officials and the bishop's retainers were to be seen not only in the diocese, but also in the London courts when the bishop's business was being pursued. As was proper, no women were allowed in the household.

There was certainly a palace for the bishop at Hereford, if he chose to use it. However, Bishop de Vere's late twelfth-century work, advanced for its time (pages 60–1) may have been considered old fashioned and uncomfortable by 1290. Alternatively the bishop may have resided there for an extended period between July and the end of September 1290, the period for which we have no record. From the surviving portion of the roll we gain the impression that Swinfield especially enjoyed his country retreats. He was physically very active in 1289–90, a period when he was just over a quarter of the way through his episcopate and probably at the height of his powers.

From the start of the accounting year at Michaelmas (29th September) till the Christmas season was a comparatively quiet and static time. The first three weeks of October were spent at Sugwas, near Hereford, and from 21st October to 17th December the bishop and his household were at Bosbury, near Ledbury, a favourite haunt of Swinfield where, in the fullness of time, he was to die. The size of his entourage and the number of guests whom he entertained are difficult matters to resolve on the evidence we have. On the one hand we can note the number of horses being fed at any one time; never less than twenty, rising to fifty-five at Christmas, and once to seventy-six. To set against these figures are the quantites of food served up, which suggest rather larger numbers. Let us take some contrasting occasions. First a day of abstinence at Sugwas in early October, when the household were settling in. Twenty-six horses were in the stable, horseshoes were being replaced and the daily round was in progress. The kitchens provided the following: bread (in unspecified quantity); eight gallons of wine and unspecified quantities of beer; 500 herrings (300 of them salted) of which 250 were returned to store at the end of the day; four sticks of eels (three salted); one and a half salmon (the whole salmon a gift, the half later returned to store); four cod; and 300 lamperns (small lampreys, of which 100 were left over)—by any account a considerable amount of food, and to suggest 100 people fed that day does not seem unreasonable. The total cost was 9s. 2d. Second, a Sunday at the same period, with twenty-nine horses in the stable, gives us a view of a meat day. Bread, with twelve gallons of wine and beer head the list. The meat consisted of two carcases and three quarters of beef (the carcases were left over), one and a half porkers (the porker was returned), a sheep and ten carcases of mutton (eight carcases returned), twenty-nine geese (twenty-one returned), forty-eight fowls (thirty-eight returned), twenty-four pigeons (twelve returned), larks (value a penny farthing), nine partridges. Thus the meat eaten amounted to three quarters of beef, three sheep, half a pig, eight geese and ten fowls, twelve pigeons and all the larks and partridges. The cost was three times that of the day of abstinence.

Finally, the Christmas feast is well worth a glance. By this time the household had set off to trek to London, passing through Ledbury (17th to 20th December), Newent (20th), Highnam (21st), with the Christmas period spent at Prestbury where fifty-five horses rested in the stable. Christmas Eve, a day of abstinence, saw herrings, conger eels, codlings and salmon served, with a note that twelve cups, 300 dishes, 150 plates and 200 'saucers' (probably small plates) were provided. Three meals were served on Christmas day. Wine flowed freely, with forty gallons of red and four of white served up. The meat, none of which was apparently returned to store, included two carcases and three quarters of beef (no smaller joints are ever referred to) together with two calves, four deer, four pigs, sixty fowls, eight partridges and two geese, with additional bread and cheese. To set the seal on this festive day we read of a boar, served up with lemons specially provided for the occasion, in that most evocative of medieval Christmas scenes. It is possible that the 'swine' centrepiece may have been a play on the bishop's name, one of those punning allusions that clearly amused medieval people.

The journey undertaken by Richard Swinfield and his entourage to London would have been challenging in any season. In the depths of winter it must have been particularly difficult. The bishop moved eastwards by way of Coln St Aylwin (or Aldwin) near Fairford, Gloucestershire (28th December), Farringdon (29th) and Wantage (30th). After several days on the road, the travellers would have been pleased on 31st December to ride through the great gate of Reading Abbey after the twenty-four mile journey from Wantage, and to rest for several days. The Abbot of Reading was presented with four does and a quantity of partridges brought by the visitors, and returned the compliment not only with generous hospitality but also with the services of a harper paid to entertain the company. The 4th of January saw progress across the Thames by ferry at Staines and, after a stay at Bedfont from 4th to the 7th, the party arrived at the bishop's London inn near Queenhithe, west of Old Fish Street. The bishop compensated his tenant at Queenhithe for the inconvenience of his visit and while in London he attended the royal court at Westminster, and dealt with legal business while his staff enjoyed the fashionable haunts around Westminster and such additions to their diet as oysters, sturgeon and sprats from the London markets.

We know little of Swinfield's London residence, but a contemporary Bishop of Ely, John de Kirkeby (1286–90), was clearing a site at this time for a new palace in London. The hall which measured 72ft by 32ft, by 30ft high (21.9 m ×9.7 m×9.1 m), dates from 1286–90. A large courtyard led to this hall; beyond the hall was a cloistered quadrangle, a chapel (completed in 1290) and extensive gardens including a vineyard (Schofield 1984, 65). There were probably strawberries there, as Richard of Gloucester's request for strawberries he had seen at Ely Place, Holborn, reminds us (Shakespeare, Richard III, Act III, Scene 4). The chapel still exists as St Etheldreda's Ely Place, a fine Gothic edifice on two floors, although the gardens, which were passed to Sir Christopher Hatton, are now the domain of diamond dealers. Swinfield's London inn of *c.* 1290 may have been similar to, if less up to date than, that under construction for the Bishop of Ely, providing accommodation in London for the extensive party which travelled up from the country with the bishop.

Swinfield's party left London by way of Kensington on 13th January, making their way by stages back to Herefordshire, where they arrived towards the end of February. The return journey was unremarkable apart from the stay at Earley, near Reading, where the bishop enjoyed the fruits of a manor whose owner, a minor, was his ward. This provided a convenient stopping point en route and enabled the party to avoid imposing themselves again on the Abbot of Reading. Near Wantage a kitchen cart overturned with a considerable loss of dishes which had to be replaced, reminding us that medieval travellers at this level of society took all requisites with them on their travels.

March, April and May were hectic months for Bishop Swinfield as he moved round his diocese (*see* Fig. 60) visiting parishes and checking all was well with his clergy. In April he stayed in no less than seventeen different places, not counting those places he visited from day to day. For the first ten days of April

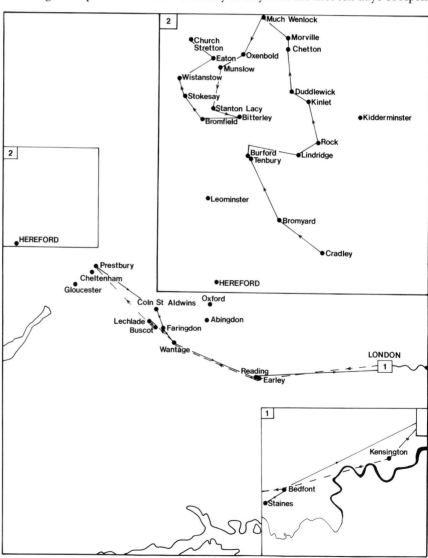

Fig. 60 Itinerary of Richard de Swinfield, Bishop of Hereford, in 1289–90. (*Drawn by Alex Turner*)

he rested at Colwall, enjoying a splendid Easter feast, which included the supply of the usual flesh but also 4,000 eggs. There were over seventy horses in the stable for this occasion suggesting the influx of numerous guests. After Easter the bishop continued on his rounds, staying at a different place every day for the remaining three weeks of the month. He enjoyed residence at seventeen places in May, apart from day trips. June saw less travel, with only three places mentioned in the first half of the month, after which Swinfield settled down at Whitborne, near Bromyard, where he stayed for the remaining period of the roll up to 20th July.

Given the seasons, the roads and the terrain of some of the areas visited (he had to take a guide through the Shropshire hills around Pontesbury and Much Wenlock), the vignette of episcopal life and activity allowed us by this fragmentary household roll is sharp and impressive. Swinfield must have been a fit and active person and his household roll probably gives a fair picture of the work of a diocesan bishop of the variety not particularly involved in the affairs of state.

When Edward II came to the throne in 1307, Westminster Abbey was by no means finished, although it had been begun by his grandfather. Building had proceeded beyond the crossing by five bays, but as it was incomplete temporary roofing had to be put up against bad weather. An extravagant coronation was planned for which considerable work was required on both abbey and palace. Writs were issued to certain abbots to supply window glass and lead workers, both for windows and roofs, and quantities of timber were ordered from as far away as Hereford. Innumerable shingles, for roofing, were requested from Surrey and Sussex. A great horn was sounded to summon and dismiss the throng of workers, who continued their work after dark by the uncertain, flickering light of candles.

A huge temporary timber hall, perhaps 500 ft (152.4 m) long was erected beside the river wall of the palace. Within this hall the central feature was a gilt and copper throne, repaired for the occasion. The building was specially strengthened to bear the press of the populace. A contemporary representation of a coronation, which may well be the coronation of Edward II, shows graphically not only the crowd of officials, clergy and lawyers round the king, but also in the background a mass of faces of ordinary people looking on from without (*see* Fig. 61). Fourteen additional temporary halls were put up at Westminster for the occasion, some newly built, others borrowed from elsewhere in the city. Two from the Archbishop of York's inn were re-erected near the palace gate as a salsary and scullery, and forty ovens were purpose-built. During the celebrations an elaborate fountain (with lead pipes) flowed day and night with 'pimento', a mixture of spiced red and white wine (Colvin 1963, 505–7). In all, £3,000 was spent at Westminster in the first year of the reign. However, the coronation and the celebrations which accompanied it were not entirely satisfactory or happy. Chroniclers, foreshadowing the difficulties which were to become even more apparent in the reign, noted that Edward spent his time fawning over Piers Gaveston and ignoring the young Queen Isabella.

Notwithstanding the great pomp of the coronation, details of work on the royal palaces under Edward II suggest an increasing desire for privacy. The

king did not choose to sleep in the great bed in the Painted Chamber at Westminster, but built a smaller bedchamber adjacent. A royal household roll of his time suggests that the king was dining in his great chamber and not, as had previously been the custom, presiding over courtiers in the great halls of his residences. This change arose in part no doubt because Edward preferred the company of his close friends, such as the unpopular Gaveston. Eating in private avoided confrontation with disapproving barons and courtiers. The trend continued after Edward II's reign, although his son Edward III relished the great feasts which occurred on occasions such as tournaments.

The king's alleged homosexuality, the murder of Gaveston and the revolt of the barons all contributed to the unhappiness of his reign. The greatest blow to the king's prestige was the desertion of his wife, Isabella, sister to the last three kings of the French Capetian line, which became extinct in the male line upon the death of her brother Charles IV (1322–8). In 1326 Anglo-French relations were at a low point, with intractable disagreements over the status of the King of England as lord of extensive lands in France. Before she deprived Edward of his throne, Isabella visited France in 1325. There she met her lover Roger Mortimer, who had been in France since he had escaped from the Tower in 1323. Isabella was apparently received cordially enough by her brother Charles IV, who gave her the palace at Vincennes as a temporary residence during her stay.

Household accounts for the queen's visit to France have survived and cast some light on the often under-documented subject of a queen's administration when away from her husband. The accounts indicate that while in France the queen lived off her own income, with funds to fall back on if necessary on deposit with the Italian Bardi bankers in Paris. Some income was derived from her French lands, for example Ponthieu in the north west of the country, which was part of her dowry. The queen was involved in intense diplomatic activity while in France and travelled about a good deal with her advisers, who included the bishops of Norwich and Winchester and the Earl of Richmond. The arrangements for the marriage of Prince Edward to Philippa of Hainault (and the supply of Hainault soldiers in Isabella's support) were successfully negotiated during her stay.

During Lent the accounts reveal that the queen was supplied by King Charles with a wide selection of fish, including pike, bream, turbot, conger eel, sturgeon, lamprey and porpoise. Later in the year he sent wild boar and rabbits. Queen Isabella both dined out a good deal and gave dinners herself. She also entertained ladies, such as the dowager queen of Louis X (d. 1316), to wine and sweetmeats. She visited numbers of shrines, making lavish donations in several cases and travelling in some state, on one occasion paying five shillings, for her suite, carriage and horses to cross the Seine. Entertainment included music, two poor *vidulatores* (fiddlers) being hired at Soissons. As the seasons progressed she bought and distributed ermine, miniver and other furs to her staff. On one occasion alone she spent £40 on coloured cloth at a Paris mercery.

Isabella returned to England in the autumn, and was based at Woodstock, although it seems likely that she would have gone to Bristol to see the Despensers, and to Hereford for the younger Despenser's trial. Christmas was spent at Wallingford. By the Epiphany she had visited Reading, Windsor, Chertsey and Merton and had arrived at Westminster (Hunter 1855, 257). Within weeks her husband had resigned his crown and on 1st February 1327 her son was crowned King as Edward III.

Chapter VI
Edward III (1327–1377)

It was traditional upon the death of a king in medieval England to lay out the body bared to the waist to show that the monarch had not died a violent death. This being the case, then a contribution is made to the historical tradition that Edward II was murdered with a red-hot poker inserted in his anus, thus avoiding mutilation of the upper part of his body. The murder was carried out in Berkeley castle by agents of Isabella and of Roger Mortimer. This cruel act was ample justification, if any were needed, of royal fears of powerful magnates and their remote castles.

The Queen and Mortimer ruled the country for a while on behalf of the young Edward III until in October 1330 the usurpers were surprised in Nottingham castle and overthrown by the young king. It is important to remember that although Mortimer was executed, the Queen Mother was treated considerately by Edward and allowed to live out her days in relative comfort, for much of the time at Castle Rising in Norfolk. She died in 1358.

Isabella has long been noted for her cultural interests, especially her interest in romance literature, an interest which incidentally she would have shared with her father-in-law Edward I, had he lived longer. Her origins at the court of France had given her a sophistication which was in contrast to the manual labour, such as hedging and ditching, said to have been the pastimes of Edward II. Exile had brought the future Edward III into contact with the artistic and stylish courts of Europe, notably France and the often underrated Hainault. These courts combined an interest in literature with the brilliant and highly developed art of the tournament, or 'hastilude' (literally a game with staffs).

William III, Count of Hainault, Holland and Zeeland in the early fourteenth century, made good marriages for his daughters: one to the Holy Roman Emperor, another to the Count of Juliers and, in the case of Philippa, to Edward III. This marriage took place in January 1328. The marriages of the Count's daughters are reminiscent of the thirteenth-century marriages of the daughters of the Count of Provence (pages 71–2). In the same way the cultural influence of Queen Philippa on her husband, and so on society at large, is significant from the early years of Edward's reign, as Eleanor of Provence had influenced Henry III a century earlier.

An unusual New Year's gift from Philippa to Edward in 1333 hints at the Queen's interest in art and the way she fostered Edward's martial enthusiasm. The gift was of a silver and enamelled set of cup, ewer and stand. The stand, decorated with leopards, bore the arms of England and the cup scenes of wars, ships and castles, including a grand castle decorated with banners. The ewer drew on different motifs, providing the young King with a gallery of real and fictional images to inspire him, including Julius Caesar, Judas Maccabeus, Charlemagne, Arthur, Roland and Lancelot of the Lake. It is these figures which encourage the belief that Edward and his household were familiar not only with historical figures but also with the heroes of romance. We know that the young Queen's family possessed a library of no less than 225 romances in 1311 (Vale 1982, 45–6). The juxtaposition of Caesar, Maccabeus and Charlemagne, respectively classical, biblical and Christian heroes, is a strong hint of the tripartite values which were to be combined later in Edward's reign in chivalric enterprises such as the founding of the Order of the Garter.

The Queen's enthusiasm for culture did not stop at presents for the King. Philippa's uncle, John of Beaumont, a familiar figure at the English court early in the reign, had been the patron of the Hainault chronicler Jean le Bel. His niece followed suit as patron of the greatest chronicler of the age, Jean Froissart, whose early chronicles derived from le Bel. Although Froissart's reputation rightly rests on his thrilling accounts of the European wars of the fourteenth century (for the early part of which he drew heavily on le Bel), he initially came to prominence as a court poet in Philippa's entourage. It has recently been argued that a set of poems by Laurence Minot, celebrating English military successes from 1333 to 1352, may have been associated with the old Queen Isabella, in residence for much of this period at Castle Rising (James and Simons, 1989). It is becoming apparent that from its earliest days the court of Edward III was dedicated to cultural and artistic interests, as well as to military matters for which it has become rightly renowned. The link between the arts and the wars is to be found in the increasingly sophisticated tournaments which were a common feature of the reign, intended no doubt to draw the no-bility together after the fragmentation and civil strife of Edward II's reign.

A great attraction of the tournament as a court entertainment was its univers-ality. Tournaments celebrated family events, royal marriages, the birth and baptism of a royal child, the churching of the Queen and religious festivals when the royal household was gathered together, such as Christmas or Easter. The religious celebrations merge into popular saints' days, such as St George's day when the Order of the Garter had their first tournament in 1349, and thence into quasi-religious festivals – the pre-Lent, carnival festivities such as those at Guildford in 1329 or Norwich in 1341, and the feast of the nativity of St John the Baptist, otherwise Midsummer, celebrated with a tournament at Smithfield in 1343. The tournament had a diplomatic function: to entertain and impress potential allies, as in the Low Countries and at home in the early years of the Hundred Years War. The war parties themselves took part in tournaments, for example in 1341 when as a result of a tournament at Roxburgh between English and Scottish nobles the Scots were worsted and returned home severely injured. Participants were quite commonly killed in tournaments. In the first thirty years of his reign Edward III attended and probably took part in at least one tournament a year (Vale 1982, 66, 172–4). These events were scattered through England and the Low Countries and no doubt attracted much atten-tion as well as sustaining the martial spirit, discovering warriors and providing a focus for splendid royal and baronial fetivities. In 1357 the first tournament to be held after dark took place, and a splendid torch-lit sight it must have been.

The often violent tournaments were not, however, the only court pastimes at the period. Court entertainments were designed to occupy and delight indoors in the evenings, particularly on special feast days. Christmas at Guildford in

1347 was accompanied by the provision of a veritable wardrobe of costumes including forty-two masks (*viseres*) divided equally into women's faces, bearded men's faces and silver angel's heads. The accompanying twenty-eight crests were more arcane, fourteen 'with reversed legs and shoes' and fourteen 'with hills and rabbits'. Amongst the other costumes, provided without exception in groups of fourteen, were peacocks' heads and pairs of wings, swans' heads and pairs of wings, and dragons' heads, together with painted cloaks and tunics, some of white and others painted with gold and silver stars. The following Christmas was spent at the archiepiscopal palace of Otford. On this occasion sets of fourteen worsted tunics of green and red goutted with gold were accompanied by a complete outfit for the king and his horse spangled with silver, the tunic and shield bearing the king's motto 'Hay hay the wythe swan, by goddes soule I am thy man'. The *viseres* included twelve heads of girls and sets of twelve heads of men variously surmounted by lions' or elephants' heads or with bats' wings. There were twelve heads of 'wodewoses' (wildmen). Away from ecclesiastical influence, during Christmas 1352 at Windsor, the costumes were this time in groups of thirteen and included devils, friars in black habits and merchants in white cloth (Vale 1982, 175).

As the royal family grew, the households of the king, queen and queen mother were joined by the households of the princes, each providing possibilities for artists and 'hastiludiators'. Leader amongst the royal children was the heir to the throne, the Black Prince who, like his great grandfather Edward I and other heirs to the throne, was provided with his own accommodation from an early age. Excavation coupled with examination of documentary sources for the Black Prince's residence at Kennington have furnished some valuable evidence about palaces in the early years of Edward III's reign (Dawson 1976). The prince obtained Kennington when he became Duke of Cornwall in 1337, following the death in 1336 of his uncle, John of Eltham, the last Earl of Cornwall. Edward the Black Prince was the first duke created in England, and although only born in 1330 found himself as titular keeper of the realm in his father's absence abroad during the preliminary stages of the Hundred Years War, which broke out in 1337. Between 1338 and 1343 documents were sealed there and despatched in the prince's name.

Kennington is important to our understanding of medieval palaces for a variety of reasons. There was already a good stock of buildings on the site when it came to be used by the Black Prince, but two major and quite well documented campaigns of building were carried through between 1340 and 1363. A series of excavations has done much to elucidate the documentary evidence and has proved very informative about building styles, materials and on the environment of the palace, which could never be known from the documentary sources alone. Archaeology and documents over a twenty-five-year period provide insights into sites elsewhere for which we now have only patchy written records and perhaps no archaeology. In particular the dramatic changes which occured at Kennington in the Black Prince's generation indicate a much more rapid rate of change and development than would otherwise be suspected.

Documents tell us of work on the hall in the 1340s and suggest from the large expenditure of some £1,500, and from other evidence, that the hall and chamber block of the 1340s were rebuilt in the 1350s. The hall itself was a first-floor room perhaps with a leaded roof, over a vaulted undercroft, used in part or as a whole as the wine cellar. The hall was aligned north-south. The undercroft hall of the 1340s appears to have come near to collapse not long after it was built. The first remedy was to fill in the undercroft to support the hall above, but this failed. The rebuilt hall was better appointed with its own buttery and pantry, three fireplaces perhaps in the style of those at Conway Castle, and two spiral staircases. The chamber and wardrobe block was extended and made more comfortable by such improvements as bath accommodation. A new kitchen was provided. The third major element of palace life, the chapel, was in existence and functioning by 1347 when vestments and towels for use therein were supplied. Work on further buildings and other features of the palace is referred to during the 1340s and 1350s.

The palace buildings lay within a park, which received a new 1500 ft (457.2 m) palisade through the activities of John Heyward in 1358–9. There were at least two areas of garden within the park. The 'great garden', into which the wine cellar opened, probably lay to the east of the hall and chamber block. Here also was the great pond, no doubt a vivarium, which afforded the luxury of fresh fish to the residents. To the west lay the private garden. A gatehouse, stables, and accommodation for stewards and other officials completed the building stock at this date. Kennington was amongst the places where Henry Yeveley worked in his early days, a man who was to be so significant in the history of English building for the rest of the fourteenth century (page 130).

Over the years 1362–71 the Black Prince shifted the centre of his affairs to Bordeaux. He returned in ailing health to Kennington in 1371, and may have died there in 1376. Certainly his widow Joan and the heir to the throne, Prince Richard, were resident at Kennington when they received the news of the death of Edward III in 1377. After the Black Prince's death Kennington was infrequently used and scarcely altered, so far as can be deduced from the surviving documentation. Richard II appears to have been the only king to make use of it, periodically visiting with his household. In 1531–2 the remaining buildings were demolished in a drive to find materials for Henry VIII's newly acquired palace at Whitehall.

The nucleus of the palace – the hall, great chamber, kitchen and stables – were excavated in 1965–8 (Dawson 1976). The excavations sampled the major ranges with work on the hall, chambers and kitchen area. The discoveries seemed to indicate that the rebuilding of the 1350s brought about a fusion of hall and chamber block into one, which had not been the case in the previous decade. This, in the excavator's view, is especially significant as it makes Kennington from the fourteenth century a point of reference for accommodation at the highest social level. Comparisons are drawn with contemporary buildings such as Penshurst (Kent), built at much the same period by the war financier Sir John Pulteney, and with subsequent buildings such as the domestic arrangements at Bodiam castle (Sussex), built *c.* 1389, and known to have been influenced by Henry Yeveley (Harvey 1987, 359).

Excavation revealed amongst the remains of the palace a wealth of evidence on structural materials and the palace environment. The building materials included chalk and Reigate sandstone from the elevations, Hassock and Kentish rag with flint rubble for the in-fill with some brick under a tiled roof. Kennington was amongst the earliest, if not the earliest, royal palaces where brick was used. Local yellow bricks, perhaps from kilns at Vauxhall, are early examples of their kind dating to *c.* 1350 (Schofield 1984, 126). Remains of interior decor included a single fragment of figure sculpture; a lone piece of Purbeck moulding indicates decorative use of Dorset stone. A small number of fragments of plaster, some whitewashed, others coloured red, red and black, and pink were also found. Broken decorated floor tiles together with fragments of coloured window glass and lead cames for supporting glass or ventilators contribute to our knowledge of the floor and window embellishment. Those remains there are hint at a richly decorated interior. They are stored and some are displayed at the Cuming museum in Southwark (*see* Fig. 62).

Environmental evidence from late medieval palace sites has always proved disappointingly elusive. This state of affairs is a tribute to increased hygiene in the post-plague era, as well as to royal organisation. It is a bonus to have material from Kennington, where a limited sample of bone evidence was secured. The variety is striking. The finds were analysed on the basis of the number of individual creatures identified. Most numerous were sheep/goat bones, 56 per cent of the sample, followed by chicken, pig, ox, fallow deer and rabbit. The bone remains demonstrated that the larger animals arrived ready jointed. Domestic animals such as a horse, dogs and cats also showed. Diet at Kennington was enhanced by fish (hake and cod), molluscs (oysters being 97 per cent of the sample, with cockle, whelk, mussel and common snail) and remains of a frog were found. A wide variety of bird remains were found: grey lag goose, mallard, carrion crow, kestrel, kite, jackdaw, rock dove and quail. Quail must have been brought in, but perhaps more surprising to the modern reader is the presence of badger and hedgehog, both, on expert opinion, probably eaten in the palace and the badger perhaps prized for its skin.

Fig. 62 Pillar base from Kennington. This is one of the few remnants of the palace which is recalled only in the name of Black Prince Road, which runs south of the Thames from the Albert Embankment. (*Cuming Museum, London Borough of Southwark. Photograph John Steane*)

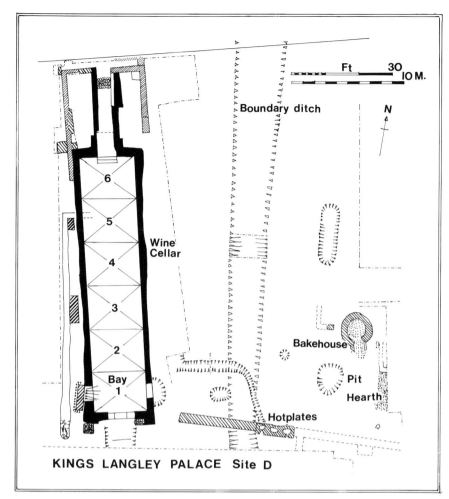

Fig. 63 King's Langley, Hertfordshire. Plan of the cellar built in 1291–92 and abandoned by 1431. (*After Neal*)

KINGS LANGLEY PALACE Site D

Some of the only comparable environmental evidence from a royal site was recovered in the excavations of the wine cellar at King's Langley, built in 1291–2 and abandoned by 1431 (*see* Fig. 63). These were not midden deposits, but fragments of bone which found their way into the fill of the cellar floor. Sheep, deer (possibly roe deer) and rabbit were the main animal remains recovered at King's Langley, together with cat, dog and rat. Birds were less certain, possibly pheasant and a large water bird, perhaps a goose. Elsewhere on the site a quantity of chicken bones was recovered, filling the arch of an oven (similarly, bones were found packed into drains and other structures at Clarendon), but the date of deposition of these chicken bones is uncertain, Returning to the cellar, crab was found and some fish bones identified uncertainly as carp. If this identification is correct, this would be a very early date for the consumption of carp, which are normally believed to have been introduced into England from the east about 1450–1500 (Hickling 1971, 121; Neal 1971, 70).

Although limited in variety and less narrowly dated than the sample from Kennington, the material from King's Langley ties in well with what is known from Kennington and provides additional information, particularly the crab, which must have been brought from a distance. Analysis of charcoals from the cellar at King's Langley has identified a variety of types of wood, which were either used in the structure or burnt in a hearth or on a brushwood fire which featured in the stratigraphy. The overwhelming majority of pieces were of beech (including all the samples from the brushwood fire), but oak, poplar and ash were also identified, providing an echo of the surrounding countryside (Neal 1970, 70).

Skins do not normally survive in archaeological contexts. We have virtually nothing of the fabrics which adorned the palaces at Kennington or of the clothes belonging to the Black Prince and his contemporaries. However, the great rough-cut ruby said to have belonged first to the Black Prince and later to have adorned Henry V's helmet at Agincourt can still be seen. It is the centrepiece of the Imperial State Crown which is worn at coronations to this day (Holmes 1955, 5) (*see* Fig. 42).

Kennington was not the only palace under reconstruction in the neighbourhood of London in the central years of the fourteenth century, for the Savoy palace was extensively rebuilt in these years. Since Eleanor of Provence had given the palace to her son Edmund, the Savoy had been the London home of the Lancasters and was at this time in the hands of Henry of Grosmont, who had been elevated to the dukedom of Lancaster in 1352. Grosmont was a successful and respected commander who led six expeditions to France, and was also grandfather of Henry IV. The growing influence of Grosmont in the 1340s drew him away from his castle-base in Leicester to London where he built his new palace in the Strand. We know little of the buildings themselves, which were destroyed during the Great Revolt of 1381, twenty years after his death. The palace was, however, deemed suitable to lodge King John II of France, who had been captured by the Black Prince at Poitiers in 1356. This was a comfortable incarceration reminiscent of the loan of Vincennes to the self-exiled queen thirty years earlier.

If the chronicler Knighton is to be believed, Henry of Grosmont spent profits of war gained during the Crécy campaign of 1345–6 and amounting to £35,000, on building works at the Savoy. To gain some idea of scale of expenditure, it is noteworthy that Edward III's thirty-year building programme at Westminster palace between 1331 and 1363 cost only £30,000, as against twelve years work at the Savoy between 1349 and 1361 (page 115ff.). Only Windsor attracted more funds at this date, £50,000 spent in the 1360s. The works at the Savoy were largely complete by the late 1350s when King John stayed there, but, as was so often the case with palace builders, Grosmont died before he had much enjoyment out of his great building project (Fowler 1969, 213–4). The Savoy passed to John of Gaunt, who in 1359 had married Blanche, Grosmont's blonde, vivacious daughter.

Henry of Grosmont is one of those rare medieval aristocrats of whom we know sufficient to say something about his character as well as his lifestyle. We known a good deal of his castle at Leicester, his favourite residence. In a growing tradition of building, Leicester was more a comfortable palace than a defensive castle. The duke's own suite included a dancing chamber, later echoed at Windsor, and a feature which was to become especially fashionable towards the end of the century in the residences of his son-in-law John of Gaunt and at the royal residences of Richard II (pages 123,134). He loved Leicester for hunting. Smoking out foxes, hearing the hounds bark, enjoying the sound of the birds and the smell of flowers, and even the smell of costly clothes, are all sensual pleasures revealed in his personal writings.

It is our knowledge of such aspects of Henry of Grosmont's character as these, gained from the pages of his remarkable *Livre de Seyntz Medicines*, which singles him out from his contemporaries. He deals with the ways in which the seven deadly sins – pride, envy, wrath, covetousness, gluttony, lechery and sloth – assaulted his five senses. Such a subject promises riches to the reader eager to penetrate the medieval mind and much is candidly revealed by the duke, who gains respect for his self assessment, although he admits to a propensity throughout his life for lying to impress. A sincerely pious man, Henry finds his weaknesses painful to relate. His love of expensive clothes and strong spiced food accompanied by such quantities of wine as 'to put myself and my friends out of our senses' are failings commented on both by Henry himself and by contemporary observers. His exposition of his attitude to women goes far beyond the conventional wisdom derived from medieval liter-ature. Froissart provides a picture of the victorious general amusing himself wining, dining and entertaining the wives and daughters of citizens of French towns. On Henry's own admission he enjoyed parading his jousting skills be-fore aristocratic ladies and also loved to dance with them. He sang them lovesongs. He loved the scent of women 'or anything belonging to them'. When it came to kissing, his taste was for the attentions of a low woman 'immodest of her body' who acquiesced in his conduct, or in other words, who enjoyed kissing (Fowler 1969, 62; Barnie 1974, 61–5).

It would be surprising to find the king inactive with works such as those of Kennington and the Savoy being undertaken by other members of the royal family. Of course Edward III was an enthusiastic commissioner of buildings, and his victories in battle were to provide a ready supply of capital for major campaigns of works which dwarfed the schemes of his subjects. Edward III's reputation as a significant builder and contributor to English architectural heritage has been much enhanced in recent years. In most respects he has supplanted his grandson Richard II in the view of many as an architectural innovator. Nowhere is his architectural interest more apparent than in his palaces. His great work at Windsor is the *pièce de résistance*, together with the completion of the chapel of St Stephen at Westminster.

Altogether, between his assumption of power from Isabella and Mortimer in 1331 until 1363, Edward spent some £30,000 on Westminster Palace, where the accommodation was updated and improved in all respects. Amongst the many works done on the domestic quarters two references to innovations catch the eye, namely the supply in 1351–2 of 'two large bronze taps for the king's bath to bring hot and cold water into the baths', the first such hot and cold sup-ply known in England. In the 1360s Edward ordered a clock to be housed in a high tower facing Westminster Hall across the courtyard (*see* Fig. 64). This first great Westminster clock reminds us of the increased sophistication of time keeping in the later Middle Ages, and today the Westminster clock tower houses the national timepiece whose bell is well known all over the world (Colvin 1963, 209, 550). Ubiquitous hot and cold water supplies and both

Sala Regalis cum Curia Westmonastery, *vulgo* Westminster haall.

Fig. 64 Wenceslas Hollar's views of Westminster. Edward III's clock Tower as it stood in the seventeenth century facing the north end of the great hall.

public and private clocks today are ready reminders of how the principal of sinking, or even trickling down, culture can be exemplified: the attributes of lavish palaces in the fourteenth century becoming common throughout the land.

Edward's greatest artistic achievement was the completion of St Stephen's chapel, also at Westminster, which had been begun by Edward I and had been continued by Edward II between 1321 and 1326 (*see* Fig. 65). The interior was decorated to the most lavish specifications. In Edward III's campaign the wooden roof was vaulted to look like stone, which was a particularly English feature of late Gothic architecture in the fourteenth and fifteenth centuries, reaching a high point in the suspended vaulting of Henry VII's chapel at Westminster *c.* 1500. The roof was also diapered and stencilled in a rich variety of colours, including many thousand foils of gold and quantities of silver as well as red, blue, green and yellow. Highest quality materials were obtained for brushes made of materials ranging from pigs' bristles, squirrels' tails, and feathers of geese, swans and peacocks. The decoration was carried down the walls to the foot of the large windows. In the spandrels between the windows large gilded statues of angels were to be seen. One group of angels was shown

Fig. 65 Westminster from the Thames. St Stephen's chapel is the tall, narrow building to the left of the picture

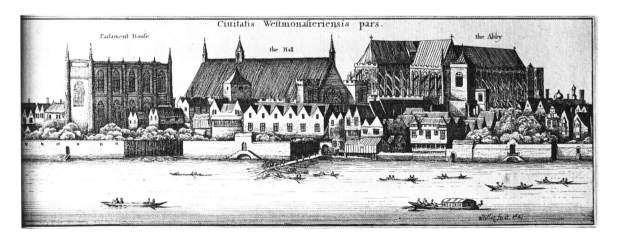

Ciuitatis Westmonasteriensis pars.

Parlament House   the Hall   the Abby

censing, and for these actual thuribles were supplied and suspended from their hands by wires. Below the windows were no fewer than eighty panels depicting religious subjects. Purbeck stone was the material of the altar and floor, and at the east end the religious themes were supplemented each side of the altar by depictions of St George and Edward III himself, together with Queen Philippa and their ten children (Colvin 1963, 518–9) (*see* Fig. 66). The chapel was raised on an undercroft, which had been completed by Edward II, and which still survives (*see* Fig. 67). The lower chapel is strikingly similar to its counterpart in La Sainte Chapelle in Paris. The court style was influential and what William Ramsey created at Westminster was soon copied in the provinces, for example at Gloucester Cathedral.

The upper chapel was converted for use as the House of Commons in the sixteenth century and over the years the decoration was steadily covered over with layers of whitewash and with wainscot, which masked the paintings from view. Sir Christopher Wren was responsible for truncating the remarkable height of the chapel by removing the clerestory and covering over the roof (*see* Fig. 68). The chapel was gutted in the great fire of 1834 and was subsequently demolished. However, in rebuilding the Houses of Parliament the arrangement of stalls facing one another was reproduced in a ghostly legacy of the arrange-

Fig. 66 Westminster. Drawing of Edward III's family as it appeared in St Stephen's chapel. Virtually all this mural painting was destroyed when the chapel was demolished, but a few painted stones were saved and are preserved in the British Museum. (*Society of Antiquaries of London*)

Fig. 67 Westminster. St Stephen's chapel elevation section. (*Britton and Brayley*)

ments which had obtained in St Stephen's chapel. Thus, as Colvin has suggested, the requisitioning of the remains of this unique medieval chapel, which was designed for prayer, not for politics, reinforced the British two-party political system, as the opposed ranks of stalls allowed little scope for the accommodation of politicians of a middle persuasion who elsewhere in Europe might find their places more readily in semi-circular chambers.

The rebuilding of St Stephen's chapel was surely envisaged by Henry III, in the thirteenth century, to echo Louis IX's Sainte Chapelle which was a token of admiration for the French monarchy in general and St Louis in particular. The work which Edward I put in hand gave the idea concrete form. In the style of French Gothic the building was remarkably tall, without aisles and with large windows filled with fine richly coloured glass from abroad, and plainer glass from English glassworks in Shropshire and Staffordshire. It is ironic that it should have been brought to completion by Edward III who had just presided over the defeat of the French at Crécy (1346) and at Poitiers (1356) and who held King John of France a prisoner in England.

These great military victories no doubt inspired Edward III to his greatest building project, and the ransom gained provided him with unexpected wealth to realise his plans. Windsor became the major royal residence outside London and contributed to the increasing emphasis on the royal residences in the Thames Valley. There appears to have been a false start in 1344 when an Order of the Round Table was established together with a circular building, known as the 'round table', in which the knights could meet. This was a major undertaking involving the bringing of men from far and wide: from Norfolk, Suffolk, Kent, Surrey, Northamptonshire, Bedfordshire, London and Middlesex. The whole range of skilled labourers were engaged: carpenters, masons, stone-cutters, smiths, quarrymen, chalkpitmen and limeburners, who were all provided with appropriate working space at the site and were overseen by the controller calculating the sums with counters on his chequered counting cloth. Whether there was a round table for the knights to sit round is unclear: a reference to the strengthening of the bridges at the castle 'lest they be broken with the heavy carriage of the Round Table' probably means no more than the damage evisaged by the arrival of massive amounts of building materials rather than any wooden table (Hope 1913, 112, 118–20). A Round Table, now without its legs, which hangs in the great hall of Winchester Castle may have had some connection with this knightly order, for dendrochronological analysis has indicated that the trees from which it was made may have been cut down about 1340 (page 26; *see* Fig. 69). There were sound historical reasons why an Order of the Round Table should have succeeded in the 1340s in drawing together the knights of England under their young warrior king in common cause against France. Despite the energetic execution of the royal plans it is doubtful that the 'Round Table' buildings were ever completed, and within two decades demolition took place for yet grander schemes.

Fig. 68 Westminster. St Stephen's, the lower chapel. Although heavily restored in the nineteenth century, the architectural features and proportions are still largely original. (*Photograph Sir Geoffrey Shakerly. Reproduced by permission of both Houses of Parliament*)

Fig. 69 Henry VIII depicted as King Arthur on the Round Table in Winchester castle. Now a wall decoration in the great hall, it was once a table with legs. Dendrochronology suggests that the trees used to make the table were probably cut down in *c.* 1340, but the table was certainly not painted until Tudor times, probably in 1521. (*Copyright Hampshire County Council*)

With or without buildings, invitations were issued and a splendidly lavish first gathering of the round table did take place in 1344. Details of the conspicuous consumption which accompanied it appear in the surviving wardrobe accounts. Edward III himself had two lined and trimmed suits of red velvet made for the occasion, one traditional and long, the other short in the new fashion and which was much disapproved of by conservatives as an emulation of the styles of the lower orders. To set off these remarkable suits, the velvet for which had been purchased the previous year, the king also had a cloak made up from 369 ermine skins, and a short cape made up of fifty-seven such skins. Over 100 tunics were created for the king's squires and a further sixteen for his minstrels who played trumpets and kettledrums during proceedings at the tournament. Edward opened the celebrations with a great banquet for members of the nobility, although reference to the presence of the wives of citizens of London indicates the way in which the middle class was becoming more prominent. The chronicler Murimuth summed up this banquet as being 'complete with richness of fare, variety of dishes, and overflowing abundance of drinks: the delight was unutterable, the comfort inestimable, the enjoyment without murmuring, the hilarity without care' (Hope 1913, 112). What greater tribute to any palace entertainment could be imagined? But despite this apparent blaze of success, we are reminded of the fragility of royal finances by the fact that Edward's intention to impersonate King Arthur on that occasion was frustrated in one particular respect. The King of England had no suitable crown to wear, for his great crown, lesser crown and even Queen Philippa's crown had all been pawned in the Low Countries and elsewhere in 1339 to raise money for the war then beginning against France. Edward's most strenuous efforts to recover them were only partially successful as the great crown could not be repossessed in time for the Windsor tournament (Newton 1980, 19–20).

What is surprising is that the order which did succeed, the Order of the Garter, ever came into existence at all. Only at the instigation of a king as powerful as Edward III could such a famous order of chivalry have as its symbol an article of ladies' underwear (Prestwich 1980, 205). However that may be, major works were undertaken at Windsor to provide a centre for the new order. Although these works included the demolition of the 'Round Table' building, the Order of the Garter in its personnel and royal sponsorship was the true successor of the various round tables held in the early 1340s, but under a different name. The king began by instituting work in the Lower Ward for the Order of the Garter. Henry III's chapel became their centre at Windsor and other buildings were converted, including Henry III's former domestic suite. The works included the supply of the earliest mechanical clock known in England. Begun in the shadow of the Black Death in 1348, these buildings were completed in 1358, reflecting the glow of success which followed the great victory at Poitiers, and the happy conclusion of the work was celebrated with a magnificent feast and tournament designed in part to impress the captive king of France with whose subjects hard bargaining was in progress relating to English territorial and regal aspirations in France.

By 1358 an even greater scheme of works for the king's own use was in progress in the Upper Ward (*see* Fig. 70). The Chancellor and Bishop of Winchester, William Edington, was chaplain to, and a prelate of, the Garter order from its foundation. In charge of the works in the Upper Ward between 1356 and 1361 was William of Wykeham, who was in time to succeed Edington in all four capacities, bishop and chancellor, chaplain and prelate of the Garter. Little now remains of Edward III's residential quarters at Windsor, but they were contained in first-floor suites raised on vaulted undercrofts of the type already described at Kennington from the same period, although at Windsor the scale of the works was much more grand (pages 110–111). Detailed accounts survive for Wykeham's work and for that of his successor William of Mulsho, who put into effect plans which were already decided when Wykeham left Windsor in 1361.

The king's apartments at Windsor included a set of five chambers, one of which was called '*la Rose*', also a closet, a chapel, a painted chamber and a great chamber which received no fewer than twenty windows, suggesting it

was substantial and lit from both sides. Some idea of the interior appearance in '*la Rose*' can be deduced from surviving accounts for its decoration. By far the most valuable item was '1,400 of gold leaf at six shillings per hundred', then '*vertegris*' (green), red lead, white lead, '*azure de Bys*' (blue) and brown. With these commodities, which were measured by weight, there were twenty-two gallons of oil, presumably as a base for the paint (and discrediting the popularly held notion that medieval art was only pursued with water-based paint), and two qualities of varnish. To this impressive suite can be added the great hall (Hope 1913, 194–7). The hall and chapel were end on, in a manner later reproduced by Wykeham at his New College in Oxford. At Windsor they were later knocked through to make the single, very large, St George's Hall (*see* Fig. 71).

Queen Philippa was provided with a more limited range of accommodation, four chambers plus a chapel. Two noteworthy features of her suite were a sizable room distinguished by reference to mirrors, for which boards were purchased for the mirrors to be fixed to in 1363–5. Such luxury fittings may have been added as an afterthought, perhaps financed out of ransom monies which flowed more freely after 1360. There was also a 'daunsyngchambre' which lay adjacent to the 'queen's tower', perhaps a garderobe tower, at one end (Hope 1913, 195). The enthusiasm for dancing shown in this special provision was passed down to Philippa's grandson, Richard II, who added dancing rooms to his favoured residences (page 134). The queen enjoyed her suite at Windsor for only a few years, as she died in 1369.

The detailed accounts which survive for Windsor in the reign of Edward III give a clear picture of the scale of works and materials used. This has already been hinted at in the works on the 'Round Table' building in the 1340s. As the works on the royal suites moved towards completion in the 1360s, the accounts abound with evidence of intensive use of materials and lavish attention to detail. Stone came from far and wide, virtually all the major sources being tapped,

Fig. 70 Windsor castle from the air

Fig. 71 Windsor castle by Wenceslas Hollar. Edward III's end-on chapel and hall knocked through into one. A feast is shown in progress in this seventeenth-century view and the laden tables and ranks of retainers are very reminiscent of medieval banquets

suggesting varieties of stone used for visual effect and for different structural purposes: Caen (from France), Taynton, Reigate (in this case vault stone quality and other 'for divers works' stipulated), Quarr, Wheatley, Sherborne, Roche, Purbeck (both from Dorset and from the London Friars Minor, the latter perhaps suggesting reuse), and 'heathstones' from Collingley in Windsor Forest. For the king's suite alone 820 oak trees from 'Combe Park' were ordered in 1362–3, but this was found to be an insufficient quantity and a further 110 were required from Pamber forest as a supplement. These were in addition to 2,125 oaks from Combe already devoured by the works in the previous year. As the buildings were largely of stone these must have been for interior works and roofing, the supply of £1,087 worth of lead at the same time, lending support to such speculation. Glazing was also going on: 46½ ft (14 m) of painted glass being purchased for the great chapel and 923 ft (289 m) of glass, partly coloured and with a border of the king's arms, for the king's and queen's suites, while the following year a further 1,336 ft (391.1 m) of glass was bought. With the windows up and roofing complete, the scaffolding was removed and tiling of the floors could take place: 214,000 paving tiles were provided for the king's chambers alone, and literally tens of thousands elsewhere in these suites. Wainscot boards were much in evidence in the interiors, arriving in large quantities at a late stage in the proceedings (Hope 1913, 178ff).

In all, Edward's works at Windsor cost over £50,000. Coupled with the convenient situation of Windsor, the sheer scale of the expenditure and the solidity of the buildings where Wykeham was clerk of works may have resulted in the almost unique position of Windsor as a royal palace inhabited almost continuously from the Middle Ages to the present time. It may be no coincidence that other great works initiated by Wykeham at Winchester and Oxford have also stood the test of time. It is noteworthy that the furniture obtained to grace these splendid rooms was rudimentary in the extreme, for example trestle tables, stools and benches. This is a further reminder of the itinerant existence of the court, for as the inventory of possessions of Edward's daughter Joan shows (page 125), the furnishings carried from place to place were all-embracing and luxurious even for this king's daughter.

Edward III maintained and improved other residences besides Windsor and Westminster. From 1343 he held Eltham where he carried out a major rebuilding programme which included new chambers, kitchen, roasting house (replaced in the 1360s), saucery and larder. References to work on the king's chapel and the queen's chapel remind us of their separate establishments, while repair of the 'halls' at Eltham in the 1350s suggests that there may have been private as well as public hall accommodation, or perhaps that Queen Philippa enjoyed a separate hall as well as chapel and chamber. Internal details included the provision of fireplaces in the great hall and , in 1376, a screen for the organ in the chapel. Outside, defensive measures included a drawbridge, perhaps reflecting the growing dangers of the French wars. Vines flourished in the garden and the buildings were embellished with a weather cock in 1369, which may mark a symbolic conclusion of a phase of works (Colvin 1963, 930–3).

A good deal is known about palace buildings from this period, but something needs to be said of the life of a royal household in the later Middle Ages.

Fortunately, it is from about 1350 that we have some most helpful documentation. Edward III intended to strengthen links between England and Spain through the marriage of his daughter Joan to Pedro the Cruel of Castile (d. 1369). In 1348 Joan, a young girl, set off to make the long journey via English possessions in Gascony down to Spain. An inventory survives of everything she took with her, and complements a source such as the Windsor building accounts, which reveals so much about palatial buildings, but helps little with an understanding of the kinds of furnishings introduced into palaces and other residences by visiting royalty.

Princess Joan's baggage fell into two categories. First, there were the necessary materials for Joan and her household to make themselves comfortable in various manors along the way, where the accommodation she was expecting to use was clearly unoccupied. Second, there were the items to impress her husband-to-be and to demonstrate the wealth and prestige of the English royal house from which she came. The accoutrements of the elements of royal domestic living are all included in the surviving inventory of her possessions. These consisted of the complete furnishings for a chapel and two sets of hangings for a hall (one of worsted decorated with popinjays or parrots and the other embroidered in the main with roses), hangings for two beds, and two chairs, of which one was designated for washing, the other for use while the princess was having her hair done. A considerable amount of kitchen equipment followed, including pots, pans and cutlery. Equipment was also transported for the buttery, pantry and spicery, including a supply of spice to suit the English royal palate (Evans 1967, 172, 174). Items to impress Pedro included a set of three ceremonial saddles. (A suspicion is aroused of a certain element of English national pride in sending leatherwork to Spain, always so famous for its leather goods).

Joan unfortunately died of the Black Death in Bordeaux before ever she reached Spain. Pedro subsequently married a French princess whose possessions and gifts were much more extravagant than those sent from England with Joan, and included a veritable sea of fur. King Pedro's life was cut short as Joan's had been, not by plague but by murder. A civil war in Castile in the 1360s was fuelled by Anglo-Gascon intervention under the Black Prince who, in support of Pedro, triumphed over the rival claimant Henry the Bastard of Trastamara at Najera in 1367. As was so often the case in English military activities in the fourteenth and fifteenth centuries, having won the battle he failed to win the war. With French support Henry overcame and murdered King Pedro in 1369. English interests were kept alive by the marriage of John of Gaunt to Constanza of Castile. Gaunt took a considerable interest in Spanish affairs, campaigned there and lived to see the unification of the two sides from the civil war in the marriage of his daughter to Juan I, son of Henry of Trastamara, who succeeded in 1390. Thus three of Edward III's children were involved in Castile, playing a variety of roles in this theatre of European activity.

Apart from the inventory of the Black Prince's sister, Princess Joan, another valuable source which casts light on royal daily life survives from the mid-fourteenth century. This is the *Libro del Infante* written by Juan Manuel, nephew of Alphonso X of Castile who, like Joan, died in the Black Death. The work was based on a scheme originating in the reign of Louis IX (d. 1270), that fountain of many ideals of medieval kingship and royal protocol (page 118).

For the Spanish prince the morning was occupied by religious observance and military training. Dinner, in the middle of the day, was taken with the whole royal suite and was accompanied by singing and reading from epics. The Mediterranean siesta followed and then the prince proceeded to Vespers. Affairs of state were attended to until nightfall. Supper was the last meal of the day, after which lighter pursuits were enjoyed until bedtime. Further passages from the epics were recommended as bedside reading. In the cooler north business was usually pursued before dinner, but practice changed from reign to reign and some kings, such as Henry II, were notoriously irregular and indecisive in their habits (Evans 1967, 170).

In 1348, the very year of Joan's death, tragedy struck the royal family again when Prince William was born but died so soon that the accounts record his funeral expenses before the lavish clothes ordered for the reappearance of the queen in public at court, an event which usually took place forty days after the birth of a child. For the vigil and the day of the churching itself the queen's clothes included an ensemble embroidered with gold birds, each bird encircled by large pearls, the background powdered with a pattern worked in silks and small pearls and spangled with 10,000 doublets or counterfeit jewels. The weight of the garment must have been prodigious, for apart from 400 large pearls, there were thirty-eight ounces of small pearls, thirteen pounds of plate gold, eleven pounds of gold thread and seven pounds of embroidery silks, as well as the 10,000 doublets and not to mention the 2,000 bellies of miniver used in the linings and an estimated 150 ft (about 50 m) of velvet and sixty skins of ermine. An outfit depicting oaks and other trees with lions beneath them was worn on the day of the churching (Newton 1980, 34).

The reign of Edward III changed character somewhat in the king's later years. His long marriage of some forty years ended with the death of Queen Philippa in 1369. After the treaty of Calais of 1360, which brought lands in France as well as a king's ransom for John II of France, Edward withdrew from active participation in military affairs, a role eagerly adopted by the Black Prince. After Philippa's death, and on some accounts before, the ageing king began to lose his way. This has in part been blamed on Alice Perrers, who became his mistress around the time that the queen died. As Edward's mental health was affected by senility and his physical health by what seems to have been a series of strokes, Alice became more firmly entrenched at court. Chroniclers give a picture of general oppositon to Alice's influence, but as the king enjoyed her company and indulged her whims there was apparently nothing to be done. She began to appear in public with the king and even the stoical Londoners were shocked by her outfit as the sun in a pageant in the 1370s. The evident power of the young woman over the old man, in gaining lands and privileges, and in reducing public occasions at which the couple appeared to a travesty of the chivalric extravaganzas of the 1340s and 1350s, was obvious for all to see.

The failure of the court to displace Alice was amongst the grievances which surfaced in the so-called 'Good Parliament' of 1376, which came at a difficult time for the old king, his family and officials. Royal officials were impeached for mismanagement of the war against France and for financial misconduct. Alice was banned from court after moves initiated by the House of Commons.

Edward himself was too sick to preside over the parliament and delegated the task first to the Black Prince, who himself was dying and indeed died during the sitting, and then to John of Gaunt. Despite these efforts to reform the royal household, Alice soon made her way back to court and was present at the death of Edward III, from whose fingers it is claimed she wrenched the valuable rings with which she fled the palace of Sheen where she and the king had spent so much time away from the concerns of state in the closing years of the reign. The wheel of fortune had turned full circle from the horrible events which brought Edward III to the throne in 1327.

Chapter VII

Richard II and the Lancastrians (1377–1461)

The reign of Richard II, the Black Prince's surviving legitimate son, opened with a splendid coronation, reminiscent of that of his ill-fated great-grand-father, Edward II. There was a magnificent procession in which the young king walked by the side of his uncle, Gaunt, who carried the *curtana* or the sword of state. Behind them came the other royal uncles followed by the Archbishop of Canterbury and other prelates. After the coronation the unique authority of the king and the allegiance of the nobles was symbolised as each of the great men touched the crown (McKisack 1959, 398–9). The ten-year-old king who had lost his father and grandfather in the previous two years found himself sud-denly elevated to the throne in a blaze of glory and a great deal was expected of him after the decay of the court of Edward III in recent years. At the corona-tion banquet a knight rode into Westminster Hall to challenge anyone to dispute the new king's title. This was not, as might be expected, a special event designed to delight the young king, but was already an ancient custom in 1377; indeed two knights claimed the right to be hereditary challengers. This piece of pageantry survived until 1821.

As was usually the case in minorities, the country ran well enough without the king insofar as residences were maintained and updated. However, the at-tempt to introduce a new form of taxation, the poll tax, was amongst a variety of grievances which led to the Great Revolt of 1381. On this occasion, Richard, confronting the rebels, showed outstanding courage. Amongst the casualties of the revolt was John of Gaunt's Savoy Palace in the Strand, which was destroyed by rioters as a protest against Gaunt's general unpopularity, especially with the Londoners whose mayor he had threatened to replace with a royal nominee. This destruction of his London base, coupled with other problems of the king's minority, persuaded John of Gaunt not only to stay out of politics, but to be seen to stay out of politics, and led to his retirement to his country properties, especially Kenilworth.

Gaunt rebuilt Kenilworth in a most splendid fashionable Perpendicular style. The imposing remains, including a first-floor hall from this campaign of works, attracted interest at the time of the Gothic revival when the celebrated architect Pugin made some brilliant drawings of the remains of the hall, and in particular of the windows. The buildings at Kenilworth are in keeping with Gaunt's international reputation and with his pursuit of royal status for him-self in Spain (*see* Fig. 72). The new roof at Kenilworth may even have provided one of the models for the great new roof of Westminster Hall (pages 133–5), and is a fine example of noble building in Ricardian England.

The royal family were not the only castle builders at the time, and it is not

Fig. 72 The ruins of John of Gaunt's innovative great hall at Kenilworth. It is raised on an undercroft with wall-set fireplaces and all part of his 'spacious and showy' rebuilding there. (*Copyright English Heritage*)

surprising to find that the castle building and palace building activity of wealthy men outside the royal family has much in common in design, style and in the use of particular masters of works with what was done to royal buildings. Of the castles that survive from the late fourteenth century, Bodiam (Sussex) is the most spectacular, set in a fine moat. A licence to crenellate was issued to Sir Edward Dallingridge in 1385. Old soldiers from the French campaigns of Edward III and the Black Prince, such as Sir Edward, followed their king's example of spectacular castle-palace accommodation at Windsor, but appropriate to their means. In the south of England they also built against the possibility of invasion from France, and in the north from Scotland.

Sir Richard Abberbury, formerly a knight in the service of the Black Prince, was appointed a guardian of the heir to the throne after the Black Prince died in 1376. The fine gatehouse of Abberbury's castle at Donnington (Berkshire) survives, dominating a section of the old road from Winchester to Oxford, and the east-west route from London to Bath. As Edward III had built a castle of chivalry at Windsor, so in France the Duc de Berry, amongst others, was building similar structures which are so beautifully illustrated in his 'Book of Hours' (Platt 1982, 117ff). Cannon were capable of making short work of such traditional castles, as the French showed in Normandy towards 1450. Castle builders knew that the days of the stone keep were numbered and so, in the late fourteenth and fifteenth centuries, no doubt spent more on embellishments to create impressive rather than impregnable structures.

A feature of the building and design of Donnington is that royal servants may well have been involved, and this influence of royal servants upon aristocratic and episcopal building may also be observed in the case of palaces. William of Wykeham, the clerk of works at Windsor, had projects in hand both in Oxford and Winchester at the time that Donnington went up in the wake of a licence to crenellate in 1386 (Platt 1982, 118). Both William Wynford and his friend Henry Yeveley were royal servants, and Wynford was also involved in building works at Winchester and Oxford. More immediately, Wynford was at work on Wykeham's residence at Highclere near Donnington. Establishing links between buildings and clerks of works, in order to show an aspect of royal culture (in this case the introduction of spacious and comfortable castle-palaces) filtering down to the knights and gentry, is notoriously difficult. Thus it is not surprising to find architectural detail in the gatehouse at Donnington which is consistent with work done elsewhere by Wynford, and also with work by Yeveley's assistant, Walton, at the better preserved and palatial accommodation at Portchester castle where a major building programme was carried out for Richard II in the 1390s (Wood 1965, 15–18).

Fig. 73 Dartington Hall, Devon, as it appeared to Samuel Buck in the early eighteenth century. (*Society of Antiquaries of London*)

Dartington Hall (Devon), constructed for Richard II's half-brother John Holland, is as fine in certain respects as Kenilworth (*see* Fig.73). It is plainly undefended, as a proper palace should be. Much has been written about Dartington, and excavations were carried out there by Colin Platt. The scale and

THE EAST VIEW OF DARTINGTON-TEMPLE, IN THE COUNTY OF DEVON.

splendour of the buildings are exceptional and sufficient survives or has been reconstructed to give a good impression of what the buildings consisted of in the late fourteenth century when Holland's builders were at work. The hall measured 70 ft ×38 ft (21.3 m×11.6 m), matching the somewhat earlier Penshurst (Kent) 62 ft×39 ft (18.9 m×11.9 m) and the ground floor hall of 1381–96 built for Archbishop Courtenay's summer palace at Croydon 56 ft×38 ft (17.1 m×11.6 m). The significant measurement in these buildings is the width of the hall, the area to be spanned by the roof. The original hall roof at Dartington has long since been replaced, but may well have provided a model for Hugh Herland's great new hall roof at Westminster. The three unscreened arches between the hall and the kitchen and service areas at Dartington are still in use, and are an impressive sight, matching similar work elsewhere, for example at the archbishop's palace at Canterbury, and at the bishop's palace at Lincoln.

A notable feature of the buildings at Dartington is the considerable provision of accommodation for guests (*see* Fig. 73). Provision of adequate guest accommodation was always a problem in the Middle Ages, especially when kings held major congregations in their rural residences. However, for Holland, whose social circle was more circumscribed than that of the king, the matter of scale was not a problem. No doubt he wished to retain links with his friends in London. Thus it is perhaps more likely that it was through this guest accommodation that Dartington represented 'the importation into the country of metropolitan fashions', rather than in the roof structure. Dartington was highly innovative in a variety of ways.

Another good example of guest, or perhaps retainer, accommodation was to be seen at Ewelme (Oxfordshire) where now much-mutilated accommodation similar to that at Dartington is to be found. The block in question at Ewelme was put up after 1430 by William de la Pole (d. 1450), one of that family of Hull merchants who climbed the social ladder to become bankers to royalty and eventually Dukes of Suffolk. William de la Pole's wife Alice was a granddaughter of the poet Geoffrey Chaucer. Substantial remains of the guest block, including individual suites of lodgings, were still standing in 1729, although today only the hall end of the block survives (Barley 1986, 99).

Richard II's reputation as a builder and leader of aesthetic taste has come under close scrutiny recently and this account bears out that research. It is emerging that while Richard enjoyed and beautified his royal buildings, which had been very much enhanced by his grandfather, Edward III, his reputation as a builder has rested largely on one major and comparatively late scheme, the restoration and reroofing of Westminster Hall in the 1390s. There is no doubt that this work on Rufus's great hall, which had stood almost unaltered since the eleventh century, was a remarkable achievement, still to be seen today (*see* Fig. 74). Viollet le Duc's drawing of it provides a clear exposition of its form and structure (*see* Fig. 75). The span is 69 ft (21 m) and stability is provided by the interlinking of two different types of roof design, the hammer beam and the arch-brace. The creation of this structure at Westminster, perhaps based on prior models at Dartington and Kenilworth, enabled the floor of the hall to be cleared of any roof supports and so maximise the space. This roof was created by the royal carpenter Hugh Herland and is estimated to weigh 660 tons, covering almost half an acre. The wood was cut in Hampshire and Hertfordshire

and prepared at Farnham in Surrey, itself famous for the early timber work in Bishop Blois's hall (page 36). Stone was brought from near Doncaster for the corbels which were cut into the walls to carry the timber. The only major change to the structure of the building was the walling-in of the Norman gallery passages. No roof project on such a scale was ever attempted subsequently.

The work on Westminster Hall was modern in its style. It was not really a household hall but a hall for grand occasions such as coronation feasts and parliaments. The heyday of the great household was over. The rebuilding of the roof of the hall was matched by a rebuilding of the north façade of the palace, which hints clearly that Richard was interested in making a show of power by

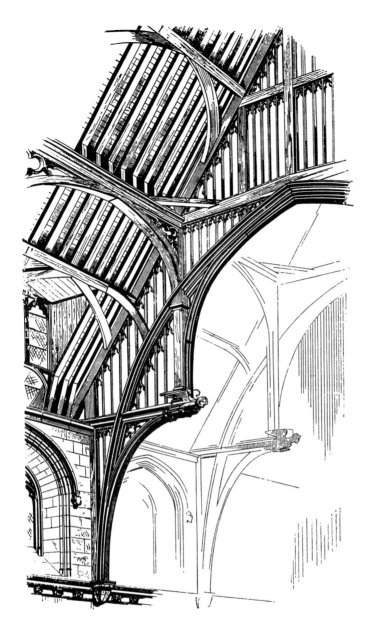

Fig. 75 Detail of the hammer beam arch brace structure of the roof of Westminster Hall, redrawn after Viollet le Duc. (*HMSO*)

his works. Already in 1385 he had ordered thirteen large statues of kings representing his predecessors from Edward the Confessor to his own reign, no doubt to bolster his ideas of kingly power (Colvin 1963, 528) (*see* Fig. 9).

Further evidence of Richard's desire to impress with his power is to be found in Adam of Usk's account of the Westminster Parliament of 1397. This was held in a temporary hall, with an especially high throne for the king, built in the palace yard while the great hall was out of commission. The occasion was most spectacular with the enthroned king flanked by his noble supporters who were dressed in red silk robes embroidered with gold and bordered with white. The culmination of the proceedings was the beheading of the Earl of Arundel, adjudged a traitor, on Tower Hill in the presence of, amongst others, John Holland of Dartington. Meanwhile, during the proceedings the open-ended hall was surrounded while the parliament was in session by Richard's Cheshire archers, fingering their bowstrings menacingly, in a show of force designed to persuade agreement to the king's plans. Without a doubt there were other matters to the fore in the 1390s, apart from mere architectural considerations.

It is not the achievement of the rebuilding of Westminster Hall which has been challenged – the achievement is beyond doubt – but the timing and precedents. It has been strongly argued that works such as Gaunt's Kenilworth and Holland's Dartington provided the inspiration and the experience for the king's great work. The archbishop's hall at Canterbury (126 ft ×42 ft, 38.4 m×12.8 m) and especially Gaunt's hall at Kenilworth (90 ft×45 ft, 27.4 m×13.7 m) are strikingly wider than Dartington, although at almost 70 ft (21.3 m) Westminster dwarfed these schemes. This does not destroy the argument that the roofing techniques which improved building potential in the last quarter of the fourteenth century, by obviating the necessity for pillars, were pioneered in noble and episcopal rather than royal buildings. Compared with his uncle John of Gaunt in particular, Richard II was by no means a substantial innovator, his contributions arising from the enhancement of particular aspects of many royal residences, for example the addition of a dancing room (*camera tripudiancium*) and other refinements at Clarendon and elsewhere. In Richard's defence, however, it should be recalled that he did undertake some substantial building schemes, in particular his work at Westminster and in the provision of residential accommodation which included an upper hall and chambers within the defended area at Portchester. Although the remains of this range to be seen at Portchester today are impressive enough, the most recent analysis of them concludes that Richard's buildings at Portchester were 'quite in contrast to the spacious and showy rebuilding' at Kenilworth (Cunliffe and Munby 1985, 101–8).

Particularly during the lifetime of his first wife, Anne of Bohemia, Richard seems to have enjoyed a sophisticated and happy family life. Anne's father, the Emperor Charles IV, presided over a court of considerable intellectual and artistic distinction. His daughter brought elements of this background with her to England. The palace at Sheen, which had been favoured in his later years by Edward III, who had died there in 1377, was similarly popular with Richard and Anne, who preferred a more intimate social circle to the great jousts and orders of chivalry which had characterised the early years of Edward III's reign. To the main buildings at Sheen Richard contributed a superb new bathroom lined with 2,000 ceramic tiles. On an island called '*La Nayght*', in the Thames beside Richmond, Richard erected a pavilion which he and the houshold used as a summer house. It was a timber-framed structure on stone foundations. Contemporary accounts refer to trestle tables, benches and other details of its interior. The idea for the island retreat in the Thames may have come from Gloucester. At Gloucester, where the castle ditch joins the Severn, an island similarly called '*Naight*' existed beside the priory gardens, which had been enjoyed by Eleanor of Provence in the thirteenth century (page 84) (Harvey 1981, 86). Richard petitioned for access to the gardens at Gloucester by way of the bridge originally constructed in 1277, giving an undertaking that no right of way should be thereby established. So attached was the king to Sheen that when Queen Anne died there in 1394 Richard in his mourning gave orders for the whole palace to be demolished and the ground levelled. This was done, providing a remarkable insight into the personality and exercise of power of this king. The king's uncontrollable grief spilled over into an unfortunate scene during the funeral in which he became involved in a struggle with another mourner whom he believed to be behaving in an unseemly fashion (*see* Fig. 76).

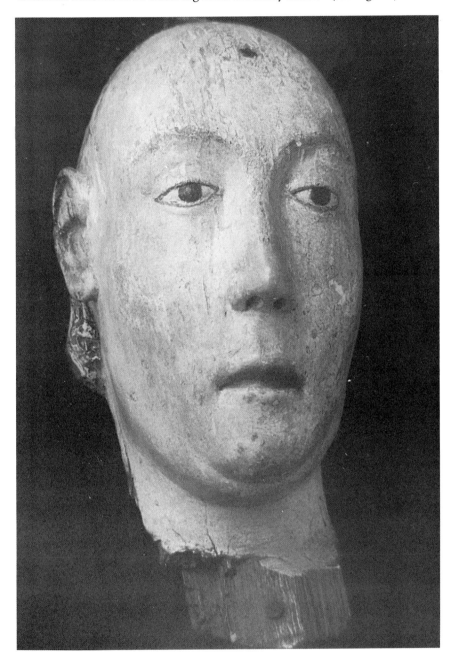

Fig. 76 The wooden head of the funeral effigy of Anne of Bohemia, one of several from the later Middle Ages which are displayed at Westminster. (*By courtesy of the Dean and Chapter of Westminster*)

As Richard's civil servant with special responsibility for buildings, and subsequently as bishop of one of the wealthiest sees in the land as well as holding senior government posts, William of Wykeham was presented with an ideal opportunity and environment to develop his architectural interest. This great Bishop of Winchester's career spanned the reigns of three monarchs, those of Edward III, Richard II and Henry IV. Wykeham is best remembered for his royal works at Windsor under Edward III (pages 121–3) and for his college works at Winchester and Oxford, begun during the latter part of Richard's reign. These grand college schemes were to be the inspiration for Henry VI's Eton and King's College Cambridge.

Wykeham's work on his own residences is less well known, but highly significant nonetheless. Major campaigns of works are recorded in the bishopric pipe rolls, for example at Bishop's Waltham and at Highclere, where existing ranges of buildings were enlarged and beautified, and at East Meon where the complex of buildings he created still substantially survives and has recently been matched by Edward Roberts with the original accounts in the pipe rolls which detail the provision of materials still readily visible. The bishop had spent his life on the move, and his lordship in the Winchester diocese witnessed no diminution of this activity (*see* Fig. 77). At his main palace at Wolvesey in 1372–3 the expenditure, at £199 10s 9½d, was almost the highest recorded on this building in any year of the thirteenth to fifteenth centuries. The main focus was the refashioning of the bishop's own chambers at the south end of the west hall, which took some four years to complete. A new salsary was constructed and, as elsewhere in the south of England in those troubled years, considerable sums were spent on the defences: on the moat and drawbridge and on a curtain wall for the palace and also on the rebuilding and re-crenellation of the adjacent runs of the city wall for which the bishop took responsibility.

These works made Wolvesey a more commodious place for welcoming royalty. Wykeham, who owed his fame and fortune to royal patronage, was prepared to repay his benefactors generously when the opportunity arose. As a senior and respected royal servant, it was appropriate that, in 1393, Wykeham should invite Richard II and Queen Anne to Wolvesey for two great feasts: the first, for 210 guests, cost £10 1s 2d, and the second, held on the following day for 367 guests, cost £39 15s 3d. On a normal day the bishop's household expenses did not exceed two or three pounds. Richard and Anne probably stayed at Wolvesey during the Winchester parliament which occasioned these feasts.

Wykeham was perhaps too old and experienced to fall foul of Richard as did Archbishop Arundel, who was deprived of his office and banished in 1397. Indeed Wykeham survived the revolution of 1399 when Henry IV deposed Richard II. Henry was active in politics and building in the early years of his reign, although from about 1405 he began to suffer from nervous prostration. At first there was much to be done to consolidate his position. He reinstated supporters such as Arundel and he quelled rebellions, such as that led by the great Percy family, who were defeated at the battel of Shrewsbury in 1403. Meanwhile work was carried out at both provincial palaces and those in and around London.

Henry favoured Eltham, where he was married by proxy to Joan of Navarre in 1402. Work concentrated on the domestic accommodation, first that of the

Fig. 77 William of Wykeham's battered mitre case, solidly built to withstand the rigours of medieval travel from manor to manor and on royal business. (*The Warden and Scholars of New College, Oxford. Photograph M.C.T. Mitchell*)

king and subsequently of the queen. These were timber buildings with stone fireplaces and chimneystacks. A study and parlour were included in the king's suite. The study is worthy of particular note. The roof of this room contained sixty-eight carved wood bosses of angels and archangels bearing scrolls and scutcheons. It was a cosy room, measuring 16½ ft×13 ft (5.05 m×4 m). Furnishings included two desks, one of two stages 'to provide accommodation for the king's books'. Natural light came through seven glazed windows depicting saints and the Virgin Mary. Unlike the great chamber, the windows of which were decorated with royal badges, scutcheons and the like, the parlour was a much less formal room. Here the windows were decorated with birds and grotesques (*baboueny*) (Colvin 1963, 935–6). Parlours varied from place to place. One suggestion is that they grew out of the bay windows which began to appear at the dais ends of great halls in the later Middle Ages (Wood 1965, 103). However, this can hardly be said of Archbishop Arundel's great parlour of 51 ft×21 ft (15.5 m×6.4 m), sited west of the great hall at Croydon (1397–1414), since it stood in addition to big bay windows.

Henry IV spent five Christmases of his reign at Eltham, which was so convenient to London. But rural palaces such as Clarendon were not entirely neglected at this time. A spacious new stable block 63 ft (19.2 m) long and with a substantial timber roof of '*xlvj couplez rafters*' and other timber was ordered. This hints at the preoccupations of the king moving with a large retinue round a potentially hostile realm (James and Robinson 1988, 41). One of those by whom he felt threatened was Roger of Clarendon, an illegitimate son of the Black Prince, born at Clarendon during the Poitiers campaign in the 1350s. Roger, as a half-brother of Richard II, unwisely plotted against Henry IV. He was executed for treason although it was his proximity to the thone which really hastened his end.

Richard's reign is usually depicted as a period of great expenditure and that of Henry IV as one of retrenchment and parsimony. Like all generalisations, this is only partly true; the early years of Henry IV's reign saw some lavish expenditure, by no means all by the king. An example of this was a splendid feast held at Wolvesey palace for Henry and Queen Joan to celebrate their marriage when the queen arrived in 1403. Old Bishop Wykeham welcomed the royal couple to stay at Wolvesey and lavished a feast costing £522 12s on them, or some fifteen times as much as had been spent on Richard II ten years earlier. Admittedly it was a more auspicious occasion, but the contrast is startling and, of course, the bishop paid on both occasions. The feast included cygnets, capons, venison with frumenty (a dish composed of hulled wheat boiled in milk and spiced with cinnamon, sugar and other ingredients), griskins, rabbits, bitterns, pullets, partridges, woodcock, plover, quail, snipe, fieldfares, roast kid, custards, fritters, creams of almonds, pears in syrup and 'subtleties with crowns and eagles' (Biddle 1986, 18–19). This was certainly a more sumptuous and varied offering, from what evidence we have, than William Ralegh's feast for St Edmund's day in the same diocese 150 years earlier. Here also we find an echo of the bone remains from the Black Prince's palace at Kennington, where the remains of quail and assorted meats had ended up in the middens around 1350 (page 112).

The pressures of maintaining the position Henry had usurped were considerable, and it is not surprising that his mental health suffered. Matters were not made easier by the pressure applied by his son, the active and able Prince Hal, who not only had fond memories of Richard II but who had different ideas about the pursuance of the French wars, to the extent that father and son allied with different factions in France and Hal even attempted to take the throne for himself from his ailing father.

Henry V (1413–22) spent much of his short reign abroad campaigning in France. He admired Richard II greatly and had the remains of the deposed king reinterred at Westminster. It is possible that certain aspects of his building activities may have derived from this fondness. The rehabilitation of Sheen, a favourite place of Richard II until he had it demolished on the death of Queen Anne in 1394, is perhaps one aspect of this. Another is Henry's work at Kenilworth on his 'Plesaunce', an isolated spot approached only by water, analogous to Richard's island retreat of '*La Nayght*' in the Thames off Sheen (page 134). (*see* Fig. 78).

Building accounts for Henry V's reign are not as detailed as those in previous centuries, but it is evident that Henry intended to make Sheen one of the great

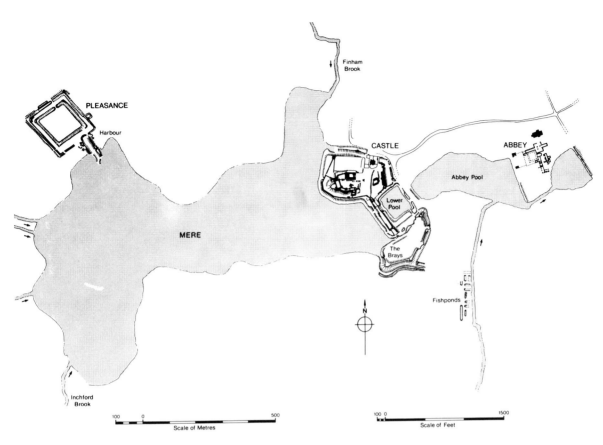

Fig. 78 Plan showing Henry V's 'plesaunce' at Kenilworth. It was remote from the castle but accessible by barge across the lake. Excavations have revealed timber framed structures to accommodate the royal parties. (*Copyright English Heritage*)

palaces of the land, although he was prevented from completing work there by his early death. Sheen was the product of the prestige and profits gained in the Agincourt campaign in 1415 and in the subsequent conquest of Normandy. The work at Sheen at the height of Henry's success is strongly reminiscent of Edward III's work at Windsor at the equivalent point in his reign. Sheen was intended to be very grand, in keeping with the extravagant pageants which welcomed Henry back to London after Agincourt and which so impressed the Holy Roman Emperor, Sigismund, in 1416. A distinctive feature was construction material of brick. The use of brick on such a large scale was unusual in the early fifteenth century in England, and may have popularised its use in London. There was a great courtyard 208 ft × 175 ft (63.4 m × 53.3 m). The buildings included a great hall 77 ft × 40 ft (23.5 m × 12.2 m) and a chapel of similar proportions raised in an undercroft. Many other details are lost to us although we do know that there was much reused material at Sheen palace, notably from Sutton and Byfleet.

Sutton was a comparatively new site, where a manor had been built late in Richard II's reign and work was still apparently in progress on the accession of Henry IV. Apart from the loads of Reigate stone, ashlar, moulding and other stone, 120 Surrey oaks, 20,000 rooftiles and 28,000 'flaunders tyle' (brick) were used at Sutton to build, amongst other things, a spiral staircase. Henry V held a council there in 1413, but in 1415 he gave orders for the demolition of the manor (Colvin 1963, 1004).

In addition to the Sutton materials, materials from Byfleet were used at Sheen in the construction of a curious building which was actually called Byfleet. This was no mere hash of old timbers but a major residence immediately beside Sheen, complete with bath-house and royal chambers, which cost nearly £6,000 to build compared with some £2,500 spent on the refoundation of Sheen. The detailed decoration of Byfleet, with a great antelope surmounting the kitchen quarters, eighty antelopes and swans costing twenty pence each decorating the parlour and chamber, and with lions and fleur-de-lys cresting the beams, has led to the suggestion that it may even be that Byfleet was the main residence and Sheen the administrative quarter (Colvin 1963, 1000). However, the function of Byfleet as a separate residence immediately beside Sheen is unclear. Its early completion suggests it may have been rapidly erected to provide accommodation for the royal household while the new palace next door was under construction. This double residence foreshadows those of Henry VIII.

At Kenilworth, where John of Gaunt had done so much work, Henry contented himself with the addition of 'the Plesaunce in the Marsh'. This was sited a distance from the castle across the lake and approached by a waterway sufficiently wide to admit the royal barge. This pavilion had a hall and chambers and was soundly constructed. The 'Plesaunce' lasted a century or so until it was demolished by Henry VIII (Colvin 1963, 685; Thompson 1971, 206).

The long reign of Henry VI is chiefly remembered architecturally for the royal building of Eton and King's College Cambridge, but these works came later. The early part of the reign was dominated by the king's uncles, chiefly the Duke of Bedford, regent of France, and the Duke of Gloucester, regent in England. Humphrey of Gloucester obtained the manor of Greenwich in 1426 and made good use of it, notably spending Christmas 1428 at Greenwich or the manor of 'Plesaunce' as it was called, an echo of Kenilworth. A licence to crenellate the house was granted in 1433 and permission given for Humphrey to build a stone tower in the park (Colvin 1963, 949). The tower was much developed by Henry VIII as a remote site within the palace grounds (page 158). After Gloucester died in 1447 the manor passed to the queen, Margaret of Anjou, whom Henry VI had married in 1445. Precise accounts survive of some of the works carried out under Queen Margaret and from these we learn a good deal of the finer details of the residence. The king and queen each had a separate courtyard. The queen's chamber overlooked the garden and was embellished with heraldic glass, much of it ordered by the queen herself. The king's and queen's flowers, hawthorn buds and daisies (margarits) decorated one of the bay windows, and the royal arms of both king and queen were inserted in the chapel windows (*ibid*).

In the same year, 1426, that he gained Greenwich, Humphrey set about rebuilding his burnt-out London palace at Baynard's castle, south of Thames Street and fronting the river (Schofield 1984, 132). So many major residences relied on river transport for access and egress and in Humphrey's time Baynard's castle seems to have enjoyed its own dock, carved out of the embankment to the west of the property. Baynard's castle remained in royal hands for the rest of Lancastrian and Yorkist rule in England and was the scene of stirring historical events: both Edward IV in 1461 and Richard III in 1483 were offered the crown of England there. Thus the residence of Henry VI's warlike uncle Humphrey passed to Richard of Gloucester, the most notorious wicked uncle of all.

There was much palace building by archbishops and bishops in the mid-fifteenth century. At Winchester the noble Cardinal-Bishop Beaufort (1405–47) and his successor, the Lincolnshire-born Bishop Waynflete (1447–86), were great builders. Waynflete undertook various works for Henry VI, such as the completion of Eton College, and was also the builder of Magdalen College, Oxford. On his own account the bishop built in brick – his striking brick tower at Farnham (1470–5) has been very favourably compared with similar structures at Hampton Court and Layer Marney (Pevsner 1969, 230) (page 20). His fine red brick gatehouse at Esher (1475–80), embellished with blue brick diapering, also survives (*see* Fig. 79). These works in brick mirror Waynflete's

Fig. 79 Esher. Bishop Waynflete's brick gatehouse today. A wooden gallery and no doubt other associated structures were removed by Henry VIII for re-use at Whitehall. (*Photograph John Steane*)

long association with Ralph Cromwell of Tattershall and John Fastolf of Caister (Waynflete was an executor at the death of each man). A connection such as this can be traced in the more copious and personal documentation of the fifteenth century, and shines brightly through the distinctive style of brick-building these old warriors pioneered in England. Indeed Cromwell and Fastolf had fought at Agincourt (1415) alongside Fiennes and Ogard who, with their buildings at Hurstmonceux and Rye (Sussex), had encouraged the use of brick in south-east England, following Henry V's example.

Further north, at Lincoln, Bishop Alnwick (1436–49) was busy up-dating his palace. His main additions were a fine gatehouse, which still stands, and a chapel block, which has disappeared. Thomas Bourchier, Archbishop of Canterbury (1454–86), enlarged the existing structures at Knole (Kent) into a multi-courtyard residence, palatial in disposition, but markedly unflamboyant in character (*see* Fig. 80). Much of his work, largely of Kentish ragstone, survives embedded in later structures. Both Beaufort at Winchester and Alnwick at Lincoln undertook work on their respective west and east halls. Alnwick added a bay window to light the dais end of his hall while Beaufort reroofed his hall (Ambrose 1980, 3; Biddle 1986, 19–20). Excavation revealed the extent of the scaffolding which enveloped the building during this work. The same programme may well have included the rebuilding of the chapel at Wolvesey, the only part of the medieval palace still in use. Both at Wolvesey and at Lincoln very considerable clearance of material remains from the site, which had accumulated during previous centuries, was done in the fifteenth century. This activity has been noted by historians and archaeologists elsewhere at the same period, for example at Clarendon where 500 cartloads of rubbish were removed from the site in about 1450. Removal of this material may have been in response to improved notions of hygiene in the post-Black Death era in which England continued to be invaded regularly and severely by waves of plague, and which reduced the population by about 1450 to its lowest point since the Conquest.

The three quarters of a century from the accession of Richard II to the accession of Edward IV were difficult times for the monarchy, characterised by minorities, failure in foreign war, civil war and plague. There were, nonetheless, significant innovations in building, especially by the nobility and by the episcopate. Henry VI devoted his energies to institutional causes, and the development of royal palaces was somewhat patchy until the reign of the flamboyant Edward IV began in 1461.

Chapter VIII

Yorkists and early Tudors (1461–1547)

Towards the end of the Middle Ages, the expenses of the war with France, the toll of civil war and the reduction in taxation brought about by the rapid decline in population all conspired to make the crown less wealthy than it had been. The impression should not be given that the crown was poor, just that in comparative terms fifteenth-century England was less prosperous than, for example, it had been in the thirteenth century, a period which enjoyed a burgeoning population and which in turn provided a large pool of labour, encouraging economic growth. Edward IV's use of palaces exemplifies this change. Fewer palaces were maintained. The palaces Edward did use were mainly near to London and included Windsor. For example, he enlarged the palace at Greenwich, which was then presented to Elizabeth Woodville, his queen. He achieved a transformation in royal finances during his reign and economising on building expenditure was no doubt one plank of this strategy. Another was negotiating large payments from France, a kind of *appatis*, for not invading the old enemy. All this added together enabled Edward to be the first English king since Henry II (d. 1189) to die in credit (Myers 1959, 11).

This Edwardian court was not, however, dull, although it could be unpredictable, as the following contrasting glimpses show. One aspect of Edward's court life which has continued to attract attention was his robust attitude to women. The king pursued women 'with no discrimination, the married and the unmarried, the noble and the lowly', a contemporary remarked, adding deferentially that 'however he took none by force'. Nonetheless the same writer recorded that when he had seduced a woman he lost interest in her and passed her down the line, often against her will, to courtiers (Given-Wilson and Curteis 1984, 10–11, 40). But this was the era of Elizabeth Shore, the merry concubine. This is not the whole story, however. A German visitor to court witnessed a very different aspect of palace life when he observed a dinner which followed the churching of the queen after the birth of a child. On this occasion, the queen sat separate on a golden chair. The queen's mother-in-law and sisters were allowed to sit after the first course had been served. Otherwise courtiers remained kneeling throughout the meal, which lasted three to four hours. There was silence throughout. This was a far cry from the boisterous tournaments which celebrated the churching of Philippa of Hainault after childbirth in Edward III's reign. The distinction in Edward IV's case seems to have been that the concubines had to be merry to retain his interest, whereas the queen, from whom he was separated for much of the time, was a fixture at court.

But what of the palaces under Edward IV? He is best remembered for his reconstruction of the palace of Eltham as it survives today, with the additions of royal apartments by Henry VII and a chapel by Henry VIII (*see* Fig. 81). In the centre of the site is the great hall which divides the public from the private court-yards (*see* Fig. 82). This hall dates essentially from Edward IV's reign, and may have been used first in 1482. It is 101 ft long×36 ft wide×55 ft high to the apex of the roof (30.8 m×10.8 m×16.8 m). This hall is a particular masterpiece with a fine hammerbeam roof and large Perpendicular windows. Bay windows were positioned to light the dais in a style found elsewhere in the fifteenth century, notably at the bishop's palace at Lincoln, and (now bricked up) at Morton's Hatfield palace. Indeed the dais bay window appears generally to have taken on a life of its own and to have grown into a retiring chamber off the dais, on occasions screened off from the hall and with its own fireplace (Wood 1965, 103ff).

The most striking parallel with Eltham is Crosby hall, formerly Crosby place, built by an exceptionally wealthy London merchant by the name of Crosby who probably employed the king's mason Thomas Jurdan, so similar are the architectural features, including the extensive use of brick. What is noteworthy about Crosby place is that the entry of a merchant into the architectural élite, his place lacking only an 'a' to distinguish it from a palace. Indeed, the future Richard III and, later, Sir Thomas More were to occupy it (Schofield 1984, 125). Crosby boldly proclaimed his allegiance to the Yorkist

Fig. 81 A view of Eltham palace across the moat in 1680

Fig. 82 The great hall at Eltham. (*Photograph John Steane*)

cause and moved in royal circles, no doubt helping to finance royal activities from Crosby place in the same way as Jacques Coeur had helped, and benefited from association with Charles VII in France from his palace at Bourges in the previous generation.

As his predecessors had enjoyed painted interiors in their palaces, Edward IV preferred warmer and more fashionable tapestrywork, such as that hung at Eltham. This was financed not by victories, as Windsor and Sheen had been, but out of the profits of the secretly-negotiated Treaty of Picquigny (1475) by which Edward promised to abandon support of the Burgundians against the French king, Louis IX. This rich pension was a valuable asset to Edward, who had spent much of his reign consolidating his position on the throne, financing his schemes with the profits of confiscated Lancastrian lands. Eltham is a brick structure with the north, or main, front faced with Reigate ashlar and the south front with squared ragstone up to the windows (Strong 1958, 11). Edward's reputation as a palace builder was recorded by the poet Skelton:

'I made Nottingham a Palace Royal,
Windsor, Eltham and many others mo;
Yet at last I went from them all
Et nunc in pulvere dormio'.

Work at Eltham was undertaken with the overt aim of matching the great Lancastrian palace of Sheen. At Christmas 1482 no less than 2,000 people were entertained at Eltham in great style. A lesser extravagance was the purchase from Spanish merchants of African lions, probably for the menagerie at the Tower.

Even greater than his work at Eltham was Edward's projected St George's Chapel at Windsor which was begun in 1473. Important buildings of the period of Henry III, to the west of chapel, were sacrificed to the chapel which had proceeded as far as the west end of the chancel, which had been roofed over, by the time of Edward's death. St George's was completed by Henry VII. Although the character of the flamboyant Edward IV contrasted very starkly with the parsimonious Henry VII, the financial reforms, reform of the household and indeed the rebuilding of St George's were all aspects of Edward's reign enlarged upon by Henry VII. After the uncertainty of the Wars of the Roses, the Yorkist victors were able, albeit briefly, to enjoy some of the spoils of war. As Edward IV, when he was able to afford it, was an enthusiastic builder, so was his Lord Chamberlain, Lord Hastings. Amongst the properties to be shared out after the Battle of Towton in 1469 was the castle of Ashby de la Zouch, formerly the property of the Lancastrian Earl of Ormonde who was beheaded after being captured in the battle. The elevation of Hastings to the peerage from the ranks of the gentry by Edward IV provides another example of many ways in which the Yorkists, and indeed all medieval kings, introduced changes normally attributed to the Tudors, in this case the promotion of so-called 'new men'.

In 1474 Hastings obtained licences to build fortified houses at Ashby de la Zouch, Kirby Muxloe and at Bagworth (Jones 1953, 6). The moated brick fortress which he built at the Hastings family seat of Kirby Muxloe is a good example of its type and era. At Ashby the existing castle, with its fine east-west aligned twelfth-century hall, its fourteenth-century kitchens and slightly later solars, was modernised and the Hastings tower was added. Ashby exemplifies the way in which the castle had developed in the later Middle Ages. The Hastings tower is a sound defensive structure with no windows on the ground floor and with walls almost three metres thick. It is an addition to the building stock for the lord and his immediate retainers, separate from the accommodation for hired soldiery who might also be needed in a seige. In classic style the tower was built beside domestic quarters and a new chapel, both of which slightly predate the tower itself. The chapel in particular, which was not served by a college of priests as at Tattershall, is considered to be a notable example of conspicuous consumption. The career of the first Lord Hastings was ended by the headsman's axe in the reign of Richard III in 1483. However, the family flourished as supporters of Henry VII, who visited Ashby in 1503, and these associations with the Tudors led to prosperity in the sixteenth century (Jones 1953, 6–9).

On the whole, as at Ashby, the tower was not the principal residence of the owner on the site. The same was the case at other castle-palaces of the nobility: at Warkworth where the lord's residential suite led off the dais of the hall and at Tattershall. A clue to the layout of tower and suites survives in a survey dating from 1647 of Buckden, where Bishop Rotherham of Lincoln had added a fine brick tower in the 1470s (*see* Fig. 83). Rotherham had been a beneficiary of the funds from Picquigny (1475) and also did well out of his association with the Woodville family. These connections fuelled his building programme. The survey of Buckden refers to the brick tower as 'the king's lodging', suggesting that great men who were wise erected strongpoints dedicated to the monarchs who had raised them up, rather than to their own defence against kings who felt uneasy on their thrones, which had been the case of the magnates in the

Fig. 83 Bishop Rotherham's
tower of *c.* 1475 at Buckden.
(*Photograph M. Barley,
Houses and History*)

reign of Edward I (page 101). Meanwhile, towards the end of the Yorkist
period, in 1489, Bishop Morton of Ely created a splendid new palace in brick
at Hatfield, much of which still survives and provides a link between the royal
palaces in brick which had a tentative beginning at Kennington in about 1350
and the huge undertakings in the same material made by an over-mighty subject such as Cardinal Wolsey at Hampton Court half a century later.

The Tudor claim to the crown was very tenuous and Henry VII, in much the
same way as William the Conqueror had been, was at pains to display continuity with the past in establishing his new dynasty on the throne. His most
favoured palace was Sheen, which had been rebuilt as a monument to Lancastrian military triumphs by Henry V and was later adorned with cupolas and

domes. Henry VII was descended from Henry V's widow, Catherine of Valois, who had secretly married a lowly court clerk called Owen Tudor, a fact only discovered after her death. Henry VI with characteristic gentleness had treated his half-brothers, one of whom was Henry VII's father, well and allowed them to remain at court. In view of Henry VII's descent through a Lancastrian queen and the court of Henry VI there were plenty of scores to be settled in the defeat of the Yorkist Richard III on 22nd August 1485 at Bosworth. So the choice of the major Lancastrian palace is not surprising.

In order to rebuild bridges with the Yorkists Henry VII married Elizabeth of York on 18th January 1486. Precisely thirty-five weeks later, on 20th September, Prince Arthur, the personification of the reconciliation, was born. Compared with the coronation of Henry VII and his marriage, much is known about the christening arrangements for this important heir, and such information as survives on this christening and on that of their second child Margaret furnish insights into an aspect of court ceremonial which is poorly known at present (Staniland 1987, 297ff). The choice of Arthur as the name for the child had a historical ring in itself and the choice of Winchester as the place of baptism reinforced the carefully orchestrated historicity. No doubt the king gave instructions which initiated the ceremonial. Whether or not the queen was involved in this is unknown. She would have retired from court some six weeks or so before the birth and not have emerged for her purification until a further rich ceremony had been enacted forty days after the birth. Given these circumstances it is perhaps not surprising that the queen did not attend the ceremony, but it is unexpected to discover that the king did not attend either – the godparents, choir, heralds and a multitude of others carried the ceremony through in the parents' absence (*ibid.* 306).

The custom seems to have been to proceed to baptism very soon after the baby's birth; Arthur's sister Margaret, for example, was baptised the morning after she was born. Preparations for Arthur's baptism were made in great detail; the silver font in which the baby was immersed as part of the ceremony was brought from Christ Church priory in Canterbury, and set up alongside Henry of Blois's Tournai marble font towards the west end of the cathedral. The baby's attire included specially made fine sheets and a mantle of cloth of gold lined with ermine, with a long train carried behind. Within the cathedral special hangings, according to custom, would have been provided together with a purpose-built closet in which the baby was to be undressed before, and dressed again after, baptism. The closet was a comfortable place with carpets, cushions, a fire and warm water, all of which would have been very necessary at Winchester on that autumn day as the ceremony was apparently relocated further west in the barn-like cathedral 'for the Wether was cowlde and to fowlle' to have it further east. However, the throng did process to the altar after the baptism to set the prince's candle on the altar (*ibid.* 306n). The bad weather may have accounted for another aspect of the arrangements, the decision to make the great procession only from the prior's hall to the cathedral, a walk of only a couple of hundred yards or so, rather than from the castle or the bishop's palace.

Although, given the circumstances of a somewhat premature birth, all the necessary people and equipment appear to have been gathered together at Winchester, one significant person did not make it in time. The latecomer to

Prince Arthur's baptism was his chief godfather, the Earl of Oxford, who was making his way from Suffolk (*ibid.* 301). The ceremony was delayed for four hours while the earl made haste to attend. Not until he was reported to be a mile off did the king give orders for the procession to begin, and the earl eventually arrived in time to join the procession to the high altar. The significance of the potential absence of the earl may have been heightened by some disability on the part of the chief godmother the queen mother (the widow of Edward IV), whose place was taken in the procession by a proxy, although she was present in the cathedral.

Prince Arthur, of whom so much was hoped and who showed such promise, died prematurely in 1502, his early death, it was said, contributing to the almost simultaneous death of his mother in childbed. The prince and his mother survived Henry's favourite palace at Sheen by only three years, for the palace, after Henry had lavished so much attention on it, had been destroyed by fire in 1499. Sheen was replaced by a fine new palace which was called Richmond in honour of the king's former earldom (*see* Fig. 84). This occupied a ten-acre site and was laid out round a series of three major courtyards (*see* Fig. 85). The layout was somewhat more formal and less haphazard than at previous palaces,

Fig. 84 The domes and cupolas of Richmond palace as portrayed by Wenceslas Hollar.

Fig. 85 Plan of Richmond. (*HMSO*)

A Possible position of Bakehouse	K Outer Gate
B Possible Offices of Plummery and Clerk of Works	L Middle Gate Building
C Possible position of Watergate	M Fountain Court
D Woodyard Lodgings, and House of Office	N Passage Building
E The Cistern House	O Royal Lodgings
F Poultry House, Scalding House	P Paved Court
Aumery Room and Ale Buttery	Q King's Closet
G Pantry and Larders	R Chapel
H Kitchen	S Queen's Closet
I Flesh and Fish Larders, and Pastry	T Galleries
J Hall	U The Friary Church

but the major structures were traditional. The hall and chapel, each some 100 ft long×40 ft wide (30.5 m×12.2 m), dominated the middle court. The windows had depictions of warrior kings of the middle ages including the Conqueror, Richard I and the victor of Bosworth, Henry VII himself. Statues and tapestries adorned the lower walls. In the chapel, cloth of gold predominated on the walls and representations of saintly kings such as the Confessor were to be found, all contributing to the Tudor sense of their own position within a laudable descent of monarchs.

The palace buildings culminated in a third courtyard which contained the royal apartments, themselves dominated by no less than fourteen towers, each with an onion cupola surmounted by a weather vane bearing the gilt and azure arms of the king. Other courtyards where the everyday work of the palace was carried out lay nearby. The whole was surrounded by gardens and an extensive park where cherry and other trees made a pretty sight in their season. The palace was well appointed for water, with elm pipes leading to intricate fountains. It was approached through a solid gatehouse on the landward side (*see* Fig. 86).

Greenwich was also favoured by Henry VII who enlarged and beautified the fifteenth-century buildings which dated from the days of Duke Humphrey of Gloucester, and subsequently Queen Margaret of Anjou. Fashionable red brick was used to face the palace, which remained essentially as it had developed in its haphazard medieval form of imprecisely aligned courts. As was the case with so many of the Thames-side palaces which were designed to be approached from the river, the main gatehouse and front at Greenwich were to the river and the frontage was extended by Henry VII to 500 ft (152.5 m). Here the future Henry VIII was born.

Despite all his work on these and other residences, Henry VII made Baynard's Castle in Thames Street his main London residence. John Stow described Baynard's castle as 'strongly fortified (and) castle-like, but far more commodious for the entertainment of any prince of great estate'. Henry wanted his major residence to be a credit to his new dynasty. It had strong associations with Catherine of Aragon, whose marriage to Prince Arthur was negotiated from here. Catherine's second husband, Henry VIII, gave her Baynard's Castle which she kept until her divorce (Schofield 1984, 132).

Henry VII was enthusiastic in his promotion of the new dynasty. He has a reputation for having been very sparing in his expenditure of money – he left a well-stocked treasury at his death – but on certain building projects he clearly

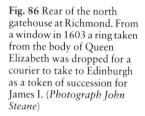

Fig. 86 Rear of the north gatehouse at Richmond. From a window in 1603 a ring taken from the body of Queen Elizabeth was dropped for a courier to take to Edinburgh as a token of succession for James I. (*Photograph John Steane*)

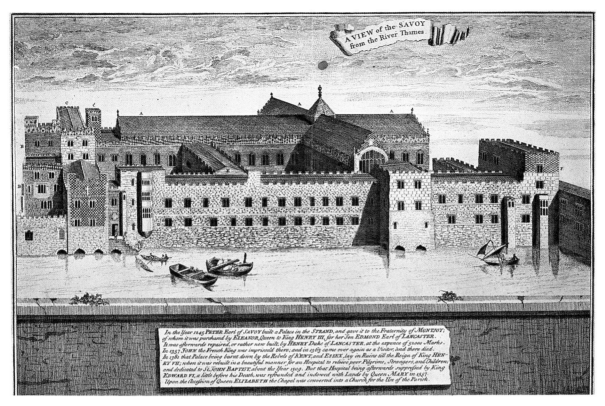

A VIEW of the SAVOY
from the River Thames.

In the Year 1245 PETER Earl of SAVOY built a Palace in the STRAND, and gave it to the Fraternity of MONTJOY; of whom it was purchased by ELEANOR, Queen to King HENRY III, for her Son EDMOND Earl of LANCASTER. It was afterwards repaired, or rather new built, by HENRY Duke of LANCASTER, at the expence of 52000 Marks. In 1357 JOHN the French King was imprisoned there; and in 1363 came over again as a Visitor, and there died. In 1381 that Palace being burnt down by the Rebels of KENT, and ESSEX lay in Ruine till the Reign of King HENRY VII; when it was rebuilt in a beautiful manner for an Hospital to relieve your Pilgrims, Strangers, and Children and dedicated to St. JOHN BAPTIST about the Year 1509. But that Hospital being afterwards suppressed by King EDWARD VI, a little before his Death, was refounded and indowed with Lands by Queen MARY in 1557. Upon the Accession of Queen ELIZABETH the Chapel was converted into a Church for the Use of the Parish.

lavished huge sums, for example on completing Henry VI's foundation at King's College, Cambridge, and on his own hospital at the Savoy (*see* Fig. 87). Through building he could elevate the dynasty in a public and permanent way, at the same time associating it with places of historic significance to bolster the Tudors' short and somewhat murky genealogy. Thus at Woodstock he built a two-courtyard stone house adorned with much heraldry and with inscriptions referring to Henry himself (Howard 1987, 214). This king's royal building works are nowhere better exemplified than at Westminster, in the splendid Gothic chapel with its superb suspended vault, and in the Renaissance tomb there, where in 1509 he was buried. In addition he completed St George's Chapel at Windsor, providing the beautiful continuous stone vault. St George's is the greatest surviving medieval royal chapel. Henry intended to be buried at Windsor alongside Henry VI, a further expression of solidarity with the Lancastrian cause, but later changed his mind, making it known that he wished Henry VI's remains to be removed from Windsor to the new chapel at Westminster, a hope which was never realised.

The Tudors strayed little from London and the Thames valley, following the example of Edward IV. Henry VII had experienced violent struggles for the throne of England and had learnt much from the failures of his predecessors to secure the throne for their own dynasties. The Lancastrians and the Yorkists had disposed of so many properties that only a handful of residences were left in royal hands in 1485 (page 164). Henry VII set about ensuring that those residences he owned provided an up-to-date and splendid expression of his

Fig. 87 Henry VII's Savoy hospital constructed on a site which had lain derelict since John of Gaunt's palace had been destroyed in 1381. The massive buildings give an impression of how the palace would have dominated this section of the river a century or so earlier

concept of monarchy. Despite debate on the topic it seems Eltham may have been considerably enlarged on his orders by the addition of new royal apartments, and appears across the river in a sixteenth-century drawing. Erasmus visited the palace in 1500, dined in the great hall and has left an account of his visit. At the same time certain more far-flung palaces, such as Clarendon, were allowed quietly to decay. The favoured residences, however, were enlarged and beautified by Henry VII and Henry VIII in the tradition which had made their royal predecessors so often the leaders of building fashion in previous centuries.

Bishops continued to flourish both as conspicuous consumers and as builders in the later years of the fifteenth century and under the Tudors. A most striking account of ecclesiastical conspicuous consumption survives from 1465. In this year George Neville (d. 1476), brother of Warwick 'the kingmaker', was enthroned as Archbishop of York and was host at a celebration of royal proportions, designed in part no doubt to bolster the Neville position in the north in those unsettled times. The scene unfolded at Cawood, where Archbishop Neville presided in his twenty-five room mansion over a gathering of seven bishops, ten abbots, twenty-eight peers, and fifty-nine knights, as well as many ladies, lawyers, clergy, leading townsmen and others, amounting to perhaps 2,500 in all. The seating arrangements from the feast tell us much about the social hierarchy of the time. The great hall was the principal focus. Here the archbishop in person presided over several hundred senior guests seated at seven tables. There were, as was customary in an ecclesiastical household, probably no women present in the great hall. The ladies dined in the 'chief chamber' with the young Duke of Gloucester (later Richard III). There were further tables in the other main chambers of the castle. In the 'low hall', perhaps sited beneath the main hall as was the case elsewhere, two sittings were required to feed the gentlemen, franklins and yeomen. The household and servants ate in the gallery.

In keeping with such an occasion the menu focused on a variety of cooked meats from droves of animals: 113 oxen, six wild bulls, 1,000 sheep, 2,000 each of pigs, geese and chickens. There were 4,000 cold venison pasties, and similar numbers of pigeons and rabbits. Twelve porpoises were consumed. Other food was provided: 300 quarters of wheat, 2,000 hot custards, 3,000 baked cold custards and 3,000 dishes of jelly. This mighty feast was washed down with 300 tuns of ale and 100 tuns of wine (Myers 1959, 2).

Such an auspicious beginning to his archiepiscopate led in the end to a fate all too common for the overmighty subject when Archbishop Neville lost the confidence of Edward IV and was imprisoned. The Duke of Gloucester did not forget George Neville, however, and by his petition the archbishop was released in 1475 after two and a half years in prison, but his health was broken and he died the following year. Nothing now remains of the halls and chambers where George Neville entertained his guests at Cawood, although a gatehouse built by a predecessor, Archbishop Kempe (1426–51), is still to be seen. An echo of the great feast was perhaps to be seen in the great banquet, which lasted for five and a half hours, following Richard III's coronation in 1485. Maybe the king cast his mind back twenty years to the great feast at Cawood which he had enjoyed in his early teens.

Bishop Rotherham of Lincoln (1472–80), who had already made his mark as a builder at Buckden, was elevated to York in 1480 and remained there until his death at Cawood in 1500. In his twenty years as archbishop he doubled the size of the archiepiscopal palace at Bishopthorpe by adding a new range in his favourite medium, brick. At almost the same time Bishop Morton of Ely (1478–86) built a brick palace at Hatfield (Hertfordshire) before 1486, when he was elevated to Canterbury (*see* Fig. 88). The surviving main range measures 230 ft×40 ft (70.1 m×12.2 m). The use of brick contrasts with the old-fashioned style and materials used by Morton's predecessor at Canterbury, Archbishop Bourchier, on his palace-building of Knole (Kent) which was created at the same time as Hatfield. The excellent building at Hatfield is described by Pevsner as the 'foremost monument of domestic architecture in the county and one of the foremost monuments of medieval brickwork in the country' (Pevsner 1953, rp. 1978, 164). Archiepiscopal revenues enabled Morton to build on a grand scale at Lambeth. Here, his formidable brick gatehouse, embellished with diaper patterns and with stone dressed quoins, survives foursquare as a monument to the financial acumen of the author of 'Morton's fork'.

Soon afterwards William Warham (1503–32) was appointed to Canterbury and began his archiepiscopate with a flourish. At the great feast which followed his enthronement the procession through the hall at Canterbury was led by the greatest magnate in the land, the Duke of Buckingham, splendidly mounted on horseback. While Warham survived the vicissitudes of political and religious life in the early sixteenth century, Buckingham was not so lucky. He over-reached himself and was beheaded in 1521, bequeathing to posterity the architectural legacy of his great house at Thornbury (Gloucestershire). Thornbury has a mighty façade incorporating six towers, but this is show. Be-

Fig. 88 Bishop Morton's brick palace at Hatfield, Hertfordshire

hind the towers lie comfortable airy domestic quarters with large windows, clearly not laid out with a view to defence. Buckingham's friend Warham converted the manorial complex at Otford into a brick palace for his own use. When Warham entertained Erasmus at Otford in 1518 the archbishop confided to his visitor that it was the use of brick which had made Otford so exceptionally expensive. Remains of the consistently-diapered brick palace with stone-dressings, and with a fine tower at the west end are still to be seen. Even in a state of abject ruin the former splendour of Otford shines through. It is to such a major monument as Hampton Court that one has to turn for a construction of similar scale (*see* Fig. 89).

Why Warham should devote so much effort to a palace less than three miles from Knole is a puzzle. The answer is in part that Warham found Knole drab. Also, as Henry VIII later demonstrated, there are advantages to having the administration and the private household separate from one another (page 160). It may be assumed that Archbishop Warham and Henry VIII had different motives for such a separation.

Many new residences were acquired and new types of building attempted by Henry VIII. Early in his reign, temporarily deprived by fires of accommodation at Westminster and at the Tower, Henry built two new residences at a total cost of £39,000; these were Bridewell in London and New Hall in Essex. Neither was particularly innovative and later Henry's son Edward expressed his views on Bridewell by turning it into a prison. Bridewell was built between 1515 and 1523 at the confluence of the Fleet and the Thames. There were two major courts with the great hall on the south side of the principal one. A third court was added on newly acquired land in 1521 and incorporated what may have been the first grand staircase in England. Recent excavations have confirmed that the now-vanished buildings were made of brick and that, although partly damaged in the Great Fire of 1666, much of the palace survived until it was demolished in 1803 (Schofield 1984, 134–6).

In the Tudor era documentation becomes broader in scope than the building accounts with their orders and responses on which the historian is so heavily dependent in previous centuries. On the other hand, as there are often fewer Tudor building accounts, so less is known of the interiors of the palaces than is the case in earlier periods. The kind of circumstantial detail which survives from the Tudor period can be illustrated by reference to Henry VIII's acquisition of Knole from Archbishop Cranmer. This transaction, if reliably recounted, is a striking example of how a monarch acquired property. Ralph Morice, Cranmer's secretary, recorded his master's surrender of property to the king:

'My Lord [Cranmer] minded to have retained Knole unto himself, said that it was too small a house for his majesty. "Marry" said the king, "I had rather have it than Otford; for it standeth on a better soil. This house standeth low and is rheumatick, like unto Croydon where I could never be without sickness. And as for Knole it standeth on a sound, perfect and wholesome ground, and if I should make abode here as I do surely mind to do now and then, I will live at Knole and most of my house shall live at Otford" And so, by this means, both those houses were delivered up into the king's hands.'

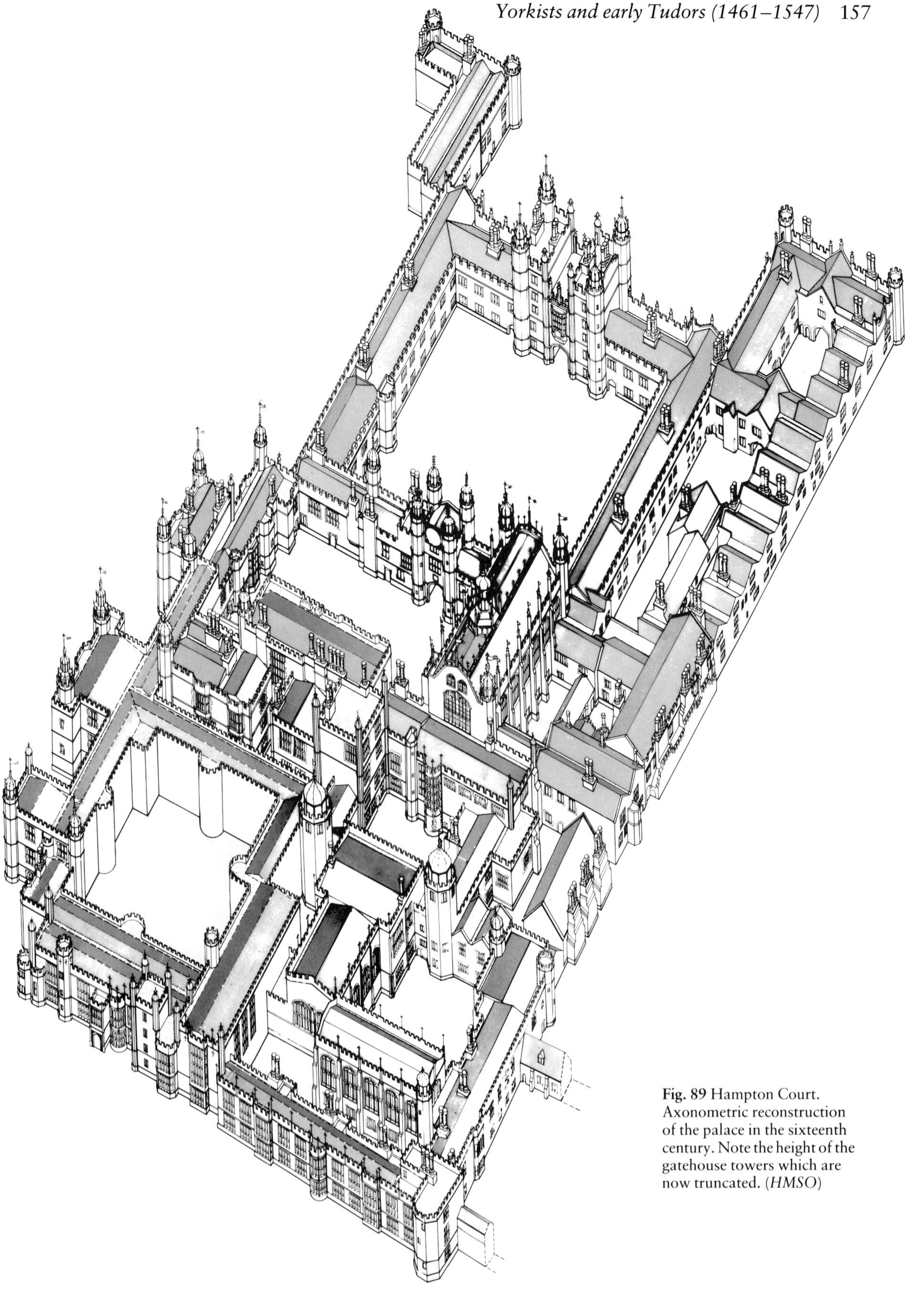

Fig. 89 Hampton Court. Axonometric reconstruction of the palace in the sixteenth century. Note the height of the gatehouse towers which are now truncated. (*HMSO*)

This take-over was just one stage in the process of reduction of Cranmer's palaces by loss or exchange of seven of the eleven palaces he started with. When his palace at Canterbury burnt down, he did not rebuild it. He was thus reduced from 'a princely to a noble style of life', a fate awaiting all the prince-bishops of the Middle Ages in the following decades of the Tudor era (O'Day and Heal 1981, 114).

Henry VIII's early building work was extended by the works carried out at Greenwich in honour of an ambassadorial visit from France in 1527. Temporary halls were erected, one for entertainment and the other for banqueting, and decorated by Hans Holbein. Each was provided with a mock-classical triumphal arch and in one hall at least, a *mappa mundi* adorned the ceiling. In the course of his reign Henry VIII improved the gardens at Greenwich by adding a water maze and creating a tiltyard and an exquisite private garden. Renaissance motifs, including cornices and spheres, embellished the fountain in the court of that name. Peacocks were introduced in the park, but only for a short time as their raucous noise disturbed the queen's morning rest and they were packed off elsewhere.

However, the acquisition of Hampton Court (*see* Fig. 90) and Whitehall (the latter formerly York Place, the London residence of the archbishops of York) from Cardinal Wolsey in 1529 opened a new period of royal works. Almost immediately on Wolsey's fall the king was taken by river to York Place, which he found excellently appointed and very much to his taste. He determined that forthwith this should be the major royal palace in London instead of Westminster. Thus the tradition which had seen Westminster as the prime royal residence in London since the Conquest and before was ended. Extra land was acquired adjacent to Whitehall, part of it was cleared and the private palace of St James's was built. This was a brick structure which included the great gatehouse of four storeys and the Chapel Royal, 70 ft × 23 ft (21.3 m × 7 m).

Fig. 90 Hampton Court in 1538, from a drawing by Antonius Wynegaard. Note the formal gardens filled with statues. (*Ashmolean Museum*)

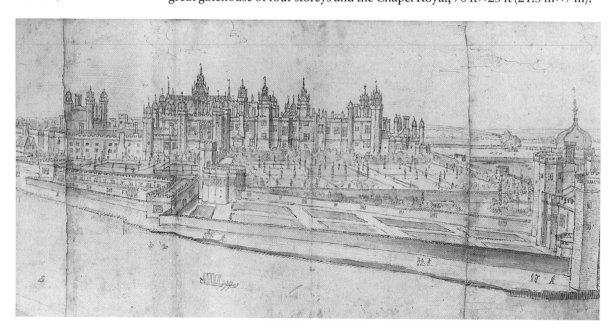

Fig. 91 Whitehall, showing the cockpit and the large scale of the structure

As at Greenwich, much was done to enhance the gardens of the palace: in particular recreational facilities were added including tennis courts, a cock-pit and bowling alley. Nothing was allowed to stand in the way of this great royal project. Houses of the nobility adjacent to Whitehall were demolished altogether with much of Wolsey's work, but use was made of the materials in the new building, including stone from the former Cardinal College at Ipswich and a wooden gallery from Wolsey's house at Esher. The galleries were used as a means of communication between the different parts of the palace, which altogether sprawled across twenty-three acres to make it the largest palace in Europe (*see* Fig. 91).

Hampton Court had already come to the king in 1527 as a gift from Cardinal Wolsey, who had created it on the site of an old medieval manor. Wolsey constructed a palace quite as magnificent and modern as anything owned at that time by the king. Hampton Court grew out of a developing English fashion for brick construction, dating back to the foruteenth century. Wolsey's palace was sufficiently large to house the entire French delegation to the negotiations in London in 1527 and Wolsey's own household may have numbered 500 in his heyday. Perhaps because he had not made the original outlay on the building of Hampton Court, which had been built since 1514, Henry felt justified in making major alterations to the buildings. He built a new great hall and considerably enlarged the kitchens, as well as adding further courtyards and reworking the gardens. All his queens visited this most splendid palace and the future Edward VI was born there.

Physically there was much that was ancient as well as modern at Hampton Court. Henry's great gatehouse with its lead cupolas and gilded weather vanes must have been reminiscent of his father's palace at Sheen. The brickwork is certainly fine but perhaps less splendid than that found elsewhere, for example at Bishop Waynflete's Farnham of almost fifty years earlier. Today, the gatehouse at Hampton Court is less splendid than it was originally, having lost two storeys. The great hall is of regal proportions, 100 ft×60 ft (30.5 m×18.3 m), with a fine hammer beam roof to preserve an uncluttered floor area. The pendants in the roof carved as lanterns are splendid examples of that famous late medieval and Tudor architectural trait of creating the effects of stonework in wood. But even as rebuilt by Henry VIII in the 1530s, a large central hearth was retained, the smoke from which would rise unhindered to be dispersed through a louver in the roof. This hearth was an essentially medieval feature, where a more modish wall-fireplace might be expected. The kitchens are on a grand scale with large fireplaces for spit-roasting, and give a good impression of the way in which a great palace needed an army of support staff to feed and minister to the throngs of guests who enjoyed wine from the ample cellars with their food. As had been the case at least since the thirteenth century, there were separate suites for the king and for the queen, as well as more than one chapel. Henry VIII, like Edward III, had a fondness for mechanical instruments. His great astronomical clock, housed in the Clock Court and dated to 1540, tells the hour, date and month, indicates the number of days since the beginning of the year, the phases of the moon and the time of high tide at London Bridge. A privy palace to Hampton Court, Oatlands, was built by Henry VIII at nearby Weybridge (Surrey). Oatlands was also of brick and served to strengthen the Tudor presence in the Thames Valley.

Nonsuch, unlike Hampton Court, was a unique structure based on building techniques which had their roots in Renaissance Italy and France. The planned courtyards, however, matched those at Richmond and Hampton Court (*see* Fig. 5). As Henry III had admired Louis IX in the thirteenth century, so it was Henry VIII's admiration of Francis I which led to the building of Nonsuch. *Nonpareil*, as it was otherwise known, was a suitable French name for this unique structure with its timber frame, ornate slate and *stucco duro*, on which King Henry lavished £50,000. Nonsuch was an entirely new venture. Work began on 22nd April 1538. The village of Cuddington, complete with its church, was destroyed to make way for the new palace and its park. The remains of the former priory at Merton were tossed in as foundation rubble, in a manner reminiscent of the demolition of Chertsey Abbey for the foundations of Hampton Court. The inner court was completed by 1544, when Queen Catherine Parr died there, but the outer court was unfinished at Henry's death in 1547. There were in all three courtyards and the whole site measured 377 ft×202 ft (114.9 m×61.6 m) overall. The inner and outer courts matched one another in size, 132 ft×115 ft (40.2 m×35.1 m), while the third was a smaller kitchen court to the east (Biddle 1961, 7).

From a distance Nonsuch resembled a castle in form (*see* Fig. 92). The nearest parallel in respect of its exterior form was the Duc de Berry's early fifteenth-century castle at Mehun-sur-Yévre. Closer examination, however, reveals that the structure belies the form. This was no old-fashioned stone castle, but a light, highly decorated structure drawing on Renaissance Italian models and built under the supervision of continental craftsmen, such as Nicholas Bellin of Modena, who was already known as a royal craftsman from his work on certain stucco fireplaces at Whitehall in 1537. It is to Italy and France, to Mantua and particularly to Fontainebleau that we should look for parallels (Biddle 1966).

As contemporary pictures show, the palace was decorated both on the exterior and the interior with highly ornate stucco work (*see* Fig. 93). There were life size figures at ground floor level with emblems and cartouches above. There were slate plaques gilded and incised in the style of the buildings of the Loire. The interior courtyards contained panels with representations of Roman emperors and classical scenes. They were, in part, a heroic history lesson for the future Edward VI. Martin Biddle's excavations of thirty years ago and historical research have revealed the lost glories of Nonsuch, both in material form and in the excellent exposition of continental parallels (Biddle 1961, 1966). The materials from the Nonsuch excavations are now held at the Museum of London.

In its essentials, for all its up-to-date sixteenth-century art and iconography, Nonsuch retained an ancient purpose. It was built and developed as a private hunting lodge where Henry could enjoy the pleasures of the chase away from the public eye (no accommodation was provided for courtiers), just as his Norman and Plantagenet predecessors had done elsewhere before him. It remains a matter of debate how appropriate to English conditions the structure of Nonsuch was. The damp must have wrought havoc with the fabric, which was much better suited to the warmer climate of Italy. Despite lavish expenditure

Fig. 92 View of Nonsuch palace in 1568, by Hofnagel. (*Trustees of the British Museum*)

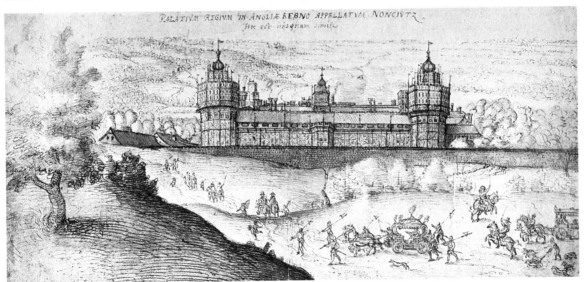

on this favourite building project, for £25,000 had been spent by 1545, Henry VIII never lived to see the palace finished. After his death in 1547 it passed to the Earl of Arundel, who had completed it by 1556. It was popular with Elizabeth I, which may have accounted in part for Arundel's son-in-law, Lord Lumley's decision to dispose of it in 1592, so that he would no longer have to entertain the impecunious queen there.

The palace stood for a century or so, but declined in the seventeenth century, eventually providing accommodation for the admiralty, devolved from London in the time of plague and Pepys in 1665. John Evelyn was surprised that the stucco work had survived so well to 1665, but remarked that it should be removed to a dry place! This was not to be, for the palace was shortly afterwards demolished on the instructions of the Duchess of Cleveland, a mistress of Charles II.

By the death of Henry VIII there was a traditional stock of royal palaces such as Windsor and Woodstock, variously developed from medieval predecessors, and Clarendon was in decay. In addition, there were 'modern' buildings strongly influenced by European models, such as Hampton Court, Whitehall

and the incomplete Nonsuch, creations of Henry's own lifetime. After half a millenium, Westminster, the centre of royal life since the reign of Edward the Confessor, had been set aside as a major royal residence in favour of new palaces such as Whitehall and St James's. Truly, a new era of royal palace life had begun. As for the episcopal palaces, they had been plundered by the self-appointed head of the church in a way which might have been the envy of many of his predecessors who had struggled against wealthy bishops and coveted their fine residences. Bishops' residences were no longer to be known as palaces; the old links with the Roman past were severed for ever. Some bishops' palaces, along with confiscated religious houses which had been converted into residences, formed a new strand of noble living which developed into the country houses of the sixteenth century. But the development of these familiar great houses in more recent times is another story.

Chapter IX

Lost palaces

This survey of palaces and palace life in the Middle Ages and early Tudor period has identified a number of trends and themes through time: changes in numbers and distribution of properties belonging to the monarchy and the associated changes in mobility which redistribution brought; development of household size; change in layout including a trend towards privacy, signalled by an increase in private chambers; changes in the materials used. Additionally, there were structural alterations to the buildings: to windows, floors, water supply and also in decorative taste and disposition. If royal palaces and the use made of them is the yardstick, similarities and contrasts through time can be drawn with other palace dwellers, the nobility and the higher clergy.

Most clearly there was a change in the numbers of palatial residences (*see* Fig. 94). The highest number possessed by an individual king before 1500 was the twenty-nine or so inherited, or taken by force if he chose, by King John before he died in 1216. The figure, so far as traditionally held palaces was concerned, fell to its lowest point, under ten, in 1485. These were Westminster, Baynard's Castle, Eltham, Greenwich, Sheen, Woodstock, King's Langley and Clarendon. Henry VII added five to the list, including the finely appointed Minster Lovell (Oxfordshire), the recently rebuilt home of William, Lord Lovell, who was attainted of high treason after Bosworth when his lands were confiscated by the crown. This property was quickly passed on by Henry VII to his uncle Jasper, after whose death in 1495 it returned to the crown until it was sold off in 1602 (Taylor 1985, 7). These transactions epitomise the continually shifting sands of property transactions beyond the handful of palaces which remained in the care of the crown or an individual lord over a long period.

To the dozen or so properties inherited or taken over by his father, Henry VIII added a further ten in the early years of his reign, to give a total of perhaps twenty-four. In the period from 1535 to his death in 1547 this number was doubled, largely at the expense of bishops but also of nobility, to the highest number of royal residences ever in the history of the English monarchy (Colvin 1963, 120; 1982, 2; James and Robinson 1988, 44). The sum of episcopal residences remained at around a total of 150 through the period until Henry VIII's incursions (Colvin 1982, 2; Barley 1986, 83).

The pattern of distribution of royal residences changed appreciably between the end of the Saxon period and the death of Henry VIII. There was a tendency as the period progressed to greater concentration of residences in and around London and in the Thames Valley, at the expense of residences in the north and west. It is not surprising to find Clarendon, one of the more westerly royal residences, virtually abandoned in the Tudor age after 400 years of more or less regular use as a base for hunting and for the transaction of business.

At the beginning of the period, in the eleventh century, feudal society and the

Fig. 94 Maps showing the distribution of royal residences: a) Henry II, Richard and John, 1154–1216; b) Henry III, 1216–72; c) Edward III, 1327–77; d) Tudor, *c.* 1550. (*After Colvin*)

164

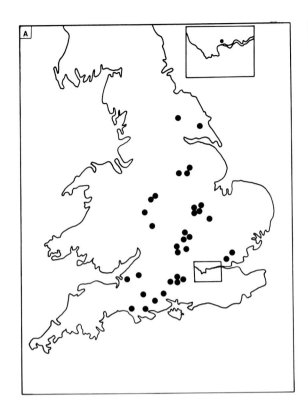

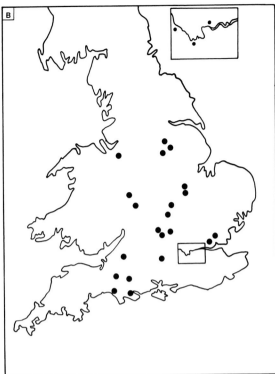

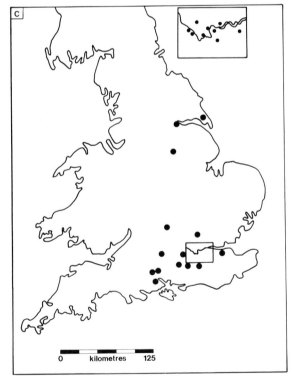

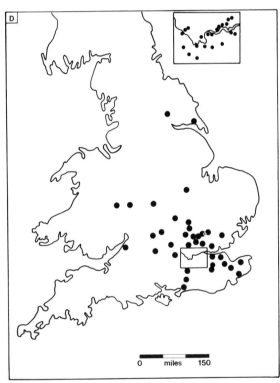

0   kilometres   125

0   miles   150

feudal economy were essentially rural phenomena. Towns were of comparatively little significance in the sum of economic, political and military activity. However, that is not to say that all towns were insignificant. William the Conqueror could not capture London outright, but, after being invited in, established a stronghold there at the Tower. The combination of political power vested in holders of feudal fiefs, and the concomitant necessity of being seen by rural tenants in chief and feudal vassals, rather than in development of urban links by the Normans and their successors was one reason why they made use of country retreats. The pursuit of hunting as a major pastime strengthens this view of kings as lords who felt more at home in the countryside, although they were more and more obliged to take account of towns and urban residences. Kings and their households sought freedom from the cares of the state in very remote places. Richard FitzNeal, successively treasurer of the realm and Bishop of London in Richard I's reign, summed this up well when in his *Dialogue of the Exchequer* he wrote:

> 'the forest is the sanctuary and special delight of kings, where, laying aside their cares they withdraw to refresh themselves with a little hunting: there away from the turmoil inherent in a court they breathe the pleasure of natural freedom' (Johnson 1950, 60).

Thus the court was particularly mobile in the eleventh to fourteenth centuries, moving from manor to manor, from hunting lodge to lodge and from rural retreat to town and back again. Mobility can similarly be traced in the examination of the nobility and the higher clergy, for very much the same reasons, to be seen within the lands of which they were lords and to enjoy the proceeds and profits, with the additional responsibility of keeping in touch with their own lord and patron, the king. However, distinctions can be made through time and between groups. Thus bishops visiting the parishes in their dioceses and conducting business in London remained more peripatetic than the nobility. Nobles were perhaps less mobile than the monarchs they served, partly because of their regional power bases and partly because as the monarchy settled more and more in the south east of England a proportion of royal servants, often 'new men' in addition to traditional noble administrators, moved south with them. But even in the same period there were always those who moved about and those who did not; thus Gilbert de Clare moved once every two weeks in 1309, while Hamon le Strange moved not at all in the eleven years between 1341 and 1352 (Mertes 1988, 15).

If changes in feudalism, for example the rise of towns and the lessening necessity to consume the excess produce of manors on site, were amongst the reasons for a decline in mobility, there were also political reasons which led to the development of a lifestyle focused on the south east of England. From about 1300 onwards the struggle with France became more intense, which encouraged kings to spend more time in the south and east. As the wars progressed in the fourteenth and fifteenth centuries into the Hundred Years War (1337–1453), there were certainly occasional major English victories in pitched battles, as at Crécy (1346) and Agincourt (1415). However, these successes were interspersed with setbacks and fears of French invasions and inexorably the tide turned against England until, in 1453 all their French lands – which from time to time had, on paper at least, amounted to half of France and more – were lost, apart from Calais. Militarily France triumphed and English history books which discuss the 116-year conflict fail to acknowledge that the concept of the Hundred Years War was dreamed up by post-medieval French historians to encapsulate a conflict in which France defeated England and virtually drove the English from French soil after centuries of struggle. So royal properties in the north and west declined. Care of these regions was left to powerful magnates and prelates, while the kings pursued their French enterprises.

Mobility of major households and their support staff in any period had to be carefully planned. Henry I in the early twelfth century, for example, announced where he would be going a month in advance in order to allow the household and suppliers to prepare themselves. The four royal bakers were sent ahead to purchase corn. The household was comparatively small in Henry's reign, perhaps 150 (Given-Wilson 1986, 4). Under the Normans, Angevins and the early Plantagenets, the surviving evidence enables royal itineraries to be charted with some certainty. The nature of the evidence, however, changes from the reign of Edward III onwards, partly because of the onset in earnest of the French wars which demanded that the administration of the realm should be able to function without the personal presence of the king. Such arrangements as were made began with the Walton Ordinances of 1338, and made it much more difficult to be certain where the king was thereafter in relation to his administration as documentary sealings no longer signalled the actual presence of the monarch.

With the decline in numbers of royal palaces towards 1485 some decline in the mobility of the royal household must have taken place, although it must be said that the monarchy continued to exercise vigorously the right to stay in noble households. The bunching of royal residences in the south east further contributed to this development. This tendency is already apparent in the reign of Edward IV, who moved little from the Thames Valley. So the Tudors, as in so much that they did, merely continued a tradition already established by their predecessors. The dramatic increase in residences in the later years of Henry VIII is paradoxical. To have used all fifty of his residences in a year even for a week the king would have had to move on virtually continuously, which he clearly did not do, not least because his health declined towards the end of his reign and his corpulence argues against the kind of mobility displayed by an energetic monarch such as Henry II. A partial answer of course is that the king took on residences in close proximity to one another, as at Knole and Otford (Kent) (page 156). The overall drift towards the south east, apparent in the later Middle Ages and under the Tudors, was not an entirely straightforward exchange of residences more distant from London for those near at hand. The Black Prince's palace at Kennington, for example, was rebuilt twice in the middle of the fourteenth century, but was rarely used thereafter by the royal family and so was a ready quarry of materials for Henry VIII's Whitehall works in the 1520s.

These developments in royal ownership and usage appear to contrast sharply with the continuity of ecclesiastical distribution and occupancy of residences, which continues at much the same level throughout the period, and with the experience of the nobility. The higher clergy were able or well connected men who came to enjoy sees for their lifetime only; the nobility lasted several generations, but it is well known that many of the noble families of the twelfth and thirteenth centuries died out, or were dispossessed. 'New men' replaced these families in the fourteenth and fifteenth centuries, and this group was enlarged to include those who benefited from allegiance to the Tudors in the late fifteenth century. In the sixteenth century a further group of noble families emerged to benefit from royal policy. These were the 'augmentations' men, gaining the lands and property of the dispossessed monasteries at the Reformation. Monastic houses and their estates did not long remain in royal hands for long. One of the reasons for the unpopularity of Queen Elizabeth in the 1590s (page 162) was the expense of entertaining her and her household. It is a surprising fact that hardly an acre of monastic lands remained as part of the royal estates by the later years of the sixteenth century. Many former monastic estates are still today grouped together in the hands of the descendants of beneficiaries of the dissolution.

The size of the royal household seems to have been about 150 in Henry I's reign and there seems to have been little change between the beginning of the twelfth century and the early thirteenth century. A similarly numerically slim and fit household accompanied King John to that which had supported Henry I a century earlier. The comparatively short reign of John, coupled with his loss of the French possessions gained by his father, meant that John probably spent more time in England than any of his predecessors since 1066. The comparative brevity of his reign has resulted in detailed studies which have focused attention on his royal itineraries in England. This has shown in sharp relief just how very mobile an early thirteenth-century king could be, never in the same place for more than a month.

John's son, Henry III, and grandson, Edward I, continued this mobile lifestyle. Towards the end of Edward's reign, when the numbers were apparently at their greatest to date, the royal entourage had six long and seven short carts, each with a carter and fore-rider. In addition there were forty-one packhorses, quite apart from the assembled mounts of the courtiers. The transport outlined here carried the royal belongings, which were all embracing as was usual, from plate and clothes to beds and chapel furnishings. The king took steps by the statute of St Albans (1300) to limit expenditure on his entourage by cutting down the numbers of those who ate in his hall (Prestwich 1988, 159, 162). Although the motives for this were partly political, military expenditure on such matters as castle building in Wales was cripplingly expensive and was to become more so over the remaining two and a half centuries with which this study is concerned.

During the reign of Edward II, however, household size was increasing. A household ordinance of 1318 shows that it had grown to perhaps 450–500 members. A perceptible shift to a more sedentary style of life is appearing. In the fourteenth and fifteenth centuries this trend becomes more clear. Fewer royal palaces are decked out and, perhaps as a result, there is more extravagance at individual sites, for example at Windsor. Although overall expenditure on buildings was probably lower in the fifteenth century than it had been in the thirteenth, much extra money must have gone on the household which rose in size to perhaps as many as 800 in the reign of Henry VI, although the numbers fell again under Edward IV. However, it must be said that, despite the onset of dire economic, military and political circumstances in the fifteenth century, the wealth of the crown remained exceptionally large in a compact and administratively well organised country such as England. The increasing scale of palace building in the Tudor period testifies to growth in household size once more, apparently to the level where the court and household needed more than one residence in an area to settle itself.

In the five centuries from Edward the Confessor to the death of Henry VIII, palace life became ever more comfortable. Palaces, court entertainments and dress were designed more and more extravagantly to impress. The Tower was designed to dominate London with its impregnability coupled with palatial accommodation overlooking the city and the Thames. Rufus's great hall at Westminster was the largest building of its kind in Europe. The welcome afforded to visitors to court was increasingly glittering. Henry II's welcome of the Scottish King Malcolm to Woodstock was one such occasion; Edward III's tournaments were equally extravagant, and after King John of France was captured he was housed in the splendidly rebuilt Savoy palace as his prison. The Londoners' magnificent pageantry for the victorious Henry V was intended to impress the Emperor Sigismund in 1416. By the later years of the fifteenth century English royal christenings had become extravagant affairs, but already at the beginning of the century concern was being expressed that in France the lying-in of a merchant's wife had become in one case as extravagant as that of a queen. Thus the royal family were continuously pressed towards more sumptuous displays not only to impress their own subjects but to compete on the European stage, as the glitter of the Field of the Cloth of Gold in 1520 showed. The 'mountains of plate, cutlery and glass' to furnish a complete fairy-tale palace built of wood and canvas on a brick foundation created an effect described by a contemporary as the eighth wonder of the world. In effect the ephemeral pleasure-palace that Wolsey created in France for Henry VIII on this occasion was a demonstration of the wealth of England at peace, to impress the old enemy (Scarisbrick 1968, 76–9).

Palaces were not only provided by English monarchs, nobility and prelates for the benefit of foreign potentates. English society at all levels, to a greater or lesser extent, would have known palaces at first or second hand, in a population which may never have exceeded six million in England before 1550. Nobles and higher clergy came with their retinues to counsel the king, London merchants and their wives joined the royal banquet at the 'round table' in 1344. Lower clergy such as the friars served in the royal chapels and hundreds, even thousands of these poor clergy were fed by Henry III (page 87). Even the poor and lepers came to benefit in John's reign from the king's penance for breaking fast days, or to join Henry III's feast days, or to benefit from Edward I's alms given as he developed an increasing inability to attend chapel towards the end of his reign. There is no proof that Henry III lived up to his intention to feed 500 poor a day (182,000 a year), but when he gave orders for his hall at Westminster or Windsor to be filled with poor, officials no doubt obeyed him. Such alms givings were potentially violent affairs as the deserving poor, the sick and lepers mingled with those whom the Tudors were to dub 'sturdy beggars'. Officials at the distribution associated with the coronation of Queen Eleanor in 1236 were empowered to sentence to be burnt lepers who knifed one another during proceedings. Edward I certainly gave alms to 75,000 on church festivals in 1296–7 alone and provided for 4,000 paupers in the week following Christmas 1299. Queens, and other members of the royal household, as well as nobles and clergy, according to their status, dispensed alms on appropriate scales which attracted the poor to their residences wherever they happened to be (Johnstone 1929, 149–67; Prestwich 1988, 112).

So far as palace buildings were concerned, after Henry III and Edward I's work at Westminster, Edward III's Windsor and Henry VIII's Nonsuch were the most lavish in overall achievement and speed of execution. Works at Windsor were funded by the huge ransom of John II of France and Nonsuch by the windfall of the monasteries and their lands. Richard II's Sheen and Henry IV's Eltham are small scale reflections of Windsor. It is at once apparent that different monarchs liked to stamp their character on different palaces, as George III did in purchasing Buckingham House (now palace) as a private residence next to St James's palace, or Victoria and Albert did in creating Balmoral and Osborne. The most obvious example of this is Henry III and Westminster, where he attempted to create an English royal monastic-cum-palace and coronation complex, to roll the functions of the French St Denis (monastery), Vincennes (palace) and Rheims (coronation site) into one. This vision, which was based around admiration for Edward the Confessor and for the French monarchy, was ultimately realised, a major addition being the royal mausoleum established by Edward I towards 1300.

Despite the enthusiasm of kings from Edward the Confessor to Henry III for public display and living, this attribute of court life began to change after 1300 in Edward I's reign, when it can be seen that the king favoured living at smaller manors, for which he is best remembered, rather than at the great castles. At Windsor he preferred the manor in the park to the castle. Clipstone (Nottinghamshire) and Woolmer (Hampshire) were manors where he spent much time, perhaps because they were good places for him to enjoy falconry (Prestwich 1988, 164). These were no doubt comparable in function and accommodation to the royal sporting estate at Sandringham (Norfolk) purchased for the Prince of Wales (later Edward VII) in 1861 for its excellent pheasant and partridge shoot. As Edward I had done at his residences, so Sandringham was rebuilt in 1870, and although this latest royal residence has stood for over a century it is now viewed as undistinguished architecturally (Robinson 1982, 187), which may lead in time to the same oblivion which was the fate of hunting manors such as Clipstone and Woolmer. What binds these places together through time is the combination of royal devotion to the chase in its various forms, coupled with desire for seclusion.

In the Tudor age the form of the palace changed: old 'organically developed' rural palaces such as Clarendon and Woodstock declined or were subjected to major rebuilding programmes. The great Tudor palaces, now readily recognisable by the comparative symmetry of their Renaissance form, are confined to the hinterland of London. Buildings were used in somewhat different ways as the period progresses. The great hall of Rufus's day gave way more and more to a variety of halls with different names: the great hall and the lesser hall, the winter hall and the summer hall, the upper hall and the lower hall. Ranges of private chambers developed alongside 'wardrobe' government; the king and his immediate family and guests had meals and passed their time away from the throng. The great hall was reserved for public displays, otherwise it was abandoned to retainers and servants. The description of this as a division into 'upstairs' and 'downstairs' is an apt one (Given-Wilson 1986, 30). Thus Hampton Court is characterised by a series of audience chambers, privy chambers, bed chambers and so on.

In the eleventh to thirteenth centuries, the golden age of great hall culture, the nobility spoke one language and the serving people another. It appears that all sat together in the great hall, the nobles speaking French amongst themselves and the servants and retainers, no doubt at separate tables (or sittings), English. This is perhaps hinted at in Professor Jespersen's observation that while living animals – ox, cow, sheep, swine, boar and deer – are named in English, they arrive at the table in French guise as beef, mutton, pork, bacon and venison. The swineherds and retainers were no doubt English while the culinary performance which was enjoyed, at least by the élite, French (Jespersen 1935, 82–3). However, there is some evidence that, predictably, there was a different menu for different social groups, for example in Bishop Swinfield's household in 1289–90.

By the fifteenth century, when English was the common language, chamber politics were more to the fore and the great halls were used less. It may be over speculative to suggest that the linguistic homogeneity which emerges in the age of Chaucer (d. 1400) was a factor in the break-up of the great hall culture, but it may have been. More significant than these speculations about linguistic groups at table in the great hall were the social upheavals of the later Middle Ages in the wake of the Black Death (itself blamed for the decline of French, quite apart from the enmity with France), when opportunities for new men arose. The administration attempted from the 1360s onwards to keep people in their place by a series of sumptuary laws, which laid down detailed parameters of dress and diet at all levels of society and the penalties for infringement. In their residences kings, nobles and bishops all siphoned off unwanted visitors and valued their privacy more highly. The series of inter-connecting rooms in Tudor palaces, which excluded people at various distances from the monarch, epitomise this development well.

Changing architectural style and acceptable levels of comfort led to continual change in medieval palaces. Where they were too *démodé* they were demolished and replaced. Dark Romanesque interiors gave way to light and airy Gothic structures, with their pointed and gabled windows filled with coloured glass which carpeted the floor in a kaleidoscope of colour as the sun moved round. Rush strewn, rammed floors gave way from about 1200 onwards to tiled floors, exceptional not only for their exciting designs, but also for their ease of cleaning – water supply and sanitation were always problems. Even the King of England relied on well water in his palaces and this helps to explain the great consumption of other drinks, mostly wine and beer, always a feature of palace life throughout the period.

Climatic deterioration set in from around 1300 when a mini ice-age swept western Europe bringing the great European famine of 1315–22 which had weakened men's resistance to disease when the Black Death carried off perhaps half the population in the years immediately after 1347. Although the sum of the evidence can be read in different ways, the bad weather may have affected buildings and so have led to a requirement for increased measures against the cold and wet. Improved technology may have helped, as in the case of ceramic roof tiles which succeeded the myriad wooden shingles which had been the predominant covering for royal and noble buildings up to about 1250. It is difficult to disentangle fashion and improved technology from measures forced on clerks of works by worse weather. What is certain, however, is that deteriorating or not, the English climate is notoriously unkind to buildings in any era. Wall paintings, for example, were especially at risk from rising damp in structures with no damp course. So the weather, and particularly that colder period after 1300, must bear part of the blame for the scrappy remains we have today. Palaces in southen Europe have stood the test of time much better.

Throughout the Middle Ages the influence of southern Europe on English palaces is considerable. Norman links with Sicily are well known, and Edward I was called upon to arbitrate in Sicilian wars. Links with Spain are a continuing thread from the marriage of Henry II's daughter Eleanor to the King of Castile, reaching an apogee with the marriage of Eleanor of Castile to Edward I, continuing with John of Gaunt's aspirations in Spain and carrying down to Henry VIII's marriage to Catharine of Aragon. Spanish influence is to be found in the illumination of the beautiful Winchester Bible of the cosmopolitan Henry of Blois (d. 1171). Henry II's water-palace at Everswell in Moorish or Sicilian style was unique, and the introduction of the 'gloriet' as a feature of palatial residences from the reign of Edward I onwards hints at further Spanish influence (page 54).

Influences from France are strong throughout the period. The castle-palace at the Tower, drawn from a Norman model, is dominant in the eleventh century. Henry III modelled his palace and abbey complex at Westminster on French lines. Fifteenth-century builders in brick similarly introduced the style from Burgundian models seen in the wars. These are among the best examples, along with St Stephen's chapel at Westminster, copied from La Saint Chapelle in Paris. Henry VIII, always an ardent admirer of Francis I of France – he copied the French king's affectation of a beard – also drew on Franco-Italian exemplars and craftsmen for his magnificent palaces at Nonsuch and Whitehall.

Painstakingly detailed study of often very fragmentary remains is opening doors on new possibilities in the understanding of many aspects of medieval buildings, whether they are of stone, timber or brick. Similarly, detailed scientific and artefactual analysis of sites such as Clarendon and King's Langley show a continuous trickle of more exotic materials and crafts into palaces. The lapis lazuli from Afghanistan tinting the blue plasterwork at Clarendon has already been mentioned and azurite, perhaps from Hungary, found its way into the scriptorium for manuscript illumination, and thence into the archaeological record. In addition to the local Chilmark stone, early work at Clarendon includes Caen stone. A wine glass of Low Countries origin complements documentary references to imported wines from France. Coins from Scotland and the Low Countries as well as from England found their way into the archaeological levels at Clarendon; at King's Langley a series of English and

French coins dating from the period of the Hundred Years War appears in the finds (Neal 1971, 56–8). Fragments of maiolica pots of Mediterranean origin at both sites hint at medicaments or spices, which undoubtedly arrived at the site, coming ready packed (James and Robinson 1988, *passim*; Neal 1971, 65). Documents help to provide a fuller picture of the use of spices by an individual monarch. A list from Edward I's reign mentions almonds, rice, ginger (which the king particularly liked), galingale, pepper, saffron, caraway, cumin, sugar and much else besides (Prestwich 1988, 159).

Microcosmic analysis such as that carried out on the Clarendon finds provides a background to the clear documentary evidence of the widespread interests and links of the greatest families and churchmen in the land. The royal family itself was always cosmopolitan: apart from Rufus, John was the first post-Conquest king to be buried in England (although his heart was buried at Fontevrault in Anjou), a century and a half after the Conquest. Royal marriages were usually to foreign princesses who did much to civilise the forbidding accommodation offered by the kings of England to their brides from sunnier climes. The international influences found in art, architecture, court hastiludes and other pastimes are legion and the records abound with the detail as brilliant and intricate as the medieval illuminations and tapestries which have occasionally survived the centuries. Edward III's obvious enthusiasm for embroidered mottoes on his clothes for tournaments and other occasions emerges from scrutiny of the household and wardrobe accounts. '*Honi soit qui mal y pense*' is well known, but 'It is as it is' and 'Hay hay the wythe swan by goddes soule I am thy man' are two other examples. Lavish clothes and bedcovers spangled with clouds and suns, garters, Catherine wheels, trees, animals and many other devices abound in the records. The suits in red velvet and fur prepared for Edward III for the Round Table celebrations in 1344 were remarkable, but are eclipsed by the amazing outfit prepared for his Queen Philippa in 1348, covered in hundreds of pearls and thousands of doublets and incorporating pounds of gold thread and hundreds of animal skins. Thus documentary and archaeological evidence combine to recreate the palaces, their occupants and their functions, but there is much yet to be discovered.

Who was responsible for the building of the palaces? On the whole, royal palace building projects were overseen by officials of whom some were and some were not churchmen. Appointment to ecclesiastical office in the Middle Ages was as often as not a result of royal favour and not infrequently was a reward for royal service. William Giffard was William Rufus's treasurer before he became Bishop of Winchester. It may be no coincidence that the west range at Giffard's Wolvesey alone matched Westminster Hall for size. Elias de Dereham was employed both on royal contracts, as at Clarendon, and on major ecclesiastical work, as at Salisbury and Wells cathedrals (in both of which cathedrals he held a canonry) and at Canterbury. Anthony Bek, around 1300, experienced both royal approval and disapproval, but left his palace at Eltham to the crown. William of Wykeham (d. 1404) was successively the royal clerk of works and creator of Edward III's Windsor Castle, Bishop of Winchester and ultimately Chancellor of England. Cardinal Wolsey's Hampton Court was given to Henry VIII in 1527 (in an unfinished state), but did not prevent him falling from royal favour two years later, thus allowing the king to gain York Place in London and many other property assets from the cardinal.

The linking of royal, noble and eclesiastical palace building projects is a feature of the whole period. The great Norman bishops such as Roger of Caen at Old Sarum were great church and palace builders. Roger, unfamiliar with local materials, preferred his native Caen stone to English equivalents, in itself implying the great financial resources available to the conquerors of England. On the whole, however, materials used in palaces were local: Kentish ragstone in London, Reigate stone from Surrey at Kennington and King's Langley, Chilmark stone from Wiltshire at Clarendon, Taynton stone in quantity at Windsor, Purbeck 'marble' in the south, Frosterley 'marble' at Bishop Auckland. There were exceptions, as already noted in early days when Norman builders were unfamiliar with English quarries. Later, as the fine qualities of certain materials became known they were moved further. Purbeck stone from Dorset was used in quantity in thirteenth-century works at Lincoln cathedral and in the bishop's palace. Those working on the re-roofing of Westminster Hall in the 1390s specifically asked for stone for corbelling from a place called 'le Mar' (Marr) near Doncaster in Yorkshire (Baines 1914, 4). The clue here is that the material was to be brought in ships arrested for the purpose. In the Middle Ages water transport was inestimably more easy than transport overland.

Much less is known about the nobility than about royalty and leading churchmen, but undoubtedly the magnates were significant builders and conspicuous consumers and the greatest medieval magnate of all was John of Gaunt (d. 1399). Although the shell of his beautiful work at Kenilworth survives, his Savoy palace was destroyed in 1381. It is noteworthy that the most recent analysis of Richard II's palace work at Portchester interprets the king's work, impressive as it is, as unflamboyant compared with Gaunt's contemporary 'spacious and showy' work at Kenilworth (Cunliffe and Munby 1985, 108). The cross-fertilisation of royal and ecclesiastical projects can be forcefully argued for at Winchester, Salisbury, Clarendon and elsewhere in the twelfth and thirteenth centuries. What was formerly seen as a general 'episcopal style' of architecture used in cathedrals and associated buildings in the first half of the thirteenth century, is now being broken down into regional groups, such as 'southern Gothic' and the influence of individual bishops and archbishops is being identified (Jansen 1985, 97). The inspirations and origins of these Early English style developments are still matters of debate, but it is certain that the laity were involved and that continental influences were present from the great flowering of Gothic, at that time especially in France.

Medieval churchmen usually travelled, studied and spent their lives far from their birthplaces. This is not surprising amongst the Norman episcopate following the Conquest, but remained a significant feature in the twelfth and subsequent centuries. The great Bishop Blois (d. 1171), Abbot of Glastonbury and Bishop of Winchester from 1128, spent his early life and a lengthy period of exile at Cluny in Burgundy. Bishop de Vere (d. 1198) of Hereford, a former courtier of Henry II, is credited with the creation of a fashion for sumptuous halls in his buildings at distant Hereford (Blair 1987, 61). The Gothic builder, Hugh of Avalon (d. 1200), Bishop of Lincoln, responsible for the rebuilding of both the cathedral and the great hall of the bishop's palace nearby, was a Burgundian by birth who served elsewhere in England to establish the Carthusian order before arriving at Lincoln in 1186. He died at his diocesan London residence at the Old Temple in 1200 (Srawley 1966, 9, 25). Archbishop Langton, credited as a driving force in Early English Gothic after the death of King John in 1216, had spent much time in Paris where Richard Poore had been amongst his pupils, successively Bishop of Chichester and Salisbury and whose monument is the great cathedral church of Salisbury.

Undoubtedly the most prolific builder bishops were those who served both king and diocese. Wykeham has already been mentioned, but a successor at Winchester, William Waynflete (d. 1486), was also an impressive builder, excelling in the use of a novel material, brick. Waynflete assisted as an executor in the completion of Ralph, Lord Cromwell's great brick tower at Tattershall (Lincolnshire). He also oversaw Henry VI's project at Eton College (Berkshire) and enhanced the stock of episcopal residences in the Winchester diocese with brick gatehouses embellished with glazed diaperwork patterns at Farnham and Esher (Surrey). He finally left his own monuments of Magdalen College, Oxford, and his legacy of the fine brick school in his native Wainfleet (Lincolnshire), a miniature version of what he had achieved elsewhere. Able men such as Wykeham (said to have been the son of a bondsman from a Hampshire village) and Waynflete, also from obscure origins, show just how open the medieval church was to men of talent and ability, provided of course that they could find patrons. Waynflete's career provides a striking example of how an individual was involved in the spread of a particularly innovative building style far and wide through the country.

The distinctive contribution by lay magnates to the architectural wonders of the Middle Ages is also becoming ever more apparent, especially as records improve from about 1250 onwards, although it remains a very under-researched topic. Richard II's half-brother, John Holland, rebuilt Dartington (Devon) and this may have been one of the models, with John of Gaunt's Kenilworth (1392), on which the king drew for the greatest roofing project of the era, the rebuilding of Westminster Hall in the 1390s. There is much yet to be learnt in this respect. Where a magnate's or chuchman's property fell into royal hands, as at Eltham, Knole, Greenwich or Hampton Court, the evidence survives, but elsewhere it is too often lost. This study has concentrated on residences which can be associated with individual kings, nobles and prelates, but there is still much to be done, for example to tie individual buildings to patrons.

Palaces from the eleventh to the mid-sixteenth century have almost entirely disappeared. A number of reasons can be put forward to explain this, of which changes in building materials and building fashion are but two. Exterior woodwork of the eleventh to thirteenth centuries has all too often rotted away or been reused, although occasional interior work has survived, such as the remains of wooden arcading in the bishops' halls at Farnham and at Hereford. Stone buildings have stood the test of time rather better, but have tended to fall prey to demolition for re-use, as happened to the Black Prince's palace at Kennington. Brick comes late on the scene and a good deal of brick has survived, partly because of its late date, partly because of its durability and partly because, except as rubble, it is difficult to reuse. Experimental materials such as the stucco façades of Nonsuch proved unsuited to the English climate and, when available as rubble, highly attractive to limeburners and so have vanished almost entirely. Changes in the climate, which was better in the eleventh to thirteenth centuries and worse from the fourteenth century on, may have played its part in bringing about the dearth of remains today. Fires are recorded at all major sites from time to time and were clearly a major hazard even for the wealthy.

But probably the major reason for the poor survival rate of palaces has been the continuous desire of patrons for modernity and rebuilding. This arose from building and decorative fashion developments and partly from changes in the needs of those who commissioned the buildings. The small mobile court and household groups which moved around England in the twelfth and thirteenth centuries become larger and less mobile by the fifteenth. In the sixteenth century a grandee like the Duke of Buckingham would have had a household of 500. Wolsey had 300 attendants in his retinue at the Field of the Cloth of Gold, compared to Archbishop Warham's seventy. Stephen Gardiner, Bishop of Winchester (1531–55) and who succeeded Wolsey, travelled 'in his satin, aloft upon his mule trapped with velvet and golden stirrups and bridle' followed by a retinue of 140 (O'Day and Heal 1981, 113). Henry VIII's entourage appears to have needed two residences at any one location for accommodation, particularly after the dissolution of the monasteries whose distribution had guided the king's itinerary in pre-dissolution days.

Political demands tended to keep the monarchy in the south east after 1300 and so enhanced the building stock there. This growing need for residences in and accessible from London took its toll of bishops' residences, and during the Reformation the episcopate was plundered for its residences, losing such prime sites as York Place (Whitehall) and Knole to the king. But despite changes of fortune and dynasty all aspects of palace life and use did not change. Most notable was the connection between royal residences and hunting. As Edward the Confessor hunted from his residence in Bernwood forest, so Henry VIII sought new sites for palaces in areas where he could hunt, as at Nonsuch. The difference between the two kings, apart from the scale and symmetry of their buildings, was that the Confessor probably chased the game himself, whereas Henry VIII had the game driven to him for the kill. This decline in mobility in hunting, as much as anything else, exemplifies the changes in palace life between the years of 1050 and 1550, by which date the era of the medieval palace in England had gone forever.

Bibliography

Abbreviations

BAR: British Archaeological Reports.
Ant. J.: Journal of the Society of Antiquaries.
Arch. J.: Archaeological Journal.
JBAA: Journal of the British Archaeological Association.
Med. Arch.: Medieval Archaeology.

Addyman, P.V. 1973: 'Excavations at Ludgershall Castle, Wiltshire, England (1964–72)', *Chateau Gaillard*, 6.
Alexander, J.G. and Binski, P. (eds.) 1987: *The Age of Chivalry* (London).
Altschul, M. 1965: *A Baronial Family in Medieval England: The Clares 1217–1314* (Baltimore, John Hopkins UP).
Ambrose, T. 1980: 'The Bishop's Palace, Lincoln', *Lincolnshire Museums Information Sheet*, Archaeology Series, no. 18.
Anderson, J.C. 1879: *The Archiepiscopal Palace at Croydon* (London).
Arts Council of Great Britain 1984: *English Romanesque Art 1066–1200* (London).
Aston, M.A. 1979–2: 'Earthworks at the Bishop's Palace, Alvechurch, Worcestershire', *Transactions of the Worcestershire Archaeological Society*, Series 3.
Aston, M. (ed.) 1988: 'Medieval Fish, Fisheries and Fishponds in England', *BAR* 182.

Bacon, F. rp. 1900: *The Essays: Colours of Good and Evil, and Advancement of Learning* (London).
Baines, F. 1914: *Westminster Hall* (HMSO).
Barley, M.W. 1986: *Houses and History* (London).
Barlow, F. 1983: *William Rufus* (London).
Barnie, J. 1974: *War in Medieval Society, Social Values and the Hundred Years War* (London).
Bertelli, S., Cardini, F. and Zorzi, E.G. 1986: *Italian Renaissance Courts* (London).
Biddle, M. 1961: 'Nonsuch Palace 1959–60: an interim report', *Surrey Archaeological Collections*, 58.
—— 1966: 'Wolvesey Palace', *Arch, J.* 123.
—— 1966: 'Wolvesey: the *domus quasi palatium* of Henry of Blois in Winchester', *Chateau Gaillard*, 3.
—— 1966: 'Excavations at Winchester 1965', *Ant. J.* 45.
—— 1966: 'Nicholas Bellin of Modena', *JBAA* 29.
—— 1973: 'Winchester: the Development of an Early Capital', in Jankuhn, H. *et al.*
—— 1975: 'Excavations at Winchester 1971. Tenth and Final Interim report: Part I', *Ant. J. 55*.
—— 1986: *Wolvesey: The Old Bishop's Palace, Winchester, Hampshire* (London).
—— and Clayre, B. 1983: *Winchester Castle and the Great Hall* (Winchester).
Binski, P. 1986: *The Painted Chamber at Westminster* (London).
Blair, C.H.H. and Honeyman, H.L. 1936: *Norham Castle, Northumberland* (HMSO).

Blair, J. 1987: 'The Twelfth Century Bishop's Palace at Hereford', *Med. Arch.* 31.

Blaycock, S.R. 1987: *Observations in the Bishop's Palace, Exeter, 1985* (Exeter).

Bond, C.J. and Tiller, K. (eds.) 1987: *Blenheim, Landscape for a Palace* (Gloucester).

Borenius, T. and Charlton, J., 1936: 'Clarendon Palace: an interim report', *Ant. J.* 16.

Brayley, E.W. and Britton, E. 1836: *The History of the Ancient Palace and Late Houses of Parliament at Westminster* (London).

British Archaeological Association, 1982: *Art and Architecture at Canterbury before 1220* (London).

Brown, R.A. 1954: *English Medieval Castles* (London).

—— 1964: *Orford Castle, Suffolk* (HMSO).

—— 1969: *Rochester Castle* (HMSO).

—— and Curnow, P.E. 1984: *Tower of London* (HMSO).

Campbell, M. 1988: 'The Shrewsbury Bowl', *Ant. J.* 68.

Chapman, H., Coppack, G. and Drewett, P. 1975: 'Excavations at the Bishop's Palace, Lincoln 1968–72', *Society for Lincolnshire History and Archaeology*, Occasional paper 1.

Charlton, J. 1954: 'Auckland Castle', *Arch. J.* 111.

—— 1964: *The Banqueting House, Whitehall* (HMSO).

—— 1987: 'Eltham Palace', *Ancient Monuments Society*, 31.

Coad, J.G. 1984: *Castle Acre Castle, Norfolk* (HMSO).

Colvin, H.M. 1983: 'The 'Court Style' in Medieval English Architecture: a review', in Sherborne and Scattergood (eds.).

Colvin, H.M. *et al.* 1963: *The History of the King's Works. The Middle Ages*, 2 vols. (HMSO).

—— 1982: *The History of the King's Works, 1485–1660*, 2 vols. (HMSO).

—— 1986: 'Royal Gardens in Medieval England', in MacDougall.

Cooper, I. 1938: 'The meeting places of Parliament in the Ancient Palace of Westminster', *JBAA*, 3rd Series, 3.

Cunliffe, B. 1971: *Excavations at Fishbourne: The Site,* vol. I (London).

Cunliffe, B. and Munby, J. 1985: *Excavations at Portchester Castle*, vol. iv (London).

DAMHB 1975: *Archaeological Investigations in New Palace Yard 1972–74* (HMSO).

Dawson, G.J. 1976: 'The Black Prince's Palace at Kennington, Surrey', *BAR* 26.

Detsicas, A. (ed.) 1981: *Collectanea Historica: Essays in Memory of Stuart Rigold* (Maidstone).

Dictionary of National Biography.

Douglas, D.C. 1964, rp. 1977: *William the Conqueror* (London).

Drewett, P. 1971: 'The Archiepiscopal Palace at Croydon; a further contribution', *Arch. J.* 128.

Drinkwater, N. 1955–7: 'Hereford Cathedral: the Bishop's Chapel of St Katherine and St Mary Magdalene', *Transactions of the Woolhope Naturalists Field Club*, 35.

Ducarel, 1783: *Biblioteca Topographica Britannia* (London).

Durham, B. n.d.: *Witney Palace, Excavations at Mount House* (Oxford Archaeological Unit).

Eames, E.S. 1988: 'The Tile Kiln and Floor Tiles', in James and Robinson (eds.).

Emery, E. 1958: 'Dartington Hall', *Arch. J.* 115.

Emmison, F. and Stephens, R. (eds.) 1976: *Tribute to an Antiquary. Essays presented to M. Fitch* (London).

Evans, J. (ed.) 1967: *The Flowering of the Middle Ages* (London).

Eyton, R.W. 1878: *Court, Household and Itinerary of King Henry II* (London).

Faulkner, P. 1971: 'Some Medieval Archiepiscopal Palaces', *Arch. J.* 127.
Fowler, K. 1969: *The King's Lieutenant* (London).

Gem, R. 1975: 'A recession in English Architecture during the early eleventh century and its effect on the development of the Romanesque style', *JBAA* 3rd Series, 38.
Girouard, M. 1978: *Life in the English Country House* (Yale).
Given-Wilson, C. 1986: *The Royal Household and the King's Affinity* (London).
—— 1987: *The Nobility of Later Medieval England* (London).
Given-Wilson, C. and Curteis, A. 1984: *The Royal Bastards of Medieval England* (London).
Gostling, W. 1825: *A Walk in and about the City of Canterbury* (London).

Hallam, H.E. (ed.) 1988: *The Agrarian History of England and Wales, 1042–1350* (Cambridge).
Hare, J. 1988: *Bishop's Waltham Palace* (London).
Harvey, J. 1948: *The Plantagenets* (London).
Harvey, J. 1954, rp. 1987: *English Medieval Architects* (London).
—— 1987: *Medieval Gardens* (London).
Henderson, G. 1961: 'Giraldus Cambrensis's account of a painting at Winchester', *Arch. J.* 118.
Hesketh, C. 1915: 'The Manor House and Great Park of the Archbishops of Canterbury at Otford', *Archaeologia Cantiana* 31.
Hickling, C.F. 1971: 'Prior More's Fishponds', *Med. Arch.* 15.
Hind, A.M. 1922: *Wenceslas Hollar* (London).
HMSO 1922: *Old Sarum*.
Hodgson, J.: *Southampton Castle* (Southampton).
Holmes, M. 1955: *The Crown Jewels* (HMSO).
Holt, N.R. 1964: *The Pipe Roll of the Bishop of Winchester 1210–11* (Manchester).
Hope, W.H. St. J. 1913: *Windsor Castle, An Architectural History* (London).
Howard, M. 1987: *The Early Tudor Country House* (London).
Hunter, J. 1855: 'Notices of the Old Clochard or Bell-Tower of the Palace at Westminster', *Archaeologia* 37.
Hurst, J.G. 1961: 'The kitchen area of Northolt Manor, Middlesex', *Med. Arch.* 5.

James, T.B. and Robinson, A.M. 1988: *Clarendon Palace. The History and Archaeology of a Medieval Palace and Hunting Lodge near Salisbury, Wiltshire* (London).
James, T.B. and Simons, J. 1989: *The Poems of Laurence Minot* (Exeter).
Jankuhn, H. *et al.* 1973: *Vor- und Frühformen der europäischen Stadt in Mittelalter* (Gottingen).
Jansen, V. 1985: 'Lambeth Palace Chapel, the Temple Choir, and Southern English Gothic Architecture of *c.* 1215–1240', in Ormrod (ed.).
Jespersen, O. 1935: *The Growth and Structure of the English Language* (Oxford).
Johnson, C. (ed.) 1950: *Richard Son of Nigel: Dialogus de Scaccario* (London).
Johnstone, H. 1929: 'Poor relief in Thirteenth Century England', *Speculum* 4.
Jones, M.K. 1987: 'Collyweston – an Early Tudor Palace', in Williams (ed.).
Jones, T.L. 1953: *Ashby de la Zouch Castle, Leicestershire* (HMSO).
Jope, E.M. (ed.) 1961: *Studies in Building History* (London).

Kingsford, C.L. 1916–20: 'Historical Notes on Medieval London Houses', *London Topographical Record* 10–12.
Kipps, R.K. 1934: 'The Palace of the Archbishops of Canterbury at Charing, Kent', *Arch. J.* 90.

Kusaba, Y.L. 1983: *Architectural History of the Church of the Hospital of St Cross, Winchester* (University of Indiana, unpublished PhD.).

Labarge, M.W. 1965: *A Baronial Household of the Thirteenth Century* (London).
Lethaby, W.R. 1906: 'The palace of Westminster in the eleventh and twelfth centuries', *Archaeologia* 40.
—— 1927: 'Medieval Paintings at Westminster', *Proceedings of the British Academy* 13.
Lloyd, N. 1925: *A History of English Brickwork* (London).

MacDougall, E.B. (ed.) 1986: 'Medieval gardens', *Dumbarton Oaks Colloquium on Landscape Architecture,* No. 9. (Dumbarton Oaks).
McIntosh, K. 1986: *The Royal Manor of Havering* (Leicester).
Mackenzie, F. 1844: *The Architectural Antiquities of the Collegiate Chapel of St Stephen, Westminster* (London).
MacLean, T. 1981: *English Medieval Gardens* (London).
Mango, C. 1980: *Byzantium: The Empire of New Rome* (London).
Marshall, E. 1875: *The Early History of Woodstock* (London).
Mertes, K. 1988: *The English Noble Household 1250–1600* (Oxford).
Moorman, J.R.H. 1955: *Church Life in the Thirteenth Century* (Cambridge).
Myers, A.R. 1940: 'The Captivity of a Royal Witch: The Household Accounts of Queen Joan of Navarre, 1419–21', *Bulletin of the John Rylands Library* 24.
—— (ed.) 1959: *The Household of Edward IV* (Manchester).

Neal, D.S. 1971: 'Excavation at the palace and priory of King's Langley', Hertfordshire *Archaeology,* 3.
—— 1977: 'Excavations at the palace of King's Langley, Hertfordshire', *Med. Arch.* 21.
Newton, S.M. 1980: *Fashion in the Age of the Black Prince* (Woodbridge).

O'Day, F. and Heal, R. (eds.) 1981: *Princes and Paupers in the English Church 1500–1800* (Leicester).
O'Neil, H.E. 1956: 'Prestbury Moat: a manor house of the bishops of Hereford in Gloucestershire' *Transactions of the Bristol and Gloucestershire Archaeological Society* 75.
Ormrod, W.M. (ed.) 1985: *England in the Thirteenth Century* (Harlaxton College).

Parker, J.H. 1882: *Some Account of Domestic Architecture in England* (Oxford and London).
Peers, C. 1955: *Richmond Castle, Yorkshire* (HMSO).
Pevsner, N. and Cherry, B. 1978: *Hertfordshire* (Hatfield/Harmondsworth).
Pevsner, N. and Lloyd, D. 1969: *Hampshire and the Isle of Wight* (Harmondsworth).
Platt, C. 1962: 'Excavations at Dartington Hall', *Arch. J.* 119.
—— 1982: *The Castle in Medieval England and Wales* (London).
—— 1986: *Renaissance Britain* (London).
Poole, A.L. (ed.) 1958: *Medieval England* (Oxford).
Post, J.B. and Turner, A.J. 1973: 'An Account for Repairs to the Westminster Palace Clock', *Arch. J.* 130.
Pound, N.J.G. 1979: 'The Duchy Palace at Lostwithiel, Cornwall', *Arch. J.* 136.
Powicke, M. 1962: *The Thirteenth Century* (Oxford).
Prestwich, M. 1980: *The Three Edwards* (London).
—— 1988: *Edward I* (London).
Pugin, A.W. 1838: *Examples of Gothic Architecture* (London).

Radford, C.A.R. 1946: *Grosmont Castle* (HMSO).
—— 1958: *Goodrich Castle, Herefordshire* (HMSO).
—— 1961: 'Acton Burrell Castle', in Jope (ed.)
—— 1962: 'The Bishop's Palace and Ecclesiastical City of St. David's', *Arch. J.* 119.
Rahtz, P.A. 1969: 'Excavations at King John's Hunting Lodge, Writtle', *Society for Med. Arch. Monograph Series* 3.
—— 1979: 'The Saxon and Medieval palaces at Cheddar: excavations 1960–62', *BAR* 65.
Rait, R.S. (ed.) 1910: *English Episcopal Palaces* (London).
RCHM 1910: *Hertfordshire*.
—— 1926: *Huntingdonshire*.
Renn, D.F. 1972: *Portchester Castle* (HMSO).
—— 1973: *Kenilworth* (HMSO).
Rigold, S.E. 1966: 'Bishops Waltham Palace', *Arch. J.* 123–217.
—— 1971: 'Compton Wynyates', *Arch, J.* 128, 218–220.
—— 1978: 'Structures within English Moated Sites', in Aberg (ed.).
Roberts, E. 1986: 'The Bishop of Winchester's Fishponds in Hampshire 1150–1400', *Proceedings of the Hampshire Field Club* 42.
—— 1988: 'The Bishop of Winchester's Deer Parks in Hampshire 1200–1400', *Proceedings of the Hampshire Field Club* 44.
—— 1989: 'Bishop Raleigh's Banquet, 1244', *Hampshire Field Club Newsletter* 12.
Robinson, J.M. 1982: *Royal Residences* (London).
Roche, T.W.E. 1966: *The King of Almayne* (London).
Ross, C.D. 1951: 'The household accounts of Elizabeth Berkeley, Countess of Warwick', *Transactions of the Bristol and Gloucestershire Archaeological Society* 70.
Rothwell, H. (ed.) 1975: *English Historical Documents*, Vol. III (1189–1327) (London).

Saunders, A.D. 1959: *Barnard Castle* (HMSO).
Scarisbrick, J.J. 1968: *Henry VIII* (London).
Scattergood, J. 1987: 'Fashion and Morality in the Late Middle Ages', in Williams (ed.).
Schofield, J. 1984: *The Building of London from the Conquest to the Great Fire* (London).
Sherborne, J.W. and Scattergood, V.J. (eds.) 1983: English Court Culture in the Later Middle Ages (London).
Shirley, E. 1867: *Some Account of English Deer Parks* (London).
Simpson, W.D. 1937: 'Buckden Palace', *JBAA* 3rd Series, 2.
Smith, A. 1776: *The Wealth of Nations* (London).
Smith, J.T. 1837: *Antiquities of Westminster* (London).
Sneyd, C.A. (ed.) 1847: *A relation of the Island of England about the year 1500* (Camden Society).
Srawley, J.H. 1966: *The Book of John de Schalby, Canon of Lincoln 1299–1333* (Lincoln).
Staniland, K. 1987: 'Royal Entry into the World', in Williams (ed.).
Steane, J.M. 1988: 'The Royal Fishponds of Medieval England', in Aston (ed.).
Strong, D.E. 1958: *Eltham Palace, Kent* (HMSO).
Sweeney, M. 1981: *A History of Buckden Palace* (Buckden).

Tatton-Brown, T. 1980: 'Excavations at the "Old Palace" Bekesbourne, near Canterbury', *Archaeologia Cantiana* 96.
—— 1982: 'Interim Report on Excavations in 1982 by The Canterbury Archaeological Trust', *Archaeologia Cantiana* 98.
Taylor, A.J. 1958, rp. 1975: *Minster Lovell Hall, Oxfordshire* (HMSO).
—— 1976: 'Royal Alms and Oblations in the later Thirteenth Century', in Emmison and Stephens (eds.).
—— 1985: *Minster Lovell* (DOE/HBMC).

Thompson, A.H. 1941: 'Master Elias of Dereham and the king's Works', *Arch. J.* 98.
Thompson, M.W. 1966: 'Merdon Castle', *Arch. J.* 123.
—— 1971: *Conisburgh Castle* (HMSO).
—— 1971: 'Kenilworth Castle', *Arch. J.* 123.
—— 1972, rp. 1987: *Kenilworth Castle* (HMSO/HBMC).
Tudor-Craig, Pamela 1957: 'The Painted Chamber at Westminster', *Arch. J.* 114.

Vale, J. 1982: *Edward III and Chivalry* (Woodbridge).
Venables, E. 1895: *Episcopal Palaces of England* (London).

Webb, G. 1956: *Architecture in Britain: The Middle Ages* (London).
Webb, J. 1854–5: *A Roll of Household Expenses of Richard de Swinfield, Bishop of Hereford, during part of the years 1289–90* (Camden Society).
West, J.J. 1981: 'Acton Burnell Church and Castle', *Arch. J.* 138.
—— 1981: 'Acton Burnell Castle, Shropshire: a re-interpretation', in Detsicas (ed.).
Westminster Abbey information sheet 1989: *Westminster Abbey: The Great Pavement* (London).
Wight, J.A. 1972: *Brick Building in England from the Middle Ages to 1550* (London).
Williams, D. (ed.) 1987: *England in the Fifteenth Century* (Woodbridge).
Wood, M. 1950: 'Thirteenth Century Domestic Architecture in England', *Arch. J.* 105, Supplement.
—— 1965: *The English Medieval House* (London).
Wright, F.A. (ed.) 1930: *The Works of Liudprand of Cremona* (London).

Index

See London *for residences in and near the capital*